The Boy From

The Corner House

By Colin R Park

Text copyright © 2013

Colin R Park

Dedicated to my parents
and grandparents

Thanks to Carol and Vickie
for their help and support

Preface

The Boy From The Corner House is an account of my childhood. It is therefore autobiographical. But more importantly it is told from a child's perspective, thereby concentrating on the complex boyhood condition with no holds barred and warts and all.

Born into a rural, small-town, proletarian environment in 1953 my early years were not on the whole unpleasant, but perhaps a little unusual as opposed to common.

There was a massive generation gap and I was an only child witnessing the advent of the rock 'n' roll era from the sanctuary of the ramshackle, semi-derelict Corner House.

The often solitary and emotionally intense boyhood that seemed so ordinary at the time was in fact rich in extraordinary, sometimes surreal experiences.

I'm sure my book will serve well as a social documentation with which to measure and compare our rapidly changing lifestyles and attitudes. At the same time I hope it will also provide an insight into an only-begotten boy's world.

Chapter   Page

1

Nestledown

Brilliant bright light flashed randomly on to my closed eyes. The light was intense enough to penetrate through my eyelids illuminating blood and blood vessels. Between the flashes, patterns stayed on in a visual stew of kaleidoscopic after-image.

There was the thunder too, mighty crashes that rolled around overhead. They reminded me of a sound I'd heard somewhere in the past but this time it was a thousand times louder. I imagined a giant man chucking heavy balls across floorboards in a world above; and then there'd be another crash and clatter as a ball struck home yet again.

Unlike the past there were no men shouting and cheering but two familiar voices. These voices were the reason I was not in the slightest scared; as I lay there semi-conscious and feeling warm and safe. It was the worst storm for decades but I was far too young to either know or care. I had no idea what the words meant, but just the tone of my parents' voices were calming and comforting enough.

As the storm worsened I was able to pick up on a slight hint of panic, but I wasn't at all aware of its significance. It was just a barely detectable deviation from the norm; and anyway my parents, being masters of the universe, as I knew it, would sort things out.

It seemed there were more spherical missiles and they were rolled and hurled ever closer. Sheets of rain, sea spray and the angry wind pounded the tiny tin caravan's walls and windows, but the rocking motion encouraged further unconcerned, semi-slumber. I must have drifted off into real sleep but then was suddenly aware of being swept up and my cheek was thrust close against Mother's bosom. I was aware of a large broach in the shape of a butterfly displayed on her spotted frock just an inch from my eye.

The voices were now more serious – even Father's. Despite becoming drenched as we escaped to Father's massive black motorcar, I still didn't cry, didn't even wake properly. The familiar smell of luxurious leather meant definite safety as the V8 Ford Pilot was driven away to leave 'Nestledown' the rented holiday caravan, to its fate at the mercy of the terrible storm there on the precarious cliff-top.

This is my earliest significant experience and the ferocity of the storm has been recounted many times by my father. A year or two later I still didn't realise recognise any real danger from thunder and lightning, but I had begun to be aware of and understand words. I believed anything my parents told me like the existence of tooth fairies and Father Christmas and that lightning only ever struck places in far away lands. It was the secret bogeymen in their cubbyhole on the landing at the top of the stairs that I feared far more.

Apart from that rare holiday and the cliff top experience, my infant childhood world had scarcely begun to extend beyond the boundaries of the walls of our home. But my mind often wandered freely whilst pondering over increasingly frequent visits to far reaches of the house. More glimpses and sound samples of the outside world gradually filtered through to make more sense and further excite an adolescent curiosity. Voids in a vast and awesome mental jigsaw, formed by the missing pieces I couldn't yet find, were often substituted by fantasies from a growing personal trove of make-believe.

Subsequent thunderstorms did indeed sound like skittle nights I must have heard emanating from the pub across the road. But in my mind, thunder was still a noisy game that God played with his friends in their gigantic world.

My world and the bogeymen's cubbyhole existed in a house called The Corner House, which is still situated on the eastern edge of the town of Sherborne in Dorset, England. It is by a junction where six roads meet in a staggered, untidy fashion: Long Street, Newland, Oborne Road, Castleton Road, Castleton Terrace and New Road. Placed roughly on the central axis of this intersection is a small pedestrian island with a single streetlamp. In the 1950s the lamp was an old cast iron lantern type, probably converted from gas.

I spent the first fourteen years of my life living in The Corner House. The building forms the right angle where New Road and Long Street meet and on the opposite corner stood the Black Horse Hotel and bar room.

A world away, but only two hundred yards up Castleton Road on the far side of a high-walled railway bridge is a ruin of a castle and an area known as Castleton, effectively divided from the rest of Sherborne by the railway when it came to town. On the right, in the shadow of the bridge, down in the field close-by the railway line, in the left one of a pair of cottages is where my paternal grandparents lived. There are less than half a dozen other houses up there along with the tiny St. Mary Magdalene Church behind large iron gates, which squeak and screech when opened; and if you, as many do, stand and admire the tranquil surroundings just inside them, they can make you jump as they loudly and unexpectedly clank shut behind you. There are more large iron gates nearby that divide off the castle grounds and a private track called Pinford Lane continues past the church and to the left of the castle ruin. The centre of Castleton used to be a gravel area and the scrunch of the small stones gave ample warning to the residents of approaching footsteps or vehicles. Nowadays it is tarmac and provides limited parking for visitors to the church.

A vivid memory of my boyhood based at The Corner House is not so much of Sherborne Abbey's eight tons of bells pealing from way down the far end of Long Street near the town centre, but the plaintive clanging of Castleton's little church bell on Sunday mornings. The sound of the lonely bell would waft through my bedroom window; the fluctuating and quivering tone heavily influenced by changes in the direction of the wind or prevailing atmospheric conditions. The sound of steam trains also featured prominently, especially when I lay within the solitary confines of my bed. They were nearly always in a hurry and their bulldozing urgency often tipped my brain back towards consciousness. In my slumber I would sometimes become aware of the rapidly increasing sound of a train closing from the northeast, having usually missed its long, faint approach. The station lies a good distance behind The Corner House with the town in-between and the short-lived sound of the train would slide behind the buildings and diminish very quickly.

Conversely, trains from the opposite direction would suddenly burst into my consciousness as they emerged from the cover of the town, charging first under New Road bridge and then almost instantly under Castleton Road bridge. The puffing, chuffing and roar of steel would gradually dissolve into a clacketty-clack that would take ages to diminish into the far distance. The sound it eventually became reminded me of 'Champion' my old tin horse with spring loaded legs who, with eyes fixed in a wild stare, defiantly withstood my bouncing up and down on his back across the wild plains of The Corner House.

The far-off regular, rhythm of the train would die out and return several times as the rolling stock or carriages were hauled, echoing through cuttings, along embankments, over and under other bridges that 'Champion' and I had only ever dreamed of.

The Corner House is very old and its roof structure reputedly contains timbers from ancient sea-going galleons. During my time there it was also extremely basic; no central heating, two open fireplaces and just one cold tap in the whole place. Every morning there were 'slop buckets' and chamber pots from the bedrooms to empty into the solitary loo that was situated outside in the backyard.

The lived-in parts of The Corner House had simple furniture arranged with pure practicality in mind. Other areas were either totally empty and abandoned, or quite inaccessible with vast concentrations of junk, bric-a-brac and other commodities clogging things up. Unless you knew precisely where to tread it was impossible to walk on the first floor without being heard all over the house; the wide floorboards and joists creaked in an infinite variety of notes under untrained feet; perhaps in a similar way to the galleon they were once part of. The layers of gloss paint on other woodwork, dark green, brown or cream were synonymous with a period from decades earlier; as were the largely bare walls covered with the remains of pastel shades of dull primrose or turquoise emulsion. The contours of the first floor, especially within my bedroom, were not exactly flat or even. In an attempt to keep the top of the skirting boards level, their bottom edges had been custom-shaped to fit the floor. As a result the width of the skirting boards varied tremendously from about an inch to nearly six inches.

At the single window of my bedroom, simple curtains hung from taut wire, fixed with small hooks and eyelets. There was a boarded up cast-iron fireplace, quite small with a narrow mantelpiece, bare except for one tiny ceramic pot. This miniature vase bore an emblem of the town in the form of a transfer that had slipped and appeared crooked under the glaze. I had a single old wardrobe that stood a few degrees off plumb vertical in one corner. In the other corner was a marble-topped washstand; on it was a large china washbowl and jug that was only ever used if the doctor came.

My bed was made of tubular iron and painted off-white rather like an early hospital bed, it probably was. There was a particular hollow in the floor of my room where my bed, on its tiny casters, always willingly truckled back into after it had been moved. Next to my bed was an antique rickety wooden chair that served as a bedside table. On the other side of the bed and tight up to it, the wall that divided my bedroom from the corridor was made of thin tongue and groove timber swathed in plain wallpaper and daubed in fawn emulsion. This paper had been hastily hung and spanned the crevices and angles created by the joining of the boards and the thicker strengthening timber that ran horizontally midway between floor and ceiling. The small voids thus created between paper and timber had been punctured many times by my tiny fingernails, a similar odd satisfaction to that gained from popping modern-day bubble-wrap packaging.

Ill in bed one day, I had savoured the puncturing of most of the wallpaper air pockets within reach. It would have been coming up to mid-day because I was suddenly aware of the faint buzz of the small two-stroke motorcycle gradually approaching from the far distance. It got stronger and diminished then stronger again, similar to the trains, as the sound waves ricocheted off trees and the high walls of the estate woodyard beyond New Road railway bridge. It occurred every weekday at the same time and occasionally on a Saturday. It happened much quicker than the trains and no sooner had I initially heard it, the rider was easing off the throttle having negotiated his path up over the brow of the railway bridge. It had a far more raucous and aggressive sound than the trains.

Even though they often woke me, somehow the trains, delivering batches of early morning newspapers, taking passengers on excursions to the coast or maybe hauling raw materials nationwide, were strangely comforting. On the straight and level road outside my bedroom window, the motorbike rattled and spluttered by the halt sign, intermingled with random pops and explosions; and its brakes squeaked and moaned almost as loudly. Then, it seemed very reluctantly, the machine allowed itself to be coaxed into climbing the hill up Newland. I listened to the various gear changes as it disappeared into the streets of Sherborne. And then silence again.

Every weekday from nine in the morning until about midday my mother went to work as a part-time housekeeper four or five doors away in Long Street. On this particular morning as the faint chimes of the mantel clock from the room below struck twelve, I mischievously tied my dressing gown cord to the wire coat hook that was attached to the back of my bedroom door. To the cord I had tied the belt from my trousers. I practised tugging the makeshift rope as I lay back in bed to watch the door 'automatically' open and then miraculously close again by the gravitational pull created by the leaning of the wall to which the door was attached. I now excitedly waited in anticipation.

If there was no traffic passing outside I could just about hear Mother's heavy footsteps as she hurriedly rounded the corner from Long Street. I listened intently for Mother but a man had arrived outside selling fresh fish from West Bay. He'd parked his van in Newland and was shouting at the top of his voice,

"Mack row! Mack row!" It took me years to realise that he really meant mackerel.

Suddenly there was the unmistakeable sound of Mother bursting in through the front door. The door was only ever locked at night; fear of daytime intruders never existed back then. I got ready with the cord as she bounded up the stairs. I timed it just right as she approached the door. She didn't seem at all concerned when the door appeared to open all by itself and I was disappointed that my prank hadn't surprised or amused her.

"You bin gettin' outa bed again?" She didn't wait for a reply or explanation. "You know what the doctor said," she continued aiming her right index finger at me in time with each syllable she uttered. The discarded dressing gown cord and belt were left sadly dangling from the coat hook on the back of the bedroom door as I listened to my mother muttering about how Father would like the fish that she'd just bought. She thrust the parcel of fish up under her arm and the floor moaned under her weight as she walked across the room and flung the curtain back. The daylight streamed in and hurt my eyes.

My mother Marjorie was a large, well-built woman and she always insisted that she had large bones rather than being fat. Today she wore a one-piece spotted frock that had a strange familiarity about it. Even though the 'Nestledown' caravan holiday had only occurred a few years earlier, to an infant the event was already largely forgotten in the dim and distant past. However, I am sure that the familiarity of the frock stemmed from the fact that it was the same one she had worn that night when we abandoned the caravan back in a time when she used to pick me up. Over that frock she typically wore a light flowery apron that only extended from her waist down to her knees. Although the apron was tight and appeared to dig deep into her middle, it was a size too big and the ample strings formed a large drooping bow behind her.

I was oblivious to most of Mother's ranting as she peered out of my bedroom window to see who else was buying fish from the van that had now parked outside The Black Horse Hotel. Then her voice slowed to a mutter under her breath as her concentration was taken up by inspecting neighbours as they approached the fishmonger's van. Then she commented to herself about the unsuitability of a certain lady's slacks.

"I dunno what she do look like in them slacks! I wouldn't dream of wearing 'em myself!" I knew her comments were not directed at me, or indeed anyone and she probably didn't even realise that she was thinking out loud. Although I disregarded most of Mother's verbal stream of thoughts, I felt relieved that she was home. She tended to me and fed me, and all the ghosts and bogeymen had miraculously disappeared, as they always did.

"I'm gonna light the fire in the middle room," she said turning back from the window, "then maybe you can get up for a bit later on." This was certainly something to look forward to as I lay back in bed studying the wallpaper again. "I'm gonna do some nice hot beef broth in a minute," she said struggling to replace a hairgrip just above her forehead. "You've bin at that wallpaper again!" she suddenly remarked noticing my gaze. "Your father'll be angry when he gets home!" By now she had left the room and was marching back down the corridor. "You shouldn't do such a thing!" I managed to hear her say as she reached the top of the stairs. "Wouldn't be no good to decorate your room would it? You'd have it in tatters in minutes!"

When I was alone in my bedroom the murmurs of the outside world during the daytime, or at night the muffled BBC voices from Father's big radio downstairs, were occasionally taken over by the sounds of manifestations from far-flung reaches of the house. There was the shuffling spirit upstairs in the attic, the lion and tiger who lived in the very walls, the thing behind the big wardrobe in Mother's bedroom and of course the bogeymen. They were quite real but I usually remained protected by the thick Government Issue woollen blankets and flannelette sheets. Any need to leave my bed, perhaps to relieve myself in the metal enamelled chamber pot, was carried out with the rickety wooden chair close at hand to use as a shield, or even a weapon if need be. Although most manifestations were omnipresent and could crop up anywhere, it was out on the landing between my parents' bedroom and the attic stairs where the bogeymen's home was and from where they emerged and took up their various vantage positions; and to where they fled back into when Mother returned from work.

A solid door about half the size of a normal room door hid the bogeymen's headquarters. When this door was opened it revealed an odd shaped cubbyhole under the attic stairs full of thick black cobwebs, massive living spiders and the dust of past eras. Consequential of the strange and complicated construction of the upper parts of the house, this cubbyhole was somehow connected to a large mysterious void up in the roof, an extension to the bogeymen's hub that formed an ideal private playground for them all. Mother kept a battered tin dustpan and brush, feather duster and broom just inside the cubbyhole. On summer cleaning days with the bogeymen's door flung open wide, the sound of oak purlins, rafters and tiles could be heard adjusting to the changing temperature and still perhaps settling after all the centuries. In a gale the wind would race down through the bogeymen's lair to play with the doors in the corridor and then mischievously back up again, heavy black cobwebs swaying. It was to here where the ancient voice of The Corner House itself and all its resident spirits could be traced.

For some reason the promise of being allowed up that day didn't happen. But the same evening, still officially confined to bed, I discovered rock 'n' roll! The murmuring BBC voice from Father's big radio downstairs was comforting and to some extent kept spirits and bogeymen at bay. But drifting up the corridor from my parents' open bedroom window came the driving beat that positively eliminated my dark thoughts, but drove my parents crazy. The rumours that had been circulating were indeed true; The Black Horse had acquired a jukebox! I recalled Father remarking recently that trouble would inevitable follow if a new-fangled music machine appeared in the hitherto quiet bar across the road. Therefore I couldn't resist taking a peep.

Being extremely careful only to step on well-known solid and silent parts of the floor, I crept down the corridor to my parents' bedroom. I crawled; somehow thinking it would be quieter, up the two or three steps from the main landing to their bedroom. Their room was very similar in décor to my room except for thin flowered curtains and damp wallpaper that almost matched. Large areas of the wallpaper had peeled and hung in sad limpness to reveal more chalky primrose emulsion underneath. A high window incorporating a narrow seat set into the thick wall looked out over Newland and Black Horse corner. The only other window in the room was much lower with a very wide sill and it overlooked the lantern in the middle of the road junction and to its left, the main hotel entrance of the Black Horse. Mother's large wardrobe conveniently fitted in an alcove which extended over the bottom of the stairs which led up from the front door, whilst Father's little wardrobe, although matching, never seemed to have a convenient place in the room. There was a large old-fashioned double bed crammed with complicated springs and ironwork, which was always covered in a silky rose-red, quilted eiderdown.

I was obviously far too young to be actually involved in the early rock 'n' roll era and 'Teddy Boys' as my mother called them, but that night I certainly began experiencing the couldn't-care-less feeling it induced. The window with the narrow built-in seat conveniently overlooked the actual public bar entrance in Newland. With one ear on alert for the familiar screech of the homemade curtain track attached to the door of the middle room downstairs and the other mesmerised by the driving beat of rock 'n' roll, I knelt in the narrow window seat. Then with my chin resting on the sill, I cautiously peered out and witnessed the throng of the bar. The pub door opened momentarily, a window also opened for more fresh air. First the sound of Buddy Holly then Elvis Presley; Little Richard then Bill Haley and The Comets blasted out. There were couples dancing in the smoky yellow bar and occasional drunken fisticuffs spilled out into the street. It was wild and marvellous.

This was my first glimpse at planet earth. The first words I could write proclaimed me – scrawled in the back of every book I owned – as 'Colin Richard Park, The Corner House (with backyard), Long Street, Sherborne, Dorset, England, The British Isles, The World, The Universe.'

2

Alone

I was recovering well and my strength was returning thanks to more of Mother's beef broth and occasional rock 'n' roll therapy - care of The Black Horse. One morning a few days later, Mother had left for work and I realised that I really did feel a whole lot better. I also realised how desperately bored and fed up I'd become lying there in bed. It was physically impossible to puncture any more wallpaper voids and I'd exhausted all my abstract art talents by scribbling and doodling wax crayon over any bare, unbroken areas of adjacent wall. So despite Mother's warnings, I decided to brave the bogeymen and get up. Sadly there was never any music to be heard from the pub in the mornings, just the occasional faint chink of empty bottles being thrown into a bin.

I wandered down to the opposite end of the corridor from the main landing and my parents' bedroom. Here there was a drab and empty forgotten room known as the spare room that only contained cobwebs and occasional mice. The powdering walls had that familiar hint of dull primrose, one or two floorboards were missing and others were bowed and ill-fitting. Viewing the old streetlamp and junction from the different angle that this room's window offered broke the monotony for a while. After long contemplation about nothing in particular, I strolled back up the corridor.

Almost opposite my room door and similar in stark bareness to the spare room, there was an ascending grey stairway, mysteriously wider than the main stairs up from the ground floor and with much deeper steps. It wound its way awkwardly up, past a grubby window that looked out over ours and next-door's backyard.

Mr and Mrs Field lived next-door and their backyard was divided from ours with a large old red brick wall. They liked me to call them Aunty and Uncle even though they were not related to me. I was convinced that they kept hippopotamuses and other wild animals but I could never actually see them. Aunty Field would often glance up and catch me straining and staring intently as I tried desperately to see where they managed to get the animals in or indeed catch a glimpse of the elusive beasts; she would smile politely and sometimes wave.

Tantalisingly out of bounds the empty attic stairs led up to the single topmost room, which like the stairs, was a homogeneous grey in colour. This attic room was crammed full of dusty junk like a long-abandoned and very untidy saleroom. There was an even more filthy dormer window across the far side of the room that looked down on to Newland. It was too high to actually look out of and was partly hidden with all the paraphernalia. But I sometimes managed to clamber over things to inspect its sun-bleached sill and gaze up at the ancient lace curtains hung from wire and drooping heavy with black cobwebs and dead spiders. Amongst the dust were also the light husks of long deceased wasps and the fragile remains of butterflies.

Occasionally a live butterfly miraculously appeared, its origins always a mystery. My attempts to shoo the sickly looking creature to a better life, down the stairs and through an accessible window, consistently failed. They always seemed hell-bent on one single life-flutter that encompassed their entire active existence, across their attic world to that window trap. Huge eyes painted on outstretched wings and caught in cobwebs, twitched for days waiting for death.

Although fairly large to a small boy, the attic did not take up the whole of the topmost area of the building. Sealed behind lathes and plaster and on a slightly different level was the mysterious void that was the bogeymen's playground, rising up through a clutter of awkward roof timbers from their cubbyhole headquarters under the sharp bend in the attic stairs.

I lingered on the attic stairs and stared intensely into the Fields' backyard. As usual I could not see any hippopotamuses. The old red brick wall was bowed from top to bottom, bulging in the middle on our side and overhanging slightly from midway up on the Fields' side. I was convinced that the only way a wall could get to be such a shape was if large animals like hippopotamuses reversed themselves into it – perhaps to rub their rears to alleviate itching.

Then my attention was drawn to one butterfly outstretched on the cobwebs that merged seamlessly into lace curtains there before me. It was rare to see a butterfly by this window. I knew from experience, because its movements were so feeble – and may have even been caused by a faint flurry of air – that even if plucked from its predicament and carried outside it would either prove to be dead anyway or would die within minutes. I left it and clomped down the last few steps of the attic stairs. I warily passed the bogeymen's door and made my way downstairs.

There were two general living rooms on the ground floor of The Corner House; one on each side of the steep and straight staircase that descends towards the main front doorway to the outside world. The large and heavy front door was encrusted in the same plain chocolate paint that could be found elsewhere within the building; on its inside there were massive bolts top and bottom and a few smaller ones in-between.

I grew to recognise the distinctive and reassuring sound of the door being bolted each night from my bed as darkness fell. I could even tell who was securing the door. If it were Mother she would fight with each bolt in turn, every fumbling attempt resonating against the wood. Whereas if it were Father he would only ever bother with the huge top and the bottom bolts and make a quick and decisive job of sliding each one into place.

The room to the left of the descending staircase formed the actual corner of New Road and Long Street. It had a window into each street and we always called it the front room. It was by far the coldest room, probably due to it being partly subterranean – the outside pavement rises towards the windowsills as it rounds the corner from New Road.

When raking old ashes out of the dead fire early on winter mornings, the sound of the Mrs Field next-door doing the same could be plainly heard just inches away through the back-to-back fireplace. We would frequently mimic each other's scraping motions and this often turned into a game of who would be the last one to drag their poker over their cast iron fire grate. After enduring a few winters I soon became an expert in the art of successful fire lighting and I would give in easily to the raking game, desperate to light the fire to drive away the penetrating frosts that formed ice on the inside of the window panes.

The front room housed an old pianola, a three-piece suite and had reasonable carpets. There were three china ducks manufactured in halves lengthwise, flying across the simple patterned wallpaper as if frozen in individual solid lumps and embedded deep in the plaster. Comparatively the room was in an acceptable state of repair and on very rare occasions – if it was unavoidable – my parents allowed visitors in there. It was a sort of reception area on the edge of our private, almost reclusive world. Strictly no one, except close family or the doctor, was ever allowed beyond this fringe area of The Corner House.

There was a door that was always kept locked near the far left corner of the front room; it concealed a passageway that led through the rear of the building and into the backyard. It was impossible to get down this passageway because it was always crammed with junk and firewood.

On the other side of the main stairs was the second living room, which we always called the middle room. It was a cosy lived-in room but in desperate need of decoration. Upon entering this room from the bottom of the main stairs a high-pitched metallic grating sound was often emitted from the top area of the door to be heard throughout the house. The noise came from the homemade curtain track attached to the inside of the door. This consisted of a tubular steel rod on to which were threaded metal rings that suspended a heavy maroon curtain that kept out the drafts. When the door was opened each ring scraped along the rod thus producing the screech of notes.

There was a tank full of tropical fish next to the wall opposite the single window in the middle room. Other children would sometimes gawp through the window at the fish and I would stand and wave at them or if I didn't like them I'd pull faces. The middle room also had a door to the right that opened into the crammed, out-of-bounds passageway that led from the front room down to the backyard. Across the middle room near the far corner, a garden-shed type door opened down a slight incline made of concrete into the only other room on the ground floor, the crumbling kitchen-cum-bathroom. This flimsy door would always stick slightly on the rough slope making a distinctive scuffing noise, which would be much amplified acoustically through its thin wood.

That morning a cool breeze blew under the large gap between the bottom of the front door and the stone doorstep. I noticed post scattered randomly on the well-worn doormat but daren't touch any of it otherwise Mother would know I'd been out of bed. I opened the door into the middle room.

After the usual screech of curtain rings the house lay silent. Joey the budgerigar had died a few weeks earlier. I hadn't been particularly close to him but today Joey's absence made the silence all the more conspicuous. He had spent most his time chattering continuously to sparrows who lived in three cherry trees that grew up through the wide pavement outside the middle room window. If the sparrows weren't around then it was some imaginary budgie God who loitered just outside by the streetlamp to whom he'd direct his complicated tale and level his pathetic, fruitless enquiries. Joey's more desperate and frantic attempts at communication irritated Father. So much so that sometimes he'd be driven to cover Joey's cage with a tea towel to block off the outside world. The poor bird would then head-butt his tiny red-framed mirror and jangle the bell attached to the top of it time and time again. It was as if Joey had tried using his little mirror as a two dimensional crystal ball, but when no answers were forthcoming, frustration and even attempts at self-destruction took over.

I knelt in the window seat of the middle room window peering out at the road junction from yet another angle wondering if there really was a budgie God. Sparrows chirped relentlessly as if telling everyone that Joey was dead. I could also just about hear the mechanical clicks and whirs of starlings from somewhere up on the rooftop. I made a face at a rather stern looking man as he walked past the window staring in at me. Frightened that he might return, I quickly crossed the middle room to the kitchen.

As far as state-of-repair and safety was concerned, the kitchen-cum-bathroom was by far the worst room of the house. Yet being a multi-purpose area and conveniently hidden from the outside world's prying eyes, this was where we spent a large percentage of our time. It was a very dark room that only had a single, tiny and very low window that looked out into our private backyard.

There was a massive cast iron bath with large substantial feet that looked like lion's paws and right next to it, almost touching it and openly defying all health and safety regulations, was the electric cooker. The floor was blue flagstone laid in direct contact with solid earth, which made matters even worse as far as risk of electrocution was concerned. But of course I wasn't aware of such risks at that early age; I just knew that the electric fire that my mother balanced precariously on a chair in front of the bathtub made me feel a little warmer while I bathed. Little did I know that one exploratory touch of the exposed terminals that connected the wire wound element, would have meant certain death.

The flagstones were very uneven and the deep gaps between them gave refuge to roaming woodlice. Old bits of discoloured linoleum and cardboard were wedged under at least one leg of each item of furniture or appliance in an attempt to level and steady them. The cooker was antique even then, like the bath it was cast iron and very heavy. Its main body stood high on spindly legs that were constantly wearing through any floor wedge material to damage the shiny blue stone underneath.

The only other pieces of furniture in the kitchen were two almost identical wooden dressers, a flimsy Formica topped table and three rickety wooden chairs that were similar, if not the same, as my bedside chair. The dressers were made of thin, cheap plywood and painted sickly green. One had a heavily chipped enamelled metal sheet covering its worktop, while the other had thin white vinyl patterned with orange flowers stuck on to its collapsible work surface.

The plaster on the walls was crumbling leaving bits of horsehair showing. This appeared to a young mind as whiskers or other bodily hair emerging from living stuff. The bits of plaster that were intact bore the faint remains of the prevalent primrose or turquoise emulsion. The ceiling was cracked and chunks had come away revealing the wooden lathes underneath. The whistling wind through these gaping holes often encouraged more debris to fall into the bathwater. While lying in the bath and gazing up at a particular angle, chinks of light could be seen through the lathes, coming in through gaps in badly fitting floorboards in the much brighter spare room above.

Water was either heated in the kettle on the stove or in a battered, industrial electric boiler that was balanced on old scaffold planks over the end of the bath where the proper taps should be.

Either way water was put in the kettle first, because climbing on to a chair and emptying countless kettles full of water into the top of the high positioned boiler was the only way to fill it. The one consolation was that the only mains tap was nearby, sprouting from an old lead pipe over the heavy stone sink by the window. The boiler's capacity was limited and further kettles of water would always need adding directly to the bath to top it up. This was usually carried out with the person in the bath because then they could instantly judge exactly how hot or cold the additions should be. Bath times were always planned at least a half a day in advance. Not only did the boiler take many hours to heat the water, but its small tap would take another hour to trickle and splash its contents into the tub.

Mother also washed our clothes in the old bath. Agitation of the dirty washing and keeping me under control was achieved with a well-worn stout stick that Mother always called her 'poking stick.' It was about a metre long and looked like part of an extra thick broom handle that had been caressed in the sea for a hundred years. The grain was worn away more in the softer seams and was furry in places just like driftwood. It also had a tinge of turquoise from being immersed in hot soapy water for decades. The smell in our dual-purpose kitchen, bathroom and hideaway, was always a strange mixture of food, steamy washing powder and Mother's perfumed soap.

I crossed the kitchen towards the bath and the flagstones were like ice to my bare feet. As I had hoped, there in the bathtub, partly submerged in cool water, were two pint bottles of milk, one unopened and the other half full. As I eagerly reached out a huge crumpled black spider came floating from the boiler end partly propelled by at least one still moving leg. Excited, I found Mother's poking stick and soon any thoughts of rescue that the spider may have had were dashed. It eagerly reached out for anything dry but I plunged it to the depths as it clung on feebly to my prodding tool. I was amazed at the fine layer of reflective air bubbles that formed over its hairy body as I submerged it. On its second or third time out of the water it didn't want any further dunking and in a last desperate dash for freedom, it decided to run up the stick towards me. Reflex actions made me instantly drop Mother's poking stick and I left the spider on its huge floating log that it surveyed carefully from end to end. The milk tasted good.

The strange passageway on the ground floor that led from the front room to the backyard ended at an exterior wooden door that had hints of much weathered light blue paint on its surface, and long thin rust stains created from the nails that held it together. It always jammed when being opened and there were ancient, neat arks gouged into the stone floor in evidence of this. Although the passageway ended at the door, a haphazardly covered gangway continued into the backyard made of makeshift sheets of Perspex and corrugated tin. This gangway was formed between the first part of the red brick wall that divided us from next-door and the continuation of the main building there by the kitchen backdoor.

The external kitchen door was adorned on the inside with multi layers and colours of paint randomly reticulated by decades spent exposed to a cooking and washing environment. It opened into the end portion of the covered gangway directly opposite the red brick wall. The awkward bulge along the wall's middle, the crumbling bricks, many different shades of maroon and the chalky remnants of mortar between them, appeared fragile and dangerous. I pondered and consolidated my theory that over the years like farmyard cows the Fields' large beasts had gently relieved itches on their backsides up against the rough bricks and bit-by-bit the wall had gradually bowed to their shape.

As well as giving shelter when first leaving the kitchen, the roof of the gangway was also an effective rain alarm. Raindrops and especially of course hailstones, made a clattering cacophony of drumming on the variety of acoustic surfaces. This rhythm would often be syncopated with the sometimes slower, sometimes faster but always larger beats of accumulated drops from broken guttering above. The gangway ended at the backyard with the isolated toilet on the left and the red brick dividing wall continuing on the right, all the way down to Father's garage.

On the opposite side from the red brick wall the yard was separated from the street with another high wall made of large stones as opposed to brick, but equally as dangerous. There was a doorway through this wall into the street. But because the area was so unsafe it was hardly ever used – except once a week by Father to put the dustbins out. The lock had long since disintegrated and the door was only barely attached to its rusty, paper-thin hinges. Therefore it was usually left barricaded up with any available items like well-intentioned but long-abandoned building materials such as bags of sand, timber and lengths of iron scaffolding pole. There was a half-hearted attempt at a flowerbed under the stone wall kept in place with old floorboards. The rest of the yard was well trodden, compacted earth that became very messy in the wet, except that is for two or three odd shaped flat stones that lay scattered randomly in the earth, like the forgotten beginnings of crazy paving

At the far end of the yard opposite the kitchen and its grubby little window was the garage, elevated and sideways on, completing the square enclosure. Two old concrete blocks formed a makeshift step up to the locked pedestrian doorway. Beyond the forbidden entrance was Father's intriguing and largely private domain. To peep inside I would stand on the back of 'Champion' my tin horse with spring loaded legs or my posh varnished wooden horse on wheels that had no name. Then from the vantage point of one of my trusty steeds, I could stare in through the metal framed window of the garage at the substantial solid bench, the massive iron vice and the fabulous jet black Ford Pilot car that Father kept for chauffeuring people to weddings and funerals. The car had massive chrome headlamps and wide running boards down each side. I loved its smell of leather and it was a safe mobile haven.

I collected quite a few pets like Joey the budgerigar, the tropical fish, a couple of tortoises, an itinerant cat and a while ago we also had a dog. There was even a slowworm in a cardboard box locked inside the garage. When they died most of these animals were buried in the small neglected flowerbed at the foot of the stone wall. Crosses made of lollipop sticks were lovingly placed on their graves until nature's elements toppled them. Then like the remains within the grave they marked, the sticks rotted and perished into the soil where they fell. I felt this was right somehow and never dreamt of permanently removing the marking of a grave or indeed the contents of it. However, I considered a temporary inspection was fine and last summer I carefully took down the memorial to Timmy the tortoise and dug him up. I had an irresistible curiosity, just to see if the flesh had disappeared. I remember to my disappointment, the shell disintegrating as I tried to inspect it.

Now I was wondering about Joey. We had buried him about a foot in from the corner of the old flowerbed near the dangerous doorway to the outside world and his lollipop stick tombstone was still there.

It had been raining that morning and the mud from the yard soaked into the knees of my blue striped pyjamas and my old woollen dressing gown was trailing in the dirt too. I soon found Joey stiff and cold like cardboard but his bright blue feathers still stood out through the crumbly soil. I wondered if the stuff inside him that had now disappeared making him half the size and weight I remembered him, had really miraculously gone to heaven like Father had insisted it would. I thought I'd better tuck him back in his resting place so that God could arrange for the transportation of the other tougher stuff like feathers, beak and bone.

I couldn't resist having another peep at Timmy the tortoise but his remains had now truly intermingled with the soil. Any barely recognisable bits of his shell now appeared like soil anyway, just a little darker and it was apparently successfully fertilizing Mother's new recently planted rose bush. I thought about how God must be pleased with me and how he must be fairly familiar now with our 'body transfer area' there under our humble backyard wall.

When I was old enough to kick a ball with any force it was forever disappearing into next-door's space. I got to know from standing on top of the tumble-down coal bunker tucked in the corner where the red brick wall met the garage, or by gazing out of the attic stairs window, that next-door's space was a properly tended garden as opposed to a junkyard full of wonder like ours. If there was no one in next-door I would always find my garish beach ball some time later tossed back over. If it came back instantly then I knew the people next-door were enjoying their garden and I would refrain from chancing any more clumsy kicks for that particular day.

In later years a relation's misguided belief that I might like football, resulted in them giving me a far more robust, almost real football. I discovered that I could easily kick this missile high up on to the corrugated roof of Father's garage. The roof sloped back down towards the yard, therefore when it bounced off the massive wall that rose up above the far side of the garage, it would conveniently roll back down. The backyard formed a little playground and the nucleus of my early physical activities.

The two-stroke noisy motorbike broke the silence again that day. Its approaching buzz like a large mechanical bumblebee, told me it was nearly twelve. This made me drop everything and race back up to my bed before Mother returned.

3

Cigarettes For Mother
And Me

During my pre-school days and when Mother wasn't working, we would happily hold fort at The Corner House until Father got home. There would be 'Champion' the tin wonder horse, the other wooden horse on wheels with no name, a very battered family teddy bear and the tropical fish. A few years later came a new budgie and for a short while an aggressive Jack Russell dog. There was also a fluffy grey itinerant cat who could occasionally be seen scampering through the house. He avoided me at all costs for fear of getting his tail or ears pulled.

Despite the awareness of bogeymen and other manifestations, compared to the outside world the house was like a safe rock floating in a universe of mystery. There were only occasional trips into the vastness beyond the walls. I have no detailed memories of these pre-walking trips, just vague snippets of sensory perceptions like the 'Nestledown' experience.

I can vaguely recall being pushed around backwards in a large black perambulator with a high restrictive hood made of cream-coloured crinkly material that stank of plastic. It made me frustrated at only being able to see where I had been, as opposed to where I was going. It creaked and squeaked constantly as it was pushed; the large metal body hung on a crude, weak suspension. Occasionally it was swung around quickly for me to see what Mother was seeing. Having had no warning or gradual visual build-up as to what was there, it was sometimes a dreadful shock. Like being spun around to catch a glimpse of my first steam train right next to the level crossing at Sherborne station. I was sure that the living, hissing monster with wheels bigger than the pram would consume both Mother and me. The steam escaping from every tiny crevice I interpreted as extreme anger and when pistons forced those wheels to spin on the tracks the shock caught my breath and I felt my lungs would burst.

When I began to walk I don't recall a transitional period in the forward facing luxury of a pushchair, but I do remember more frustration at being tethered. I was strapped in a leather harness with reins attached. If I was good I was afforded a long rein for a short time, which allowed an occasional few quick seconds towards a taste of freedom. But Mother was always desperate not to lose her grip and more often than not I would be hauled up short and kept on a tighter-than-tight rein like a dangerous puppet or a pet chimpanzee; on display to be poked, prodded and cooed at by all and sundry.

Our first dog – a Jack Russell called Monty – had to be put down when I was finally allowed to break out of the awful reins. I guess the house just wasn't big enough for the two of us and his aggressive objections to my growing independence became a serious threat to my safety. Monty was unceremoniously escorted out of the house one day never to be seen again. He probably thought he was going for another walk rather than a one-way journey to the vets in East Mill Lane.

My earliest solitary little excursions outside the house were errands for Mother to fetch Woodbine cigarettes from the Post Office in Long Street.

"Pop down the road an' get us ten Woodbines!" Mother typically said one day. I broke away from pressing my face tight up against the tropical fish tank and stopped making grotesque faces at the Guppies and Mollies.

"Here's two and sixpence and don't be long." I could just about reach the brass handle on the huge front door. "I'm just gonna buy this ten, then I'm gonna give it up next week," Mother muttered as I left the house. The times I'd heard her say that before!

There were three shops in the first straight stretch of Long Street: Hamblin's electrical shop where Father worked on Saturday mornings, Waite's General Stores and Tom Baker's Post Office. It would have been easier and quicker one would think to go to Waite's shop as it was about a quarter the distance of Tom Baker's from home. As it happened going to Waite's usually took longer and I hated it because the girl who worked there always insisted that I calculate the change for myself, before she would give it to me. Plus the fact that Mr Waite – who reminded me so much of the big fat potato man with the stuck on ears that I'd once made – would hold an inquisition as to whether I was going to smoke the cigarettes myself.

For these reasons I very seldom visited Waite's shop. Mr Waite, wearing his extremely thick lens glasses, dressed in his grey nylon work coat and hands clasped behind his back, would watch me scuttle past his shop to Tom's. It was only superior ice cream that sometimes tempted me into Waite's shop, the taste of which was traded for an inevitable mathematical exercise, watched by all the shop staff and customers.

Although less stressful, visiting Tom Baker's could also take time and more than once Mother had become worried enough to come looking for me. Tom's shop was only about twelve feet by six, not much bigger if at all than the typical entrance hallway one would expect in the terraced cottage in which it stood. There was a substantial wooden counter running lengthwise from front to back and a quarter of it was fitted with a grill behind which Tom became a serious postmaster. He would flit from friendly 'Uncle' Tom to serious postmaster as if by magic, instantly changing as he entered or left the caged area. If a queue had formed he would even poke his head back into the shop area to apologise and then return to diligently stamp postal orders or pension books in the solemn Post Office environment. If you asked for a first class stamp, or indeed any other single item, he would always ask how many you wanted. His largely unsuccessful sales patter was annoyingly persistent, but he was still lovable and kind at heart.

He would never question if the cigarettes were for Mother but just assume that they were and eagerly take the money. Before giving change he would often gesture towards the rack of chocolates and sweets in front of him or the large jars of loose goodies on shelves behind him in a last ditch attempt at a further sale.

The shop door always needed a good shove to open it. A little sprung hammer struck the bell near the top of the door as it opened creating a sound like a typewriter bell. In actual fact the bell was hardly necessary because the cards and paraphernalia that were hung on the back of the glass door made such a racket anyway. Tom sometimes took some time to appear, especially if he was having his 'elevenses.'

I held the half crown coin tight in my hand as I crept in, tiptoeing on the blue flagstone floor that was almost identical to The Corner House kitchen floor. I always managed to brush up against the packets pinned on to the timber-clad wall opposite the counter. When other people were crammed in the shop packs of elastic bands, drawing pins or gummed labels often ended up on the floor.

Tom appeared from his private area at the far end of the counter nursing a cup of coffee.

"Woodbines please!" I said, "and sweet cigarettes."

"Do you know," said Tom, "there's a nice new chocolate bar out." He carefully placed his coffee down and came around the customer side of the counter. "There!" he said fumbling to remove a bar from the display rack in front of me. "They're called 'Bliss' and Mrs Baker says they're lovely." He held out the purple and silver bar towards me balancing it in the palm of his hand like a precious piece of jewellery. "Not too chewy," said Tom, "and not too gooey, but just right." I smiled politely but knew I would not have enough money to buy one. "You could have one now and pay for it later!" said Tom studying the bar himself and adjusting his glasses. I knew I daren't do that, I had previously ended up in deep trouble for this and Mother had nearly fallen out with Tom about it. I looked down at my feet avoiding Tom's gaze. Realising his sales pitch was not working he placed the bar back on the rack. I was desperate for an escape and prayed someone else would call in the shop.

He was now back at the gap at the far end of the counter holding up a large box of chocolates like an auctioneer selling a painting, the box did indeed have a garish print of multi-coloured roses on its cover.

"For mummy's birthday!" He gestured and peered at me for a reaction over the top of his thick spectacles.

To my great relief a lady in a gabardine raincoat entered the shop. She was a stranger and her raincoat brushed a pack of elastic bands on to the floor as she squeezed in.

"Right umm.. Woodbines," said Tom fumbling to balance the chocolates back on display. "Woodbines …. for mummy!" he continued so the lady could hear. "How many would mummy like?"

"Ten please and ten sweet cigarettes."

"Nothing else today Colin?"

"No thanks."

Occasionally if Mother didn't have enough money he would split a packet of Woodbines or even sell them singly. He sold loose biscuits by the ounce and would break them in half or even quarters to get the weight right. His thick-rimmed glasses held lenses that were even thicker than Mr Waite's and he'd smooth his fairly long white hair back from his face as he spoke to you. Near to Christmas, Easter and Mother's Day, Tom would arrange an even bigger display pile of goodies in the middle of the first room of his private quarters.

"Don't forget about the nice box of chocolates for mummy!" he whispered softly as if he didn't want the lady to hear. "And be sure to tell her about the new 'Bliss' bar," he continued while lifting a hand to shield his lips from the lady. It was as if he considered the new bar some international phenomenon only he and I should know about. Tom's silent wife suddenly appeared at the doorway of their private quarters, which hurried things along. I snatched the cigarettes and my sweets, handed Tom the money and ran out forgetting the change completely. The lady stranger had to shout up the road after me.

Of course like all children I often mimicked adults at this early age. It never really crossed my mind to try a real cigarette yet. But using Tom's thin, white sickly-sweet candies with a red tip, I would go through all the smoking rituals on my way back home. Plucking one from the pack that resembled a packet of ten real cigarettes added to the routine. I would even tap the end of each one on the packet before I placed it in my mouth, just like Uncle

Todd did with his plain 'Navy Cut' cigarettes. Then I would stroll back home with one poking from the corner of my lips. If I met anyone I would screw up my face seriously and squint as if suffering the discomfort I had seen many adults endure from having tobacco smouldering just under their nose.

When the milkman called at The Corner House he would often open the front door himself and shout, 'Milkman!' While Mother made her way to the door to shout what she wanted, he would go back to his float ready to gather the order and bring it back to the doorstep.

As I leisurely strolled back up Long Street I couldn't resist devouring another candy stick. Then as I rounded the corner I shoved another of the pretend fags in my mouth and noticed that for some reason two pints of milk were still on the doorstep. I, confident and pleased with myself, plucked them up and took them through to the kitchen where Mother, with a real fag in her mouth, was agitating the washing in the bath with her poking stick.

"Milkman!" I shouted at the top of my voice with the sweet cigarette stuck to my bottom lip. Mother turned in time to see me plonk them down hard like a proper workman on the solid stone floor. Both glass bottles shattered and I was left holding the remains of the milk bottle necks. Milk trickled everywhere into each crack and crevice of the flagstones. My heart sank and I felt sick as it dawned on me just what I had done. Different sized shards of spiky glass lay in a dangerous mess and woodlice floated out of their dark homes.

"You stupid little sod!" Mother screamed and continued a stream of other unintelligible things at the top of her voice. I ran and hid behind the armchair in the front room.

4

Jill The Dog

And Walks With Father

Immediately after Monty the Jack Russell's demise my parents vowed never to have another dog. They said they didn't want the responsibility and it would be too much heartache when the animal inevitably died. However, Father soon began to realise how much he missed walking the dog on Sunday mornings and within a month he'd changed his mind. He eventually managed to talk Mother around and I think the decision was also partially influenced by the hope that a good trustworthy dog might serve to keep me company. The decision changed my life.

It was a meek and mild-mannered, black mongrel bitch known as Jill that we adopted from an animal welfare centre near Bere Regis. I suppose the dog was the first living creature with whom I shared naive theories about the unfolding mysteries of life. When she had settled down and managed to get over the fact that we were definitely offering her a loving home for life, I introduced her to every nook and cranny of The Corner House and the relationship grew.

It was a revelation for me. The spare room was given a new lease of life as we regularly scampered through it at the expense of more debris falling into the bathtub below. Bogeymen were less threatening and I confided in her my nagging concern about whether there were really hippos in next-door's backyard.

Jill was one of those dogs who did not possess the ability to be aggressive in any way. She sometimes showed her teeth slightly but this would always be an involuntary little smile when she hadn't seen you for a while. Screwing up her upper lip in such a way would usually make her sneeze as she pranced around, her whole body writhing in sympathy with her tail. She would endure the wearing of funny hats and glasses and me tugging on her tail. Sometimes I would mimic her whining and she would become so concerned and lick me all over, whilst carefully scanning my reactions with mournful eyes. Tibby, the old itinerant fluffy grey cat left home completely for a week when Jill arrived. But after a month they were sleeping in the same bed and Tibby seemed far more friendly and relaxed.

But after two months the kind and motherly Jill was nursing a broken heart. Tibby had died of old age. I had no chance of inspecting Tibby's body or even delivering him to the 'body transfer point' in the flowerbed under the dangerous wall in the backyard. The limp bundle of grey fur had been whisked off to the vets in a cardboard box for any signs of life and was never seen again. I was never particularly close to Tibby, he was very independent and didn't relish too much human contact anyway, especially not children's. However, I certainly instinctively recognised Jill's pain. She would search the entire house for him every day for weeks looking under the beds and even braving the bogeymen's cubbyhole. She'd sit patiently by the backdoor for hours hoping for his miraculous return from some epic hunting expedition. Jill's pining eventually subsided as I comforted her as best I could. I told her he had not been delayed on some brave quest to bring his pride food or information on the wild world, but he had gone somewhere else – forever.

We came to the conclusion that there must be other 'body transfer points' scattered around outside. We consoled ourselves by coming to the conclusion that it was selfish to expect to have our own private 'body transfer point.' Without realising it we were cementing further our relationship and I suppose subconsciously I was experiencing my first taste of compassion.

Unlike my paternal grandparents who lived just up the road in Castleton, my parents were not particularly religious. The sound of Castleton's church bell on Sundays, rather than summoning my parents to worship, evolved to be a reminder that it was time for Mother to start cooking lunch and for Father and me to walk the dog.

Sunday morning expeditions with Father and Jill became the norm. A typical route would take us around New Road, over the railway and river bridges and under tall trees that grew on the right, opposite the high walls of the estate woodyard near the edge of a large field called Purley. These trees – mainly beech and sycamore – towered high above the pavement and in what was then a carefree dream world, I would stare upwards while walking and imagine we were under water. The wavering branches for some reason reminded me of waterweed that I must have noticed undulating in the depths of the river Yeo down in Purley. The sheer height of the trunks accentuated the feeling of depth and I felt I was a microscopic creature walking on the riverbed. The constantly changing shapes of the blue sky through foliage seemed like some far away hint at a bright, airy surface, even a different universe beyond.

Lagging behind Father one day I was totally immersed in my fantasy. Then something made me look down and concentrate on where I was going; I nearly stepped on a dead pigeon there on the pavement. Fearful that I was going to pick it up, Father came rushing back.

"I wondered if you'd notice that," he said, predicting my fascination with it. I did at least want a closer look at it, but Father, while fighting to keep Jill at bay, flicked it into the undergrowth with his walking stick.

"Leave it be!" he said sternly. I seldom disobeyed my father when he used that tone and Jill immediately resumed her composure.

I had an immense respect for my father from as early as I can remember. During the day when he was at work, Mother effectively dissolved any anxieties solely through the fact that I instinctively recognised her as my biological mother. But after five o'clock in the evening, on Saturday afternoons and on Sundays, Father was my first choice.

Christened Richard, Victor but always known as Victor or Vic – my father was a sensible chap who often carried a plastic mackintosh in his coat pocket in case he got caught out in the rain and more often than not he'd wear a trilby hat. From the day I first set eyes on him he was bald on top with a well-trimmed, simple moustache on his upper lip. I have heard people say that he looked a little like Adolf Hitler, especially in his younger days. However, in my opinion there was only a slight resemblance and this was definitely not indicative of his manner or philosophy.

Despite the far from ideal electrical conditions in The Corner House, Vic was an electrician. He worked for a company that conveniently had premises just a few yards up Newland and a shop an equal distance away in Long Street. He also ran a one man, posh taxi company in the very early years, usually just for weddings and funerals. On evenings and weekends he gradually allowed me into his garage domain, not only to tend to a sad captive slowworm, but also to witness the big black Ford Pilot car being polished or maintained and I'd plead every weekend to have another ride in it. In retrospect it was certainly a new and no doubt strange experience for Father to have such a persistently inquisitive young boy in his life when he was nearly sixty.

That pigeon had landed in a clump of stinging nettles and its head was bent back double poking out between the leaves.

"Why?" I asked Father as I again stared at the pigeon, "why can't I have a look?" Father held my hand tight.

"Because it's dirty," he said.

"Why?" I asked – still awestruck at the bird's gaping beak.

"Cause it's nasty and you can catch diseases."

"Why did it die?" I asked while being gently coaxed away.

"Well it was probably hit by a car." I thought for a while and shoved a finger in my mouth.

"But if it was hit by a car it would be all squashed up!"

"It don't have to be squashed to be killed … it might have just got hit……" Father hesitated. "He might've got damaged inside and we can't see it …….. because it's inside. Anyway he may have just died…… everything's got to die sometime."

"Shouldn't we bury him?"

"No he'll be alright there …… then God'll take him to heaven with all the other pigeons who've died."

Despite recent feelings that it may be selfish to have our own personal 'body transfer point,' the shock of being confronted with death and the thought of the pigeon being stung by nettles, convinced me that we should pick him up; we should abandon our walk, rush back to The Corner House and quickly bury him in the flowerbed under the stone wall ready for God to work his magic. It would be so much more convenient for God. It would save him having to look all around New Road for him. I knew God looked in our backyard regularly now and had accepted it as a recognised exit point from this world – even though Jill and I had begun to realise that there must be others.

Father eventually succeeded in dragging me away and Jill, who had now gotten over her initial excitement, was obviously quite bored and puzzled at all the continuing interest in the lifeless, deceased bird.

"Can you be damaged inside and not die?" I asked after a while of deliberation. Father chuckled.

"Yes course you can .... cause the damage might not be too bad .... Or it might be mental."

Having realised that he'd made a remark that invited further complicated enquiries, Father coughed and suggested we hurry on in case we were late home for Sunday lunch.

"What's mental?" I asked.

"I'll explain to you when you're older," he said.

Luckily for Father, I instantly forgot about the dead pigeon and the word mental when Jill was let off her lead. We both tore off together across Purley startling all wildlife in the vicinity as we went. I had a job to keep up with Jill as she raced ahead, nose to the ground. But every so often she couldn't resist stopping to sniff something. Then she'd get annoyed when I overtook her.

At the end of the woodyard, as the 'under water' trees thin out and the road sweeps gently right, on the left there is a triangular road junction with a fenced off area in the middle. On this junction is an entrance to the grounds of Sherborne's second castle, known as the New Castle. Immediately next to this entrance there is the beginning of a steep, ridged area known as the slopes. If Father felt energetic we might enter the slopes through the old iron kissing gate, climb up the very steep hill and venture some way across the public footpath into Sherborne Park, from where the lake and New Castle are visible.

Perhaps we would then return to the slopes and walk along the top, under the neatly spaced trees in front of the tall iron fence that divides the public area from the private estate. About halfway along the top of the slopes, close under the fence was an old decrepit cattle trough. The ground around it was eroded and worn away from years of animal hooves. So much so that it looked precarious, elevated high up on a pedestal equal to the level that the ground once was decades before. It was full of water boatmen and algae. We'd often gaze back down at Sherborne town and Purley while Jill would be following the scent of a rabbit or perhaps another dog.

In the summer Purley is full of buttercups, daisies and celandines. The river has coots and moorhens living on it; occasionally a flash of sparkling colour confirms the presence of a kingfisher. On our Sunday rambles across Purley Father would confirm the different species and flowers while pointing with his trusty walking stick and Jill would make full inspections.

"Do you like butter?" Father asked one day.

"Rather have chocolate!" I replied.

"Come here and lets see if you like butter .... hold yer head back." From behind his back Father produced a freshly picked buttercup. He thrust it under my chin and I giggled uncontrollably while Jill barked playfully. "There we are!" he said grinning broadly and pointing convincingly under my chin, "you like butter!"

"Why?"

"Cause it shows up all yellow under your chin…….. I reckon you eat too much butter myself."

The river Yeo takes on various personas on its journey across Purley. Back at the start of the 'under water' trees where it emerges from under New Road to divide Purley from Little Purley, it trickles gently over rounded rocks where gudgeon and bullhead dart around. Jill and I would often linger on tree trunks that are obligingly bent out over the water by many years of other curious youngsters climbing on them.

Almost immediately after it enters Purley the river widens out and becomes much shallower. There are no trees or shrubs for a while and it's airy and open. In periods with less rain, areas of dry shingle appear forming islands in the middle of the river. Jill and I would paddle there and be fascinated in the summer by the swooping aerobatic displays of swallows catching insects and twittering to each other.

The water then becomes much deeper and secretive as the river narrows. Trees and brambles shroud it from the banks. There are occasional useful small trees again that grow horizontal from the banks and out across part of the river's width before sprouting skywards at a right angle. Jill got to know the exact location of the best one and would race to it to survey the almost still and peaceful water. It was here where the fleeting glint of a kingfisher could sometimes be seen as it sped like an arrow, back from a rare excursion to the more open area upstream.

After another bend or two the river runs almost parallel with the railway line. The narrow area formed between the railway and the river is matted with dense, brambly undergrowth teeming with wildlife – I called it 'no-man's-land.'

A little further downstream, towards the station and level crossing, the river, still deep, becomes very reedy where the coots and moorhens live. Father often told of large pike and eels that could be tempted from the depths using shiny, spiky lures or hooks baited with juicy wriggling lobworms.

Immediately after the reedy pike's lair the river curves under the railway, cutting short the slender strip of 'no-man's-land.' It is here where it flows into what was then an engineering works to emerge nearer the station.

A little further around New Road a road called Gashouse Hill leads from the foot of the slopes down to the railway level crossing. Part way down this hill, off to the right, if the trees are not adorned with too many leaves, the elevated ruin of the Old Castle is visible in the far distance beyond Purley.

At the bottom of Gas House Hill, Just the other side of the level crossing the platforms and main station are on the left and there is a tall signal box nearby on the right. The Woolmington Hotel, as it was then called, is positioned in the midst of the road junction on its own triangular piece of ground.

The river Yeo emerges from the engineering works on the right behind the signal box and flows briefly out of sight under the road. It quickly re-emerges in front of the hotel to immediately turn ninety degrees left and continues under the other road that goes past the station. It reappears for a few yards before hiding under the railway again.

As it leaves the engineering works the river is quite clear and occasionally Jill and I would spot a fairly large fish, its body almost stationary against the current with fins fluttering. Jill would poke her head through the metal, latticed criss-cross fence on the bridge, focus her ears and eyes and yap playfully at it. On the other side of the road the river after a storm would appear angry at being forced around its right-angled path by the gardens of The Woolmington.

The Pageant Gardens are beyond the hotel; the main entrance is opposite the station. Maybe we'd stroll up through the gravel pathways of the gardens past the bandstand to come out further around Digby Road near the police station. I would like to linger at the bandstand; I was fascinated with the storage area beneath it where they kept chairs for the band. To me it was a hideaway dungeon that would make an excellent den. Father would be embarrassed in front of the other Sunday walkers as I always fiddled and tried to open the small wooden door in the side.

Not far away is the magnificent Sherborne Abbey and on its eastern side, standing on a wide pavement called the Parade in front of the Cross Keys Hotel, is the ancient hexagonal building known as the conduit where monks once washed. Here the bottom of the town's only main street called Cheap Street, meets the town end of Long Street. The Conduit is the central axis of Sherborne and its image has evolved to be the symbol of the town. Indeed it was an image of the conduit that appeared on my solitary ceramic pot on the mantelpiece in my bedroom.

Just a few yards into the home stretch of Long Street, on the left opposite an archway and a pub called The Castle, was Harry Hunt's pushbike shop as it was affectionately known and Jill hated it. She hated it so much because we always lingered there and she got bored. The shop sold far more than just pushbikes. Whilst Father always got silently engrossed looking at special tools and spanners, I studied in great depth and longed to own the model cars, toy soldiers and steam engines. Then across in the next window, I became fascinated with older boys stuff like knives, catapults and airguns.

Jill was such an expressive dog; after thoroughly analysing every molecule of scent there near the shop front she'd stand indignantly sulking, knowing we'd be late for Sunday lunch and that she too would suffer Mother's wrath for this diabolical sin.

If we were already late for Sunday lunch we'd take a short cut from near the station into Ludbourne Road and up through Culverhayes car park. Although this by-passed Harry's shop, it took us instead past what was then the fire station. Sometimes firemen would be cleaning their fire engine and its massive front radiator grill would be poking out on to the pavement. It was a

Dennis make with large separate headlamps and running boards. It would carry men in the open on the back and its huge ladder had large wooden cartwheels attached to aid its removal.

Once when we were hurriedly walking past – late for lunch again – it took us by surprise and exploded into life; with firemen still scrambling to get on board, the beast emerged, engine roaring and its bell being manually rung. I stood rigid with excitement as it accelerated away to a chimney fire at the top of the town. The irregular clanging of the bell and throaty growl of its large petrol engine echoed and changed tone with every street it travelled in, eventually stopping somewhere in the far distance.

"There! What did you think of that?" asked Father quite excited. I just smiled and Jill wagged her tail, glad it was all over.

On rare occasions we'd start our walk before Castleton's church bell had finished clanging its invitation. This afforded us a slightly longer walk. We'd follow New Road past Gashouse Hill and the Slopes, to its end at a crossroads with Dancing Hill on the left. The road left around the foot of the hill takes you to Dorchester via West or Sherborne Hill. Straight across is a smaller road to the villages of Thornford and Yetminster. We'd always turn right, past West Mill Lane on the left and over West Bridge that spans both the railway and the river Yeo. This road becomes Westbury and leads back to Sherborne Abbey and the centre of Sherborne.

Near the crossroads, just opposite Dancing Hill, a sign on the inside edge of the pavement proclaims the town of Sherborne. If Father and I had chosen to take this longer route I would proudly announce to Mother upon our return home that we had walked outside Sherborne, even though it was only by a few inches. Walking outside Sherborne held a strange sense of achievement for me in those days, but it didn't seem to interest Mother. It seemed important to Jill though, she would always, without fail, insist on leaving a short urine message to other dogs on the posts that secured the sign.

Another favourite walk that radiated from the security of The Corner House and its backyard in those early days was around Oborne Road. We'd leave home with the Black Horse on the left. Its bar room sash windows were often open wide and the smell of stale alcohol and smoke wafted out as staff tried desperately to refresh the place from the previous night's shindig in time for serving Sunday lunch.

On the right there is the entrance to Castleton Road and then Parson's Field dipping low to a small stream full of stickleback in the mid-ground. On the far side of the field there is the railway, beyond that Castleton Church; the nearest corner of its walled cemetery just managing to hold back its precious contents from the shiny twin tracks.

The road then curves gently with a high stone wall next to the pavement on the left. The wall retains a high bank, first with allotments elevated almost level with the top of the wall and then various styles of houses, their settings landscaped in a variety of different ways. Occasional pedestrian doorways hide excavated pathways up to secretive properties.

After Parson's Field on the right and largely hidden behind bushes and trees, there is an old water pumping station originally built to provide drinking water for the town. One of the randomly placed houses near it is called The Beeches; the sky above here was often consulted as an indication of forthcoming weather conditions.

"Tis black over Beeches!" said Father one day as we started out, "good job you got yer mack on!" Father's left jacket pocket bulged as it often did, with his rolled up ancient plastic mackintosh.

Eventually the bank on the left gets smaller and likewise the wall decreases in height. This lower wall then serves to divide the front gardens of Waterloo Terrace from the pavement. The main road then curves between the buildings of Castle Farm.

Sure enough, as we reached the farm that day a few gigantic raindrops exploded around us on the dry, dusty pavement. Jill squinted and trotted closer to Father for shelter. It wasn't heavy enough yet for Father to get his trusty mackintosh out and by the time we reached the stone walled alcove in the bank on the left it had all but stopped. There were two bench seats in the alcove and two roughly spherical, well trimmed bushes around which Jill and I would play hide and seek whilst Father admired the view across the road.

When the hedge is cut low enough to see, the view opposite can be spectacular. There is a line of trees high on a ridge in the far distance, often in semi silhouette, and the old castle off at forty-five degrees to the right. Sometimes, before the sun's rays have had time to penetrate the scene, the higher parts of the castle ruin poke up through the mist that often lingers low over the continuation of the stickleback brook. As the sun takes command the railway lines are revealed now closer to the road, on the first part of a long embankment. In those days, across the land where Cromwell's soldiers once fought, steam trains chuffed by and all in a time when people still waved at trains and passengers waved back.

"Look!" I said to Father as I excitedly thrust a large toad in his face. Jill was saucer-eyed and her ears rigid, eager for any clues about this strange creature we'd found.

"Frog!" I said urgently demanding a response.

"Tha's not a frog," said Father, "tis a toad.... where did you find him?

"Over there," I said pointing to a hole in the wall.

"Well I should put him back there otherwise his mother'll wonder where he's gone."

"What's a toad?" I asked staring at the creature intently.

"Well they'm like frogs but they don't live near water like frogs do .... now put him back quickly and hurry up about it."

"Aw dad I'd like to keep him," I whined.

"You can't keep him son, it wouldn't be much of a life for him would it?.. and like I said his family's waiting for him back down there."

"I could take him out every day."

"You're not keeping him!" Father's voice was beginning to sound angry and I knew that I didn't stand a chance and I must return him. I cupped the creature in my hands and careful not to tread on Jill prancing in front of me I returned him to his home.

"Anyway," continued Father, "what about that slowworm down in the garage? You've lost interest in him haven't you and tis I who gotta feed him and tend to him!"

The toad crawled back in his hole, any raindrops had dried up under the now baking sun and I stayed sprawled out on the warm paving slabs for a while, contemplating toad family life and my lonely slowworm banged up back in the garage back home.

Oborne Road eventually joins the A30 at an acute angled junction most people call Dodge Cross. After this junction the railway curves slightly to continue running parallel to the A30 for about half a mile. It then veers under the A30 and shoots off north, skirting west of Milborne Port.

We turned left at the A30 as we always did, back towards the northern side of Sherborne. Here there was another Sherborne sign that confirmed our steps outside the town's official perimeter and provided further opportunity for Jill to leave messages that told all other dogs of our achievement.

We continued on the pavement, up the hill past huge greenhouses on the left. At the top of the hill a narrow track crosses the A30 and this is really, officially Dodge Cross.

A little further on there was another crossroads; our route took us left here down a continuation of Castletown Way, to bring us back to Waterloo Terrace by Castle Farm. There was a high bank up on the eastern side of this lane and a smaller one on the west forming a small ravine. On the top of the eastern bank, held in place by old bedsteads, corrugated tin and old garage doors was, amongst many others, Uncle Todd's allotment. These allotments and open fields stretched across to the grounds of Foster's Grammar School playing fields and a typical suburban road called The Avenue beyond.

We were just approaching this ravine when the rain started again; overhanging trees provided some shelter as the heavens opened. Father handed me Jill on the end of her lead while he hurriedly unrolled his full-length mackintosh and pulled it on. Father's emergency procedure was well rehearsed and after only a few seconds he took Jill back from me. Our pace quickened for home as the little lane turned into a river. Quite big trickles of water were seeping through the man-made barricades and flowing off the high bank from the allotments. I ran on ahead delightedly splashing through the water. I ran so far ahead – almost down to Castle Farm and Father called me back. I ran back towards them up the slight incline. Jill hated the rain and was squinting permanently; she insisted on stopping every so often and shaking herself violently. Father looked like an official at a nuclear fall-out event in his extremely long, cream plastic mackintosh.

I too squinted in the heavy raindrops. Then suddenly from the corner of my eye I saw a small animal desperately struggling up the hill against the flowing torrent. In less then a second I thought:

Mouse! Want it! Rescue it! Before that second had passed and following some irresistible primitive instinct, I flung myself forward and caught it in a move similar to a rugby tackle. Jill had struggled so much Father had let her go, she bounded up to me barking and yapping. Father, fearing I'd tripped or was suffering a fit or something, was close behind. I looked up at them both as I lay there drenched and lying in inches of water.

"Got it!" I said as a tiny, half drowned mouse's head appeared between the thumbs of my tightly cupped hands.

Despite Father's mild protests, I carried it all the way home in my pocket. I kept it in an old fishbowl for a few days and tried to feed it cheese. Mother and Aunt Flo said it wouldn't eat because it was homesick and missed its parents. Riddled with guilt and accompanied by Father, I carried it in an old glass vase back to its home under the allotments.

5

Todd's Allotment, Shopping Jaunts And Grandparents

I would occasionally spend time with Uncle Todd on his allotment. This was a mutual arrangement between Todd and my parents, presumably when Mother and Father wanted some peace alone together and I always looked forward to it.

Todd was a jolly chap who usually wore a flat cap wherever he went. He often either rode or pushed an old heavy Rudge Whitworth bicycle while wearing trouser clips near his ankles. When going to work or to his allotment he would have with him sandwiches in a battered tin box and a flask of tea, all carried in an olive-green army haversack. He was obsessed with his prize marrows and cabbages and when concentrating on their cultivation at his beloved allotment, he would often leave me to study worms or animals drowned in an old cast iron bath that Father had helped to transport there one Sunday.

I always found the bath quite surreal with its two exposed algae covered, talon feet grasping globes larger than tennis balls. Its other two feet were hidden from view because it was partly dug into the landscape to make it level. From a particular angle it looked as though it was surfing on a wave of fertile earth. I often imagined someone in it, grasping the sides for dear life as they rode the patchwork sea of allotments.

I sometimes studied the stains dripping taps had made on its inner surface over the decades and pondered over how many people, and what sort of people had bathed in it. Resting my elbows on its smooth, curved rim I would imagine myself a desperate struggling, drowning rat and contemplate how deep and slippery the sides could be.

The actual allotment shed was a male-domain den: Todd's world, which he sometimes shared with my world. Very occasionally a bunch of big boys wandering off course and up to no good would invade the allotments. Todd and I would stand just outside the doorway of our tumble-down shack and look defiant like wild mountain men defending our log cabin. Todd was very good at conveying an air of no-messing authority. The offenders would run up through the pathways between runner beans and carrots, past an old man's immaculate floral display towards us. As they got nearer, whooping and screaming, Todd – unflinching – would coolly stand his ground, hands in pockets. He had a stony stare like a Sheriff in a western movie who was about to draw his Colt 45 on the wild villains. It always worked. By the time they reached us in their drainpipe jeans and coats with collars turned up, they would be as quiet as mice. As they nervously filed past us, some adjusting an Elvis quiff, Todd would stare at each one in turn as if inspecting them.

One day, eager for a rest from digging and desperate to sample one of Aunt Flo's sandwiches, Todd made himself comfortable in his corrugated tin-roofed shack. I was bribed into sitting still for a few moments with some surprise lemonade. Todd asked me – as he often did – what I wanted to be when I grew up – as if I really had any sensible idea in those days. But I answered instantly, as I always did.

"Pop star!" I was now regularly experiencing rock 'n' roll from The Black Horse jukebox most Saturday nights and I had no doubt that expressing oneself in such a way was extremely easy, but I'd never tried it. Todd laughed his usual laugh.

"What you gonna sing then?" he asked chuckling.

"Rock 'n' Roll!"

Todd stuffed half a sandwich in his mouth and rummaged under a pile of wooden vegetable crates for his football pools form. The form fell out on the floor, as did a glossy girlie magazine spread wide there in front of us, the centrefold beauty posing almost totally naked. I had never seen a girlie magazine before. Todd recognised my astonishment as his sandwich flopped on to the floor and he hastily announced that the girl in the picture was preparing to have a bath. He scooped the publication up and thrust it quickly into his haversack. I was puzzled at the strange reclining pose of the woman. Perhaps she was having a good stretch before climbing into her bathtub. However, what I found even stranger was Todd's beetroot red face, and it wasn't a particularly hot day.

My early recollections of pre-school weekdays involved shopping with Mother and visiting Aunt Flo. Aunt Flo was Mother's sister; she was married to Todd and they both lived in one of a row of old cottages at Newell, an area of Sherborne north west of The Corner House on the outskirts of town, where Marston Road meets the A30 near The Crown Hotel.

Occasionally, again presumably when Mother wanted a break, I would stay with Flo at 89 Newell. It had become habit for anyone visiting Flo to tap on the single ground floor window, as opposed to the door, and perhaps peer in. Flo would usually recognise whoever it was and beckon them to enter her home.

One day Mother returned to pick me up and tapped on the window. I apparently was standing behind Flo on an armchair as she strained to see who was there. Mother began gesticulating furiously as I emptied the entire contents of a tin of talcum powder on to Flo's head. Flo was completely oblivious and thought Mother was trying to convey some other information, until she started sneezing uncontrollably.

The Co-operative grocery store in the main street where Mother often shopped had two substantial, polished wooden counters, one on each side of the shop. They resembled the sort of bar counters that drinks were sent sliding down in wild-west movies. Children, including myself, would be lifted up to sit on a counter for the duration of the unhurried and relaxed ordering of goods. In those days everything was ordered from, and fetched by, the person serving you. The anonymity of self-service and supermarkets was still unheard of.

All the shop staff wore white coats with pencils or pens in their top pockets and some kept a tin of sweets to offer children. Mothers looked forward to their leisurely ramble through scrawled shopping lists and discussions with their appointed member of counter staff. In between the gossiping, the recommendations for recipes and the catching up with news, staff would busily wrap cheese, slice bacon or weigh vegetables for you. It seemed to take all afternoon and probably did. But when the order was eventually finished, neatly packaged up on the counter, and when the health update on Mrs so-and-so in Newland, Long Street or Ludbourne Road was complete, the attendant would reckon up with their pencil.

"Seventeen and fourpence ha'penny please!" They would carefully place the money and their pencilled list all totalled up, in a small container attached to a strange cable transport system. It would be whisked away suspended in the air, high up to the glass-fronted cashier's office that overlooked the entire area from the first floor. There it would be taken out, checked and the change and receipt sent back down the cable.

From time to time Mother visited the Co-operative clothes shop. I would get quite bored in there. There were no sweets and it wasn't such a social meeting place as the grocery store. The women's department, where Mother spent most of her time, was on the first floor up a flight of wide stairs. Inevitably boredom often forced a lapse into my own private world and oblivion of all other people. I often found the stairs more interesting than the shop and I would loll around on them and lean my body weight in a variety of silly poses on the metal handrail. Sometimes I would place my head upside down on a stair edge and imagine the whole shop inverted. How strange it would be to see counters and clothes in their racks hanging from the ceiling. And it'd be even stranger to be able to walk around on a clean, white floor having to step over rows of lights.

The wall adjacent to these stairs was adorned with black and white posters of ladies modelling various bras and corsets. One day I was studying deeply the area around a lacy black number that covered a lady's breast in one of the posters and feeling the texture with my finger. Suddenly I was aware of an audience. My mother and all the giggling shop girls were leaning over the top banister peering at me. I saw no reason to stop my innocent examination.

"What are you doing?" asked my mother.

"Nothing," I said.

"You're a bit young for that aren't you?" asked one of the girls.

"My Uncle Todd," I said, "he's got pictures of girls before they have a bath ……. An' they ain't got no clothes on at all!"

I never knew my maternal grandparents – they passed away long before I was born. My grandmother apparently died quite young and Grandfather was lost in the Great War. However, my father's old family home where my paternal grandparents still lived was only a couple hundred yards away from The Corner

69

House up Castleton Road, on the other side of the railway bridge near the old castle in Castleton itself. There are a pair of cottages situated away from the rest, down in the field a little closer to the river and railway line. They lived in Number 8 – the one on the left. During my early life my father would visit his ageing parents at Number 8 Castleton nearly every night and for some odd reason these visits became known as 'going for the verdict.' I would also be taken to visit them from time to time and very occasionally I'd be left in their care for an hour or two.

On the short walks to my grandparents' house we often met an old lady called Molly Hobday and I eventually got to know her just as plain 'Miss Molly.' She was an extremely small, fragile looking person with a pale complexion who usually wore a fancy pink or turquoise hat and smelled of lavender. She lived with her reclusive sister in a house called Middle House situated on the opposite side of the gravel area from the church. When not stepping quickly, yet somehow hesitantly, to or from Tom Baker's post office shop in Long Street, she would spend her time surveying Castleton through the leaded glass windows of her home or listening for footsteps on the gravel outside.

Often when we approached her domain on our way to visit Number 8, she would detect us and come out with a single sweet, a flower from her garden or a small picture she had torn out of a magazine, usually of cuddly animals. She always sent me birthday and Christmas cards, even before I really knew her, typically addressed to Master Colin, Jill the dog and Tibby the cat. Her spidery handwriting resembled the way she spoke, and indeed walked, in a sort of jerky, mechanical fashion. When she had learnt that Tibby the cat had died she went to great lengths explaining how he had gone to heaven and I would meet him again one day. Jill the dog was always an excellent judge of character and loved Molly dearly.

There was always a plentiful supply of sweets from Mr and Mrs Hart who lived next-door to my grandparents in Number 7. Mrs Hart carried a large bag of them wherever she went.

"Put some in your pocket for later." She'd say and I'd race back into Number 8 – pockets bursting.

Grandfather was a tall, well built man who always wore shirts with separate collars, black mirror-bright boots and a suit. He sometimes also wore a wide brimmed hat and a long black coat. His name was Frank and he reminded me of a kind but tough peacemaker in an old western movie, similar to Todd but more of a wise marshal than a gritty sheriff. My earliest recollection of Frank, which probably stuck in my mind through deep infant curiosity, is of him wet shaving in the open air near the doorstep of Number 8 Castleton. He would make extremely exaggerated grimaces in a mirror hung from a nail in the wall, while skilfully skimming off the frothy soap and stubble from his face and neck with a horrifyingly sharp cut-throat razor.

I was very puzzled when I first encountered the pre-shaving ritual of Frank scraping his open blade razor up and down what I then thought was an old leather belt. Of course it was a strop specifically designed for the honing of razors.

Many years before I was born Frank operated a horse and cart haulage service from Sherborne Station. Then in later years he became night watchman in the castle grounds, patrolling all night with a dog. Frank was also sexton and verger at Castleton Church for 42 years until his retirement at Christmas 1953 when I was nearly eight months old. This coincided with him giving me a pocket book of Common Prayer and Hymns. Luckily this survived through my childhood unscathed and I cherish it today.

Another vital activity that Frank and his family carried out over the years and in all weathers, was the control and regulation of the flow of water from Sherborne lake into the river Yeo. Obviously dependent on rainfall, this was achieved by manually opening or closing sluice gates near the lake, not far behind Frank's home. Frank always called this 'seeing to the hatches.'

Inside Castleton Church there is a large brass candelabrum, nowadays lacquered and only requiring the occasional dusting. But apparently in my father's youth, it was an accepted regular chore for Frank and his entire family of six children, to take down the candelabrum, carefully dismantle it, thoroughly clean it and then polish it.

When Frank retired, the mowing and tending of the churchyard at Castleton and also the private graveyard of the Digby family next-door to it, was taken over by my father. Once when I was being looked after at Number 8 Castleton, Father came rushing in from his labours over at the graveyards.

"I've got something to show you!" he exclaimed excitedly. I was ushered up the gravel footpath and across the road to the church closely followed by Frank hobbling with two walking sticks. Miss Molly was alerted by all the commotion and followed us with tightly folded arms, through the big iron churchyard gates that clang shut behind you. At the far eastern edge of the graveyard behind the church is a high ivy clad wall. I was encouraged to climb the rickety old wooden ladder up to where Father had been trimming the ivy. There in the thickest part of the untrimmed growth was a perfectly rounded nest.

"Can you see 'em?" called Father from below. As I rustled the deep green leaves four or five little heads sprang up like clockwork. I was amazed that their beaks were bigger than the rest of their heads as they quivered there synchronously. I had no idea what Father or Frank were shouting by that time. I wanted to care for them and feed them chocolate, take them home in front of the fire. I eventually realised that Father was shouting as loud as he dare.

"Come down will you, you'll scare the mother away!" After I had returned to the ground we all watched silently as the hen blackbird flew closer in bolder swoops, eventually disappearing into the ivy.

"Did ee zee um?" asked Frank in his broad Dorset dialect, grinning uncontrollably.

"Yeah," I said, utterly spellbound.

"What a lovely experience for him!" said Miss Molly to no one in particular.

The event even attracted the attention of Miss Molly's sister. I'd never seen her before – a ghostly apparition with long bedraggled white hair trying to smile through the leaded glass window.

When not stupefied by the mysteries of nature I could be a little horror. For some inexplicable reason I had an obsession of throwing toy cars at Grandma. I only witnessed Grandma's final few years of life and I can only just remember her. She always wore dark clothes, which contrasted her silvery white hair. Most of her time was spent huddled in an armchair next to the black open range in the little kitchen at Number 8 Castleton. I would put my toy vehicles through their paces on or near the table top in front of her and then launch them one after the other in her direction. I can only guess that it was my frustration at her lack of interest in a Morris Oxford doing a mid-air handbrake turn, or an American Army Jeep undergoing my extreme testing of its suspension that made me do it. It never entered my head that maybe not everyone in the world wanted to – or was indeed able to – experience the thrill of toy car aerobatics.

Quite rightly Frank could take no more one day and chased me around the table with his walking stick. He never caught me and I apparently called him a sod. I had no idea what a sod was, it was just a word that I had heard when adults wanted to express anger or frustration. Everyone – including Frank – found my first utterance of an expletive quite funny and couldn't help smiling a little. This made my tantrum worse. However, Father arrived and did catch me, and it was probably the first time that I experienced a hefty clout around the ear.

Father would very occasionally hit me hard if I'd pushed him to the limits and he felt that I needed correcting. This was typical of his philosophy; if he considered something needed doing then he'd do it full force and to the best of his ability, or not bother at all. Also, if he had made a decision that something needed doing – no matter how unpleasant, controversial or disagreeable – then he'd do it and there would be no going back. It was not wise to mess with Father because he gave little warning of his intentions and there were no half measures.

If truth be known I found this strangely tantalising. I suppose it was the adrenaline buzz of experiencing that knife-edge between him being tolerant or blowing up. But I knew when I'd crossed the line. Luckily the physical punishment was swift and I usually hadn't time to realise what had happened. His hand would meet with the side of my head with a substantial force that sent me spinning into oblivion; usually just the once – and that was enough. The blow often accompanied him shouting something like, 'I'll knock your bloody head off' or his favourite was, 'I'll knock you into next week.' It was how his father had brought him up and he knew no other way. He never ever hit me for no good reason and in retrospect I probably thoroughly deserved it and indeed benefited from it.

Once I discovered another bird's nest in one of the small cherry trees that then grew up through diamond shaped beds in the wide pavement right outside The Corner House. I was riding my tiny tricycle rather dangerously, weaving in large figure of eight patterns all over the expanse of the pavement and occasionally hurtling around the corner into Long Street and back again. Pedestrians had become wary when approaching the blind corner from Long Street for fear of me colliding with them. On at least two occasions when throwing my tricycle into the corner, I had almost hit Miss Carlisle who lived a few doors away in Long Street.

On this particular day it was a trail of ants emerging from near one of the tree's roots and up the little trunk that caught my eye and made me stop dead. After gawping at them for a while I raced in the open front door and found a piece of paper. I went back and placed it in the tracks of the ants in an attempt to divert them. After a few of the insects seemed to carefully inspect it, they just crawled right on over it.

I clambered up on my tricycle, stood on the saddle and stretched up to see where they were going. The relentless stream of black ants led to a small bird's nest. To my utter horror there were three little sparrow chicks in it, writhing around in agony and covered in ants. After my initial astonishment I ran inside for Mother. She just told me to leave them alone and forbade me to go near them. I couldn't resist going back to the tree after Mother had returned inside to concentrate on her cooking.

Father came home from work and caught me trying to hook the chicks out of their nest with a stick and away from their attackers. It was too late. The tiny creatures were plastered in a thick living carpet, the only movements of their bodies being made by the flow of ants over their featherless, pink flesh. The ants had now eaten the chicks' eyelids and eyes and I wanted to study the dark holes into their dead brains and Jill also wanted a full inspection, but Father insisted on shovelling them into the dustbin. He then boiled the old iron kettle and scalded the remaining ants in their nest by the tree.

6

School

In 1958 a new and different walking expedition took place, on a route that I would take many more times, outwards and away from the security of my Corner House.

Early one morning my mother and I hurriedly walked up the hill at the start of Newland and past the rows of little cottages on each side. Towards the end of the smaller cottages on the left and not much bigger than any one of them, stood what was then the New Inn. Almost opposite the New Inn, on the site of the old Foster's Infants School that Father had attended as a boy, were the new flats where Uncle Todd and Aunt Flo were to eventually live. Foster's Infant School had become a victim of the Luftwaffe bombings of Sherborne on 30th September 1940; miraculously all the children and teachers had just gone home when the bombs fell.

Immediately past the flats on the right is a narrow dead-end track called Tinneys Lane. Up there on the left about half way along was Foster's Grammar School for boys. Its sports grounds was watched over by a wooden cricket pavilion and was divided from private houses along its north eastern edge by a rusty chain link fence where crabapples grew; the north western perimeter adjoined the allotments and an old hedge full of scramble holes for wild animals and children provided the border. The allotments spanned as far as the A30 to the north and Castletown Way near Castle Farm to the east.

On this particular day we took the next right from Newland after Tinneys Lane, which led us into The Avenue where houses are larger and some are situated in substantial grounds behind high walls. The Avenue rises up another steady hill to a sharp right angle bend to the right. But straight ahead between more walled properties there is a narrow pedestrian passageway that eventually emerges on to the busy A30 main road.

On this and indeed many more subsequent walks up The Avenue I was fascinated with the humps, hollows and patterns in the tarmac pavement. Some areas had eroded away and crumbled forming little potholes. Others had partly melted during particularly hot summers and then set again in wavy shapes. Occasional small oblong trenches had been dug to take various services into houses and these had been re-surfaced with a more coarse and dark tarmac. As I was half dragged along, certain shapes of tarmac randomly became black hellholes and to step on one would mean a doom I couldn't comprehend. My insistence to only step on to the safe 'solid' areas meant leaping and dancing all over the place. My antics annoyed Mother intensely as she pulled me up the hill, muttering all the way that that we would be late.

My first of many encounters with the crossing patrol man on the main road instantly made me act more sensibly when he grabbed my earlobe and prepared to forcefully lead me across the busy A30. He was a small red-faced man who reminded me of a large toad. He appeared to have a constantly startled expression on his face and his flat-topped white cap was far too big for him. He mumbled unintelligible things as he rubbed my ear hard between his finger and thumb in a vice-like grip. His mumblings grew louder and his grip even tighter as he thrust his lollypop pole into the road and more cars queued for us. He dumped me on the pavement on the other side of the road and Mother was close behind.

A little further up yet another hill called Wooton Grove and amongst red brick houses of suburbia, there is a crossroads where Wooton Grove becomes Simons Road. Here, on the far right corner, stood what was then Simons Road County Primary School.

It was a fairly typical primary school of the 1950s. Its main building matched the surrounding houses in the same red brick and stood within the confines of high walls and black, wrought iron fencing. To the north of the main building on a gentle slope was the boys' playground and to the south was the L shaped girls' playground. These tarmac play areas were separated at the rear by wooden, yet quite permanent looking classrooms and more black iron fencing. In the front, bordering Simons Road was a garden with a small, white weather station in it that maintained the external separation of the sexes.

As we entered through the large iron gates of the boys' playground, I noticed one of the tallest towering windows had semi-transparent paintings by budding young artists stuck to the lower panes. We ventured across the yard to a cream painted prefabricated concrete building that housed the infants.

Miss Brown met us in one of the classrooms within this building. She seemed harmless enough and we were allowed to do anything we wanted – within reason. I can't remember any major concern about Mother leaving and I soon got used to Miss Brown's classroom world amid the mixed smells of crayons, plasticine and floor polish.

Miss Brown was good at encouraging play – even the solitary type – and before I knew it break time had arrived. I enjoyed a small chocolate bar and was rather surprised to receive a third of a pint of milk with a straw. We peered at each other sucking urgently until most bottles were empty and the straws hung damaged, limp and moist. I had never been in the company of so many other children before and I was intimidated by their stares. It never crossed my mind that I might be staring at them too.

I was far too scared to ask to go for a pee and spent most of the rest of the morning holding myself. Eventually it must have shown because Miss Brown asked me if I wanted to go to the toilet. I was terror-stricken and just stared at her wide-eyed and unable to even blink. I was about to say no; I only knew of toilet and bodily functions as a private taboo thing that happened shut away outside in our backyard. Then Miss Brown smiled and I mumbled,

"Yeah I do!" It was surprisingly simple. No one seemed too bothered. The girl at the next desk was totally engrossed in the finishing touches of her wax crayon abstract masterpiece to even notice.

I suppose I must have taken something in at infant school as play gradually included a little learning. I remember going home one day and telling Mother in great detail that there was a man who lived up in the sky and his name was Jesus. He looked down on us all and he knew if we were naughty 'cause Miss Brown said.

I soon started to notice the variety of bicycles that other children were riding to school. Very soon it became an urgent priority for me to acquire one and learn how to ride it. It was my first Christmas after starting school when Father bought me a second-hand heavy little bicycle. It had no gears and resembled a small Post Office or MOD bike. It looked as though it should be black, olive-green or red in colour, but instead it was a light shade of blue and white. I eventually learnt to ride it across the large lawn in the grounds of the house where Mother worked part-time as a cleaner.

Mother's employers were on holiday and trusted my mother to look after things. I remember wobbling nervously around, but for ages I could never manage more than a few feet. Until that is, for some reason it dawned on me that if I turned the handlebars a little left, a little right, depending on which direction I felt I was falling, constantly updating as I pedalled; then I could manage to ride the entire length of the lawn. I was soon racing to school on my bike and tearing around doing rear wheel skid-turns.

But things grew harder as school progressed, morning assembly became compulsory and interaction with other pupils was expected. The first five years of my life were seriously lacking in contact with kids of my own age. Therefore I had no idea whatsoever about playing sociably and how one should react to other boisterous children. A lot of time in my first year at school was taken up by being puzzled and mystified at social interaction, or rather the lack of it on my part. Nonetheless, it wasn't long before I started mimicking other boys, racing around the playground arms outstretched making a noise that was supposed to sound like an aircraft engine; or patting my mouth with fingers while emitting a high-pitched note. It was a while before I realised that this was what wild Red Indians did – all the time it seemed.

I suppose I was a little terror in my own way, but I never deserved the beatings, jibes and humiliation meted out to me after emerging from under Miss Brown's wing. Indeed it was immediately after progressing from the safety of Miss Brown's class that my first taste of teacher brutality occurred. I had been off school ill for a week. The doctor said I was anaemic and prescribed iron supplement medicine whilst Mother insisted on administering a daily regime of cod liver oil and liquid paraffin. This twice-daily concoction made me extremely thirsty. By now I had learnt that wanting to go to the toilet was a perfectly normal thing, so half way through an arithmetic lesson I plucked up enough courage to ask to be excused. Then on my way back across the playground I plunged my face into the drinking fountain there by the boys' entrance. I was engrossed in the heavenly quenching of the cool clean water when the boys' entrance door swung open with a familiar creak. I instantly turned my head with my body still bent over the fountain in time to see the headmaster lunge towards me and slap the back of my bare legs three times in quick succession.

"You're the pest of the school!" he shouted. I nearly choked before swinging around to face him. Instinctively I sort of stood to attention, water dribbling down my face and my legs were beginning to burn and sting. I was so shocked.

"Get to your class!" he blared - eyes wild. I had no idea we were only suppose to drink at break times.

We were encouraged to carry our PE kit in little cloth bags that had elastic threaded through the top. My favourite activity was to launch my empty bag from the back of a chair using the force of the outstretched elastic. On one occasion the bag went higher than ever and lodged on a rafter up in the open roof structure of classroom two. I received my first beating with the slipper for that – well it was always referred to as the slipper but it was actually an old plimsoll. It didn't really hurt that much but the whole class was made to watch and it was very humiliating to say the least.

I soon developed a sickening dread of the bad teachers and they a deep hate of me. I'm sure they assumed that my lack of words in the classroom was due to ignorance and shortage of intelligence, whereas if truth were known, I had developed quite a bad stammer. I would avoid speaking whenever possible and if questioned I would often pretend that I had either forgotten or didn't know the answer. I began to gradually rebel when unsupervised and retreat into my shell when in the presence of so-called authority.

Humiliation was seldom more prevalent than during morning assembly. It was of course an excellent opportunity for the headmaster to pick out individuals and make an example of them in front of the whole school. This occurred nearly every morning and there was always the fear of the ultimate slipper punishment lurking in the back of each child's mind.

I hadn't really made any true friends yet, but there was one boy called Peter who seemed gentle and friendly. I learnt years later that he was an only child too. One morning I was standing next to Peter in assembly and he seemed very fidgety and nervous. I couldn't ask him what was wrong – no talking allowed. Then the headmaster started ranting about the subject of school holidays and how we must tell our parents only to book vacations within the allotted time. Unbeknown to me, Peter's parents had requested he take his summer holidays a few days early to coincide with an important family event.

"Holidays must be taken within the six week period...." continued the headmaster thumping his reminder notes with every syllable. Then came a terrible silence when any little rustle of clothes could be heard. I looked at Peter and he was quite pale and his face was in a grimace.

"There is one boy here," said the headmaster slowly, "he knows who he is...."

To my horror from the corner of my eye I saw Peter toppling forwards. I turned towards him just in time to see him spew the contents of his stomach over the back of the boy in front of us. It gushed from his mouth with such force that it also splashed on boys two rows ahead of us. For a few short seconds Peter clung feebly to the grey jumper of the astonished boy who had taken the main blast, but then slumped to the floor – lifeless.

After the headmaster had realised that Peter did not need punishing but urgent help, the formal atmosphere turned to pandemonium. A teacher placed Peter in the recovery position as we bewildered youngsters stumbled around in pools of warm, smelly sick.

The deputy head appeared and made a hideous face as he lightly tiptoed through the awful mess like a fairy. Then while holding his nose he scattered pages of newspaper on to the wooden criss-cross floor tiles in a vain attempt to soak things up. Eventually cleaning ladies arrived from the canteen with mop buckets. Peter was fine eventually. He had fainted and been sick through sheer terror.

The Simons Road school playing fields were situated on the other side of a public footpath behind the main buildings. There was also another completely separate building on the edge of these playing fields that looked quite similar to the infant block and this building was the school canteen. I was deemed to live close enough to the school to walk or cycle home at midday. Therefore I never got to sample meals in the canteen. However, I do remember the snaking line of other children going to and from the canteen as I was leaving or returning to school. I also remember occasionally visiting the canteen to pick up a tray of tea for teachers mid-morning.

There was a rota system whereby pupils took it in turns every so often to convey tea into the staff room. When it was my turn I dreaded it more than going to the dentist. Walking back across the rough public footpath, down the slope of the rear playground balancing a tray of tea while being intimidated by other children was a nightmare. Often the rear door into the main building would be closed which of course made things quite awkward when holding a tray of precious tea. The last treacherous part was down the large three or four steps into the smoky little staff room in the very heart of the school.

Then came the inquisition rather like entering as a defendant into a courtroom. One particular day I breathed a sigh of relief as I dumped the tray unceremoniously on to the table. I looked up and shuddered at all those pairs of eyes inspecting me. The headmaster was typically lolling at the head of the assembled staff meeting and uttered forth what had become his favourite remark whenever he came across me.

"Ah..... Park the pest of the school!" Sitting next to him on that day was someone whom I thought at that time was a good teacher, an extremely tall, older woman with fluffy silver hair. She wore wire-rimmed spectacles with small, dark lenses that were a decade too soon in terms of trendiness.

"But he does write some lovely things!" she retorted. I fiddled with my fingers and gradually began to realise that the teacher's remark was indeed a compliment.

"Where are you going on holiday this year?" asked the headmaster. I had recently overheard Father expressing his interest in Llandudno, North Wales. I wasn't sure if he was seriously considering going there, but it seemed a feasible answer. So in a typical Dorset accent I replied,

"Wales." The letter W was not a particularly difficult letter for me to utter, nonetheless I was still quite pleased with myself.

"Is that Wales or Wells?" asked the headmaster precisely emphasising the correct pronunciation of each place. I looked up from my feet and again saw all those eyes. The extremely tall lady was smiling slightly, Miss Warner raised her eyebrows in encouragement and the deputy head frowned intensely and stirred his tea. I became flustered.

"Wells," I must have said.

"A fine city," said the headmaster, "will you visit the cathedral?"

"Yes sir." I couldn't be bothered to put things right – I just wanted to get out.

"OK – off you go," sighed the headmaster. It was obvious that he knew full well that I had meant Wales.

Early in primary school there were three teachers of whom I developed a healthy respect: the extremely tall woman with fluffy white hair and dark spectacles, a mild-mannered man who reminded me of Roy Orbison and another wonderful lady called Miss Warner who ran class one juniors. These were the only teachers who gave me any sort of encouragement or showed any inkling of understanding. Indeed it was the lovely Miss Warner who took it upon herself to teach me to read and write.

Due partly to my natural wandering mind in some lessons, the state of trepidation I experienced in others and the amount of time I was absent from school – sick with chest infections and bronchitis – I fell way behind. The remarkable Miss Warner, by giving up her break times, managed to encourage my reading and make it interesting for me. For this I remain eternally grateful.

To the other extreme there was the detestable so-called teacher who was the deputy headmaster. I cannot even remember what he was supposed to be teaching us. He certainly cured my wandering mind during his lessons, but at the expense of total fear. In his sessions he would make us sit for hours in silence. Often the only sound I was aware of was my own tongue desperately trying to lubricate my parched mouth. He kept that school slipper – which was actually a plimsoll – on his desk and he would regularly, purposely startle us by very suddenly grabbing it and banging it on his desk as hard as he could; his excited face – eyes bursting – would dissolve into a sickly smile. I'm convinced he needed psychiatric treatment.

A television sitcom called The Rag Trade began appearing on our very first second-hand TV at home. As far as I remember the snowy, barely watchable black and white images portrayed a clothes factory and at least once in every episode the shop floor supervisor would blow a whistle and shout 'Everybody Out!' This perhaps indicated a break, the end of the shift or maybe a call for a wildcat strike. My mother became addicted to the programme and Father found the whistle and the programme's catchphrase extremely funny. In fact Father was forever shouting 'Everybody Out!' The two words seldom made sense within the context he used them. However, I think it was the wake-up effect of the tone of voice the phrase demanded that he sometimes thought appropriate, but more often than not, just amusing.

Consequently it was not so very surprising that during a certain wet, winter break time at school, after the teacher had blown his Thunderer PE whistle to an empty playground, I spontaneously and without thinking, shouted at the top of my voice, "Everybody Out!"

The enraged deputy head in his rain-sodden gabardine raincoat demanded to know who had dared to utter a sound after his whistle had been blown and I was eagerly 'told on' by my 'classmates.' They even pointed me out as I huddled at the back of the cloakroom trying to hide amongst the wet coats.

I was dragged out in front of the whole school again and – witnessed by another awful woman teacher who wore her hair in ridiculously tight plaits that resembled headphones – I was laid across the deputy's knee and beaten with the slipper. I honestly didn't think of it as being so very wrong – breaking the ritualistic, wide-eyed silence of the pre-school whistle in such a way. In fact I thought it brought a bit of innocent fun to a dull, wet afternoon.

The whistle was always blown outside at the start of school both morning and afternoon regardless of the weather or if there was actually anyone in the playground. In the summer months when the yard was full of fighter pilots, cowboys and red Indians, each child was instructed to stop dead upon first hearing the whistle. This applied whether you were on a reconnaissance swoop near the drinking fountain, the county sheriff transporting prisoners or – as was often the case with me – racing a toy car down the tarmac slope of the playground.

"You jolly well stop what you are doing – instantly!" the headmaster had reiterated in assembly many times.

My blue and gold Ferrari or green Alfa Romeo occasionally truckled on over the storm drain near the bottom of the sloped tarmac long after the whistle had sounded, much to the annoyance of the deputy headmaster. Once in the frightening frozen moments after the whistle, my racing car continued further to collide with the wall of the main building. The last moments of the crash provided the only sound, echoing obtrusively around the schoolyard. I felt the deputy head turn towards me. I turned and faced him. He glared at me and then he insisted on a minute of utter silence as if to reiterate my stupidity and contemplate the damaged toy car there on its side.

I found this stopping what you're doing instantly procedure both ridiculous and hilarious. What if you were jumping up in the air when the whistle sounded? Would you be reprimanded for landing back down on the ground? What if you were doing handstands against the wall? Were you to remain upside down? Boys didn't seem to do handstands but girls in the other playground did them all the time. I never discovered how they got on when they heard the whistle.

Some boys really took the instruction literally. At the sound of the whistle there was often a yard full of boys stopped in their tracks and holding silly poses. Red Indians with fingers stuck on lips, pilots arms outstretched in a statuesque frozen glide.

One day I was around the back of the school walking out of the boys' toilets when the whistle sounded. I slowed to a shuffle. Another boy – I can't imagine what he'd been doing – was standing left hand on hip and the other arm outstretched. He looked rather like an effeminate policeman directing traffic and he seemed afraid to breathe. I carried on walking very slowly towards the school – nobody could see me around the back I thought. Then I heard the metallic groan of a window opening nearby in the cream painted infants' block. The woman with the hair plaits like a WW2 aircraft pilot's headphones appeared at the window.

"Stay where you are!" she shouted, "stay where you are!" she mouthed again grossly exaggerating each syllable and aiming her index finger very precisely at me.

Soon she arrived outside next to me.

"Why did you move after the whistle?" she enquired with such a frown it must have been hurting her.

"I don't know," I said. There was never any point in trying to put forward any sort of explanation, view or defence. So 'I don't know' became the standard reply. It became almost customary. Then the head and the deputy head arrived.

"He was moving after the whistle headmaster," said the woman, "I have questioned him and he says he does not know why he was moving." Like a dangerous criminal – handcuffs the only thing missing – I was escorted to the school hall for a public beating with that slipper again.

I received the slipper countless times. Once for forgetting the school sports team I was a member of – in actual fact I couldn't say the name Dickens in front of the class. Also for being caught by the headmaster inadvertently peeing directly on to a disinfectant block in the boys' urinal. Sometimes a less public beating in the headmaster's study substituted one witnessed by an audience. This meant an awful, stomach-churning wait standing in the corridor. But worse was the fact that a teacher's elderly father who seemed to live in the head's study during the day, would always watch while smoking his pipe – in retrospect highly questionable.

Another despicable weapon used by teachers – even the extremely tall woman with fluffy white hair and dark glasses – was the wooden ruler. One day we were set some sort of word exercise. I think we were given a few big words, told to look them all up in the dictionary and then include them in a short written piece. Susan was very pleased with herself. I remember vividly the proud look on her face as she read her masterpiece to the class. She retained a broad smile of satisfaction as the teacher walked to the front of the class and then approached her from behind. It was so very obvious that Susan thought she was about to be praised for her work. None of us were prepared for the teacher whipping out a ruler and slapping Susan hard numerous times across the back of her bare legs. There was the instantly recognisable mixture of utter astonishment, pain and then resentment in Susan's face as she fought hard to control her tears.

Susan was made to stand there facing the class for ages ensuring that we all witnessed the poor girl's distress and humiliation in full. I never thought the same of the extremely tall woman teacher after that. None of us knew why she found Susan's work so disagreeable – we were far too scared to ask or learn anything from such techniques. That unexpected occurrence also went some way in breeding an unfounded mistrust in other good teachers, thus ruining the learning process even further.

The same ogre who enjoyed frightening us so much with the slipper – and indeed was usually responsible for administering it – was also the PE and Games teacher. It soon became apparent to him and other pupils that there was no point in trying to encourage me to play football. I could not muster an ounce of enthusiasm for chasing a ball around a hard frosty field whilst bare legged and frozen to the bone. I was often placed in goal and would pray that the two packs would fight it out down the other end of the pitch, shake hands and leave me in peace. Even on warmer days I could be found lying on the ground between the goalposts studying a blade of grass or a strange insect – maybe just gazing up at passing clouds or far away birds. Inevitably the dispute would return to my end of the field and a ball would disturb my world by whistling past me and into the back of the net. That deputy headmaster actively encouraged the fury of some of those boys and their discomposure was almost equal to today's soccer hooligans.

In later years at primary school I began to treat everything as a joke. The 'multi-talented' deputy head began to take us for a lesson each week called craftwork. It was held at the rear of the school in one of the wooden classrooms. All we ever did was cane weaving. After the first trays had been made for parents at Christmas, the vast majority of the less than perfect ones were banned from distribution and recycled; the wooden bases used again and the scruffy, untidy mess of part weaved cane discarded.

The handful of pupils who had made trays that were deemed good enough to be given to parents were allowed to progress to proper baskets. But few were ever finished. There were abandoned and forgotten remnants of overambitious pieces of work from children who had long since left the school, strung from the high rafters of the classroom; kept it seemed, just in case some successful former pupil should ever return to claim their unfinished masterpiece.

It evolved that in our year, most of us stood at our benches and mucked around, only very occasionally bothering to do any weaving. For some reason the deputy head was more relaxed in this lesson; I think he thought of it as a feminine and pointless pursuit, something he had to contend with but had no real interest in. We received no encouragement from him. He often yawned and read his newspaper.

One day we were filing into the wooden classroom for our boring half-hearted attempt at basket weaving. The deputy head was standing at the front as usual. As I approached my area of bench I felt the need to break wind. My father had always been of the opinion that people should never hold back from breaking wind, so I bit my lip and farted. I genuinely had no idea it would be so loud. It echoed out around the classroom and I instantly dived for cover on the floor and pretended to be looking for something in the rack under the big heavy bench. I guess I thought it would save me somehow – being out of sight. But I needn't of worried, amid the sniffles of other children trying to control their giggles, I eventually peeped up over the bench at the teacher. I could feel other pupils bursting with the need to tell on me. But the deputy head carried on as if nothing had happened. He looked at me expressionless once or twice as I straightened myself up and stopped fiddling below the bench.

Maybe he'd become fed up with punishing me, or maybe he was of the opinion that a natural biological function such as breaking wind did not warrant any sort of punishment. Surely at least he should have invited me to say pardon to everyone for misjudging the loudness of my deed.

The school held a jumble sale one Saturday in the main hall and I bought a large oblong wooden radio covered in wrinkly, black vinyl. I paid sixpence for it and to my astonishment – after erecting a makeshift aerial around the picture rail of my bedroom – it worked.

One night in my room – much to Father's horror – I found Radio Luxembourg 'The Station Of The Stars.' The old medium wave reception was not exactly excellent and the broadcast would often fade and become distorted. I imagined the DJ and his friends singing 'Radio luck lucky Luxembourg' in their studio and the radio waves being battered and bashed across the sea all the way into my little room.

I guess internal combustion engines were not electrically suppressed so effectively in those days and radio design was obviously not as advanced. Whatever the reason there was much interference. My father called some of this interference 'motor boating' and it was so commonplace on mains radios at home that it hardly bothered us.

My radio replaced – at least for a short while – the need to witness the late night goings on at the pub, but Father hated it. Inevitably I would fall asleep listening to Luxembourg to be awoken by Father shouting,

"Turn that bloody thing off!" Before I had properly re-awakened Father would pull the plug himself and the likes of Roy Orbison's Only The Lonely, Brenda Lee's Sweet Nuthins' or The Dave Clark Five's Glad All Over would gradually die through lack of electricity.

After a month Father could stand it no more and the radio was confiscated. The old purple cotton covered flex that used to be the aerial still hung from the picture rail as a sad reminder and my bedroom was now always silent. Father locked the radio in the passageway that ran from the front room to the backyard. I managed to catch a glimpse of it a couple times when Father was fetching firewood. I was so sad when I noticed it was getting damp and had mildew growing on its top.

The mystery of early primary school was endured, as was the crossing patrol man's tight grasping of my ear as he led me across the A30 highway four times a day. There was in retrospect at least one sweet and touching moment at primary school I will never forget. It was my birthday and earlier in the day I had reluctantly had the fact publicised in class for some reason. I was then walking home after school along the pavement next to the low wall with black railings on the edge of the schoolyard. Around the corner ran Sandra, straight towards me. She crouched before me and beckoned that I crouch down by the wall too – so that we wouldn't be seen from the school. She handed me a scruffy little envelope and instantly kissed me on the cheek before running away. I can recall some parents laughing at us on the street corner opposite, which made me feel quite self-conscious.

When I got home the package contained a piece of bubble gum, a penny chew and a note in best joined up writing that simple read 'Love Sandra XXX.' I hardly knew Sandra and indeed didn't want to know any girls yet. Little did I know what was to come before leaving school.

7

Portland Bill

Earlier thoughts of a holiday in North Wales were abandoned in favour of a destination closer to home. The decision was I think much influenced by the fact that the shorter car journey was far more acceptable to my elderly grandparents, who Father had now invited to come with us. In retrospect it was obvious that Father was well aware of his parents' advancing years and knew it could well be their last holiday and their last glimpse of the sea.

It is the earliest holiday I can actually remember in any sort of detail. My parents, grandparents, Jill the dog and I went to Portland Bill for a week. We all squeezed into Father's Ford Pilot and took off one Saturday morning. I was far too excited to think about throwing toy cars around, but as a precaution I was kept under control on the back seat squeezed tightly between Mother and a locked backdoor. Jill was on Mother's lap and was constantly struggling to poke her nose out of the window. The thing we hadn't contemplated was Jill's inability to travel in cars. Every few miles she was sick. It was a yellow frothy sick and Mother soon ran out of tissues and patience. After a while Father managed to predict roughly how long the poor dog could go before being sick again; he would then try to stop the car beforehand.

The Isle of Portland – which is actually a peninsula connected to the mainland by part of Chesel Beach – forms a rugged, windswept extremity of Dorset, England. Near the very end, jutting even further south into the English Channel is Portland Bill. There the famous lighthouse stands proud, painted bright white and red. In those days there was just a row of fishermen's cottages, a tumble-down wooden café and a pub. Also, sprinkled randomly around on the course, rough grass – amid immovable chunks of Portland Stone – were wooden holiday huts, not much stouter than garden sheds.

Not far from the lighthouse Father nursed his beloved Ford Pilot off the main road and down a pebble covered track towards two holiday huts he'd managed to rent. Despite being driven at walking pace the car's tyres scrunched and sent small pebbles pinging.

Jill was the first to scramble out of the car and her inquisitive sniffing under the huts seemed to take her mind off the fact that she was still being sick every few minutes. After eating grass and spitting it out again she seemed to fully recover and ran off towards the cliff edge, closely followed by me.

Jill and I stopped dead in amazement. We were totally oblivious to Mother shouting at the top of her voice. Nearer the foot of the cliffs was a little fishing boat with men in it being hauled up from the deep blue sea by a wooden, hand-cranked crane that was built steadfast into a lower ledge of the craggy rock. The wind caught my breath and Jill squinted hard at the men and the new collection of fresh smells made her sneeze loudly. I hardly noticed Father arrive and put an arm around me. Jill and I had watched a large seagull land nearby, almost at touching distance. Jill couldn't resist it, she lunged forward at it but the bird effortlessly spread its massive wings and glided out across the sea. Precariously close to the cliff edge, Jill watched it for ages – mesmerised.

I wanted to go down and see the boat, the crabs and the lobsters it had landed. I wanted to climb up the lighthouse, get an ice cream from the café and throw pebbles in the sea – all at the same time. Then Mother arrived and scolded me for running off. She said we must go back to the side-by-side huts, make the beds and have a cup of tea.

Ours was a cosy little hut – a proper bed each for Mother and Father and a little bunk bed for me. The hut next-door had a little sheltered veranda with deck chairs. Grandma Eliza and Grandpa Frank spent all of their time relaxing there. It really was home from home.

The first morning Father was up early as usual. When I awoke he was stirring the pot of tea he'd made on the camping stove we had brought with us. Apparently Father had arranged to reserve a newspaper down at the café; so after breakfast – even though it was still only about six o'clock in the morning and a little foggy – Jill and I strolled with him to fetch it.

After picking up the newspaper we walked just a little further to the foot of the lighthouse, just to be able to stand right next to it for a few moments. Jill was off on the track of a hundred smells, totally engrossed in her own dog world. I was awestruck at the sheer height of the structure. When I looked up at it the passing clouds gave the very convincing illusion that it and I, were falling over.

I was studying the fragile looking guardrail on the very edge of the top walkway around the perimeter of the massive lamp when the foghorn went off. My reflexes made me sort of duck and fall over at the same time. I had never experienced anything quite so loud before and it took me by total surprise. In fact it gave me such a fright I felt quite peculiar. The first blast lasted a few seconds as it echoed out across the sea. It wasn't only the loudness, but it had a sort of grotesque tone too. Each bellow would take a couple of seconds to attain full power rather like a claxon but many octaves lower and many decibels louder. It would then stop abruptly which exemplified the echo. It was such a low note I could actually feel it with all my senses. To me it was nothing other than a hideous messenger of impending doom. Father's reaction was to force a laugh but he was obviously as shocked as I was. It went off two or three more times and even though it sounded so strange, I eventually got quite used to it. Then we turned to go and realised we had lost Jill. She was nowhere to be seen.

I ran around the other side of the lighthouse calling her name. I ran all around the edge of the rocks again shouting while Father constantly reminded me not to go too near the edge. My heart sank as I saw a lifeless form on the rough platform of rock below. The sea occasionally trickled up across this barnacle-covered ledge and gently nudged the body. We found a safe pathway down a little closer to it. I felt very sick. But I was so relieved when the tide swirled it around as we got closer and Father was able to recognise the outline of a large, dead guillemot. Father lost his paper somewhere in all the confusion as we scrambled back up the rocks. We asked in the café about Jill to no avail. I just kept calling her name.

Back at the huts everyone was up, awoken earlier by the foghorn. I was frantic and Father tried to tell me a story of a dog he had once looked after for Grandpa. He said it was a dog being trained to accompany Grandpa's nightly patrols around Sherborne castle grounds. Apparently the poor thing had been scared by thunder and had disappeared for two days. Father had left the dog's basket outside for two nights and on the second night the dog had returned and curled up in its bed quite content.

As I returned to the doorstep of the hut struggling with Jill's basket to put outside, I heard movement under the car. I rushed over and there she was shivering uncontrollably, crouched close to the ground. She eventually inched her way out still crawling with her belly skimming the short, weathered grass. I hugged her and hugged her and she cautiously licked my ear.

Soon I was collecting Father's paper on my own with Jill each morning – I think Mother and Father enjoyed the little time on their own. I kept Jill on a lead and if 'Moaning Minnie' the foghorn – as we had named it – went off, Jill was reasonable about it as long as I comforted and reassured her. Nonetheless, she would still sort of walk on tiptoe as if she didn't want to disturb this noisy great monster or encroach upon its territory.

We got to know the old chap in the café quite well and unbeknown to Mother or Father he would give us chocolate each morning. Jill and I would sit on the rocks sharing the chocolate, pondering over the vast expanse of sea.

On an early morning ramble after we'd eaten our chocolate and with Father's paper tucked down my trousers, Jill and I found a way down to a ledge of rock right next to the sea. The waves would slap up against the crevices and rock face sometimes causing a spurt of frothy surf. The sea could be heard rumbling around in caves under the rocks on which we stood. Occasionally we came across small holes and cracks down into these caves. Often the sea's only escape when forced by the tide into one of these underground sumps was up through one of these apertures. If the tide's thrust caught the water in the sump just right, this would cause a much bigger spurt in the form of a short-lived but powerful fountain high up into the air.

Apart from the fascination of getting as close as possible to the boiling surf, I had a burning, inquisitive urge to find that dead guillemot we'd seen a few days before. Jill had great problems walking on the rocks. Some rocks were smooth and slippery and others were rough and sharp. I found it much easier for both of us if I let her off the lead, that way we could pick our own individually suited routes across the difficult terrain.

My quest to find the dead bird was cut short when quite by chance we found a large dry fissure going from the seashore inland. In retrospect it was so very dangerous but as a small boy I saw little fear. The crack in the rock was just big enough for Jill and I to walk into and it seemed only the highest tide could ever reach inside.

It was eerie. It smelled of seaweed and the battering sea could be heard below and around us in those sumps and caves. Jill hesitated on each rock as we ventured further up the crevice. Father's paper fell from my belt and slipped down through a little slit in the rock never to be seen again. I did think about going back but I had heard about ocean tides and how they could trap people and I'm sure I could hear the sea entering this particular crevice back where we came in. I was in a dilemma. I kept telling myself that the walls had no water marks or algae so it would be an exceptionally high tide required for sea to enter the crevice. On the other hand I was sure I could hear the sea, not only pounding under and around us but back at the mouth of the crevice. If we went back we may meet the sea coming in and it would also use up valuable time. But was there a way out ahead?

Jill had one of her 'I told you so' expressions on her face and she was not happy jumping from rock to rock. We kept going. Daylight had all but disappeared and then reappeared as a slit above us. The floor of the crevice led down some way and as I tried to speed up our passage I noticed green algae on the rocks. The sea had indeed recently found its way into this lower section. This made me quicken up like a mechanical robot, my mind fixed on nothing else but getting out. It was now probably further to go back than carry on. I told Jill that there had to be a way out ahead and we must carry on – quickly.

A little trickle of sea reached us somehow. It just welled up and settled in pools between the rocks. I stumbled and noticed my soaking ruined sandals and trousers.

"Come on Jill!" I shouted. My voice reverberated around the cave. We soldiered on and the walls of rock opened out a little so that it made it feel less claustrophobic. However, the overhang of rock above us made the slender crack of daylight appear even further away. Then there on the floor half covered in seaweed was a small child's blue, plastic beach sandal. Jill seemed to know it was of human origin as she very carefully sniffed it and looked at me in dismay.

Eventually the floor led upwards and there was more evidence of civilisation like beer cans and ice cream wrappers. The air smelled fresher and daylight was closer above. By now it was later in the morning and I could hear voices. Around a jagged bend ahead the floor rose up sharply and the crevice ended abruptly about six feet below ground level, somewhere inland.

I felt I could just about make it out but Jill would be the problem. She hated being picked up but seemed to resign herself to the fact that it was the only way out. She grimaced as I hauled her for all I was worth skyward. I leant her as gently as I could against the crumbling rock and encouraged her to leap and make her escape. Her front paws were just about reaching the ground above. Then she plucked up courage and leapt. In the process the desperate struggling of her rear legs scraping the rock for traction meant a paw nearly took my eye out. I closed my eyes and shoved as hard as I could on her bottom while getting showered with dirt and she just about made it.

I climbed out after her to the utter astonishment of people standing nearby. Jill shook herself violently as if to permanently shake off any remaining psychological effects that confinement in the crevice had produced. We raced back to the café where my persistent begging resulted in me being given another newspaper for free.

Mother had a fit back at the hut.

"Where have you been?" she shouted, "just look at you!" She didn't give me a chance to answer. She ranted and raved about the cost of my sandals and the state of my torn and filthy trousers. She eventually calmed down a little.

"What have you been doing?" she asked again. This time she paused inviting an answer.

"Nothing," I said.

Both Jill and I were enjoying a wonderful holiday. We ran nearly everywhere on Portland Bill with the sea breeze and salt air in our faces. We were astonished at the live crabs and lobsters hauled up in those little fishing boats. We got to know the sound of the wooden crane cranking a boat from the swell of the clear sea. We never tired of inspecting those wriggling pink and black creatures from the deep. We grew to like 'Moaning Minnie's' blasts out to sea. Rather than a bringer of doom, I now likened the sound to a friendly giant blowing a much-amplified single reverberating note on a gigantic tuba or sousaphone.

Father let me stay up late one night to see the lighthouse beam stretch out across the sea and back again. Part of its warning cycle sent the beam flickering across our hut and the ones nearby, forming long dark shadows on the land. Father said it was like the searchlight in a prison camp. Jill eventually got used to it but I think at first she thought it was lightning and cowered fearfully in anticipation of the bangs.

Then one night I awoke with a start to find Father moaning and Mother whispering. Jill lay curled in her basket with her nose nestling in her tail, but she was alert with concerned eyes. The flickering oil lamp revealed Father standing on the floor but bent forwards on to the bed with his head buried in pillows. I looked at the alarm clock next to my bunk bed. It was half past four in the morning.

"Go back to sleep!" whispered Mother as Father let out another almighty moan.

"What's the matter?" I asked.

"Nothing," Mother said as she sat on the bed looking worried. I got out of bed and Jill immediately got out of her basket ready for action.

"Now look what you've done!" said Mother, "you've woken the dog up."

"She was already awake," I remarked, "anyway what's up?" I enquired again.

"Toothache!" came the just recognisable muffled reply from under a pillow. Father was in such pain he said he wanted to be left alone. It was obviously unbearable, excruciating pain. For some inexplicable reason he mumbled that he didn't even want us in the hut. I had never seen anyone, let alone my father like this. In-between moaning uncontrollably, he just kept repeating over and over again that he wanted to be alone. Even at my tender age I recognised Mother's concern for Father's predicament and what he might do.

I lit a second oil lamp and went outside. Through the thin wooden walls of the hut next-door I could hear Grandma and Grandpa snoring. I knocked on the door and opened it.

"Who's there?" said Grandpa.

"Colin!"

"Colin?" repeated Grandpa.

"Yeah – Dad's got toothache!" I said.

"Wassit bad?"

"Very bad."

Grandpa threw the covers back and swung his legs out of bed revealing his blue and white striped pyjamas.

"What's the matter?" asked Grandma from across the room.

"Nothin' to worry about – Vic got toothache thas' all."

Grandpa rummaged around in his clothes and found his tie.

"There you are look!" he said, "you tell 'im to tie this tight up round his jaw." Just then Mother appeared at the door.

"We 'ain't got no aspirins that's the trouble – I knew we should have brought some!" she said. I took the tie from Grandpa and went back to our hut. Father was kneeling on the floor, neck bent forwards as far as it would go, head upside down against the edge of the mattress.

"Dad?" I enquired.

"I can't stand it," he said. Mother arrived beside me.

"We need to tie this around your head to keep your jaw shut tight to make it better," I said. Father somehow sat up on the bed and his eyes were wild and desperate. But he would not let us near him.

"Dad!" I shouted, "will you let me tie this up around your head." He looked straight at me.

"For me!" I said, "will you do it for me?" He nodded. We wrapped the tie around the jaw on his left side and up across the top of his head. Then Mother and I pulled and made the tightest knot we could. Father collapsed in a heap leaning up against the headboard of the bed.

"Hang in there Dad!" I said. He managed a slight smile.

"I'll go and get some aspirins," I said.

"The café doesn't open until six!" said Mother.

"It's nearly five o'clock and he's always there early sorting newspapers."

I ran down to the café, Jill insisted on following. We arrived panting and it was totally deserted and no lights on. We waited an agonising ten minutes then the old chap arrived in an Austin A30

110

van with all the newspapers and sandwiches his wife had made to sell there that day. I ran up to him hardly allowing him to get out of the driver's seat.

"What ever's the matter?" he said, "I've never known you arrive this early."

"It's my dad you see," I said, "he's got toothache and we've got a tie around his head but we haven't got any aspirins or anything and he's in agony."

"Alright calm down." The old man fumbled for his keys and dropped them on the floor as he tried to open the tumble-down café and stores.

"More haste less speed!" he mumbled as the door eventually creaked open. "There you are," he said as he got inside and handed me a packet. I forgot all about paying him as I ran back to Father.

Father managed to sip crushed aspirins in water from the side of his mouth. This and the tight tie made the pain more bearable. By eight o'clock he had managed to drive to an emergency dentist in the nearest town and all was well.

I guess the Portland Bill holiday was the only time I attempted to get to know Grandma Eliza. She never left the veranda area of their hut and often just fell asleep there, black hat with a lace flower attached pulled down over her forehead. But in between my urgent explorations I did find time to show her peculiar seaweed I had found and fetch her ice cream.

One day she said she would like to wash in seawater. I had by now found an easy way down to an area where the sea was far more accessible. I obligingly took my old multi-coloured plastic beach bucket and after washing it thoroughly I brought it back brimming full with a minute sample of the English Channel.

I had rarely seen grandma Eliza without her hat and never without her glasses. She even removed her hairnet that hitherto I hadn't really noticed. She wore her usual long black dress, dark blue stockings and sensible shining black shoes. She came from an era when taking anything else off was unheard of, except in private behind a locked and bolted door. Her naked eyes were watery but seemed relieved at not having to concentrate on interpreting the world through thick lenscs. Her silvery white hair seemed to be platted at the sides and rear, she had the countenance of a wise old Indian squaw I had seen in a cowboy film.

Soon after this holiday grandma Eliza became very ill. She spent quite a long time in hospital – I can't remember where, but Father would drive us all to visit her every weekend. I hated those long hours fidgeting on the chair next to Grandma's bed and the old building smell, masked by medical disinfectant. Occasionally a kind nurse, noticing my boredom and selfish tantrums, would take me on a tour around the gardens in the fresh air.

A nurse and I returned to the ward one day and Frank was standing leaning over his wife where she peacefully lay. He was clutching his black, wide brimmed hat to his chest and softly whispering Grandma's name. She had peacefully slipped away. It was the first time that I had seen a grown man cry. Despite my tender age and being quickly whisked away and introduced to toys in a side room, I still can recall the solemnity of the moment.

Although I feel I was only just beginning to know her as I progressed from my toy car throwing stage, it was obvious she was a good woman and Frank's love for her was immeasurable. I suppose I was considered too young to attend Grandma Eliza's funeral. Life continued and Frank gradually adapted to living on his own at Number 8 Castleton.

8

Illness, Dustmen
And A Den Of My Own

The damp, cold and dusty areas of The Corner House certainly didn't help the bouts of respiratory infections I sometimes suffered. Despite the steam produced regularly by washing our clothes and bodies, the crumbling horsehair plaster that often fell from the walls and ceiling in the kitchen-cum-bathroom still created a fine choking powder. I would spend many days recovering in bed with Jill the dog as my only companion. She would occasionally patrol the house and usually looked forward to sniffing intensely any post that dropped on to the doormat downstairs. Her inquisitive deep sniffing of each envelope sounded clearly up the stairs and reminded me of an old pair of large fire bellows I'd once found up in the attic. But most of the time she'd curl up on the end of my bed and politely listen to my ramblings.

My first serious bout of bronchitis coincided with Aunt Flo and Uncle Todd coming to stay at The Corner House for a few months when their cottage at Number 89 Newell had to be demolished for road widening.

They stayed in the spare room with all their worldly possessions in cardboard boxes. An ancient and extremely noisy double bed was brought down from the attic for them, one of their stronger boxes was utilized as a bedside table and they brought their own chamber pot. Father managed to replace the missing floorboards in the spare room, but hammering them into place nearly brought down the entire kitchen ceiling. Up until now mice had lived undisturbed in the spare room but now batches of lethal mousetraps were set every night and Aunt Flo promised me faithfully she'd bury all the mouse family in the 'body transfer point' in the backyard.

Aunt Flo didn't have a job at the time and after Mother had gone to work at about nine o'clock each weekday morning, she would run down the corridor and into my bedroom singing and dancing rock 'n' roll – very badly. But I found it hilarious and I think Jill found it slightly alarming. Flo's favourite song was Bill Haley and The Comet's Rock Around The Clock. She sang all the wrong words and was grossly out of tune. Indeed her seemingly painful attempts at singing made Jill start to howl in sympathy like a little wolf. Flo's dance steps were somewhat bizarre, like some ritualistic tribal performance. The floorboards in my room had never endured such a pounding.

However, Aunt Flo entertaining me did not stop my night-time delirium when I was ill. I sometimes had nightmares and experienced hallucinations when lions and tigers came out of the walls and the hippos next-door ran amok. One evening – half asleep in bed – I remember thinking for some odd reason that it would be better if my bedside table lamp were turned off. I felt too ill – or maybe I was too lazy – to find the proper switch and I thought the electrical cable had metamorphosed into a demon snake. I took a pair of scissors left there on the bedside chair and cut through the live flex. It beheaded the snake and turned the light off – and all the lights and power in the rest of the house too. I must have become more sensible momentarily because I remember lying there in the darkness and hearing the metallic screech of the curtain rail on the middle room door as it opened downstairs; then Father trying to put more money in the shilling slot meter just by the front door.

It was a while later – after a discussion with Todd at the bottom of the stairs – that Father realised new fuse wire was required. Thankfully I did have the sense to fumble in the darkness and unplug the table lamp thereby isolating the stump of severed cable. I spent most of the night in near total darkness until the full moon appeared twinkling moonbeams through the cherry tree's branches. The following morning I noticed a huge black hole burnt in the blades of the scissors. Obviously I was extremely lucky. One of the blades must have come into contact with the earth conductor first, thereby blowing the fuse instantly when contact was also made with the live conductor, probably saving my life. The following morning I hid the damaged table lamp and scissors under the bed. The telltale evidence was soon exposed by Mother's cleaning and she left it to Father to deal with me, but he seemed far too baffled to reprimand me.

Aunt Flo was offered a seasonal job cleaning at Fosters Grammar School up on Tinneys Lane. This meant she was not able to keep me company in the mornings anymore. But she used this as an excuse to talk Father into letting me have my sixpenny radio back; but with a strict condition that I was not to use it at night. It had gotten a bit damp and its crinkly, vinyl exterior was covered in wood dust and the chrome speaker grill was showing slight rust blemishes. But it still worked and Flo managed to polish it up like new.

Living with Flo and Todd did not last long. Soon their new home was ready at Newland flats. Before they left – and as a substitute for having no bedside lamp – Flo bought me a torch which incorporated a loud horn. Why a torch should be manufactured with a horn built into it I really don't know, but it had a sliding switch for the lamp and a little red button for the horn. As it happened the horn proved very useful for me. If during the lonely twilight hours things metamorphosed or the moon's flickering light through the cherry tree's branches brought big cats scurrying from the walls, then the loud alarm emitted from my torch sent them instantly scurrying back whence they came. And bogeymen in the cubbyhole under the attic stairs were also kept under control with it.

When the doctor next came to see me he was not our usual doctor but a much older and very serious locum. He sat on the edge of my bed and peered at me. He asked me if he could use my torch to peer into my eyes and mouth. When he took it and inadvertently pressed the little red button he was so shocked he rocked with laughter. I thought my little bed would collapse. It was a great tonic for me.

One morning I must have felt better again because I got out of bed and crept across to my bedroom window desperate for a look at the outside world. Jill appeared very concerned as if she knew I wasn't allowed out of bed. Mrs Fay who lived opposite in Castleton Terrace was crossing the road. Mother must have asked her to cast an eye on our house when she could; why else would Mrs Fay suddenly turn and look straight up at me? I ducked but I knew she had seen me. Ten minutes later I heard the unmistakable sound of the front door being flung open. Jill stood up instantly and cocked her ears up. Mother came bounding up the stairs. I pretended to be asleep.

"You mustn't get out of bed!" shouted Mother as Jill gave a typical, token wag of her tail.

"I haven't," I whispered, feigning sleepiness. For years it became a talking point that Mrs Fay had seen a ghost in a window of The Corner House. Only Jill and I knew the truth.

The highlight of the week was dustbin day. Jill knew when it was dustbin day from the moment she opened her eyes in the morning. She'd be on edge the whole time constantly pricking her ears up until around ten o'clock when she'd actually detect the dustcart from streets away. Then as they got closer, it was the sound of the men constantly chucking metal dustbins up on the side of their truck and banging on them to empty completely any stubborn refuse that drove her into a frenzy. It was the one and only thing that temporarily changed Jill's character. At the first distant hint of the approaching gang of men, Jill would race down the stairs grumbling loudly, each frantic step accentuating her long throaty growls.

During the summer months the backdoor of the house would be left open for Jill and as the dustmen got closer she'd hurtle out into the backyard – nothing could stop her. As our dustbins were actually being emptied the noise Jill made could easily have been mistaken for some horrific dogfight. It really did sound like poor Jill was fighting frantically for her life. She would work herself up into such a state that she became hoarse and her mixture of barking and growling grew high pitched and squeaky.

When it was all over and the dustcart could be heard no more, Jill would tiptoe back into my bedroom still panting heavily. She'd give a little token wag of her tail and maybe a cough or two as her tongue hung flapping from the side of her mouth. She'd then crawl under the bed until she was fully recovered. When she came out she found it impossible to hide her embarrassment about her extreme behaviour.

I had plenty of time to ponder on things. Days came and went, the little two-stroke motorcycle became an integral part of my life; each day at around midday it heralded Mother's return. As the days turned to weeks I looked forward to my favourite rock 'n' roll drifting up from the pub every Saturday night.

All the while Jill's drastic change of character on dustbin day continued to puzzle me greatly and it played on my mind more and more. Docile as she was, the climax of dustbin day certainly reminded me that Jill and indeed all dogs possess a wild instinct. Not that Jill was capable of actually biting anyone, but it was made very plain once a week that she was certainly capable of a serious warning. Of course it's only natural for dogs to bark or at least object to strangers encroaching on their pack's territory; but if I hadn't known otherwise, I would have said that Jill was a mad dog suffering from rabies when that uncontrollable, hysterical state struck her.

The following week I couldn't understand why I was still told to stay in bed – I felt quite well. So when dustbin day arrived I decided to accompany Jill to the backyard. Mother had rushed out of the front door at nine o'clock that morning shouting her usual,

"I shan't be long – be a good boy!" But it always was a long time alone and little did she know some of the things that Jill and I got up to.

Jill constantly ran up and down the stairs gradually getting more and more worked up until she started panting a little. She rushed into my bedroom time and time again, occasionally stopping her panting and listening intently for the distant sound of the dustcart. Then it happened, the first distinct rattle of metal dustbins. As Jill raced downstairs I could tell by the familiar clonk shut of the metal letterbox flap that the post had arrived. Jill only gave a short uninterested sniff as she raced out into the backyard, nothing like the deep bellows type inspection that she usually carried out when less preoccupied.

I got out of bed. It felt rather peculiar; I hadn't been out of bed for two weeks. As I put on my dressing gown I felt quite dizzy but it soon passed. Jill came bounding back into my bedroom; she miraculously seemed to forget about dustmen momentarily and pranced around, her whole body wriggling in time with her tail. She even whined and then sat down by the door as if forbidding me to leave the bedroom.

The dustmen were getting closer and as I made my first steps towards the door Jill could not resist racing back down through the house again. I felt a bit shaky as I made my way downstairs. Jill came racing back and peeped around the middle room doorway at me. She was torn between the excitement of me being out of bed and her obsession with fending off the terrible dustmen. They were in the next street and Jill – grumbling intensely – disappeared again.

Soon I was barefoot in the backyard – I didn't have any slippers at the time. All Jill's senses were transfixed on the bottom of the doorway that led out into the street through the dangerous stone wall. She stood rigid with her front legs splayed in a defiant stance and her body arched across a half-full sack of sand. She was half whining, half growling and occasionally prancing forward at the door as the dustcart rounded the corner from Long Street. I heard the truck swing around the centre lamppost and park on the edge of the pavement by the cherry trees. Jill scraped and chewed at the bottom of the door in a mad frenzy as our dustbins were quickly and skilfully emptied. I thought Jill would injure herself as she fought to bite at the inch gap under the door. Then while contorting her body through unnatural positions in a psychological attempt to get under the door, she knocked over a scaffold pole put there by Father as a barrier. It clanged to the floor across the yard narrowly missing me, but Jill was oblivious to everything but the narrow space at the bottom of the door.

I thought it was all over, the dustbins had been emptied, but why was Jill still in such a state? Then I found out. Despite Father's warnings about the dangerous doorway and wall I leant over Jill and peeped through an old keyhole in the door. The driver had left his cab and he and his two mates came back towards the door. From behind his back the driver produced part of an old broom handle and shoved it hard time and time again under the door at Jill.

"Take that you little bastard!" muttered the driver. Then he handed it to his mate for a go.

"Vicious little fucker ain't he!" said the other man.

"Piss off!" I shouted without thinking, "you're the vicious fuckers!" They were completely taken aback, but would have probably retaliated were it not for Miss Molly who had just reached the lamppost. She gave a little cough to make her presence known and the men turned to see her and then coughed as well. They scratched their heads self consciously. Molly stood and glared at them hands on hips like a formidable little headmistress. As they made their way back to the dustcart I thought about telling them that Jill was a girl and not a boy. But I thought better of it and crept silently back into the house. I never discovered if Miss Molly had heard my expletives shouted at the dustmen that day, but her friendly attitude towards me never changed.

Despite hating the game of football so much, when fully fit I did occasionally get to kick a proper football around the backyard on my own. It was the frenzied pack behaviour on the football pitch at school that I didn't like. But mucking around playing by my own rules with no one shouting the odds was fine. Jill would watch but she'd never join in. She seemed far too concerned at the possible consequences of kicking a missile up over Father's garage and into the wilderness beyond.

One day in the backyard I booted the ball particularly hard, Jill stood up suddenly and looked horrified when the ball did not return back down into the yard as usual. She looked at me as if to say, 'There I told you so!'

Instead of rebounding off it, the ball had in fact sailed on over the highest stone wall that extended up about a metre above Father's garage. I had often inadvertently kicked a ball into our next-door neighbours' yard – over the much lower brick wall – but never into the secretive area beyond our garage.

The dense undergrowth into which the ball had disappeared was on land owned by an old lady called Miss Carlisle. It was part of her extensive back garden, which stretched from the rear of her house further down Long Street to sweep in an L shape to border numerous adjoining backyards too.

I had only ever noticed Miss Carlisle from afar except once when I nearly collided with her when riding my tricycle around Long Street corner. She had apparently complained to the police and the council about my tricycle antics.

That day I left Jill safe in our backyard and walked the few yards down Long Street to Miss Carlisle's front door. I pulled on a knob set in the door frame and heard a mechanical bell tinkle somewhere inside. After a while the door opened quite suddenly and there stood Miss Carlisle in the blackness of her hallway, a brown fur coat almost reaching the floor and an old knitted hat covering most of her white hair. I was surprised to see her smile slightly – when I had nearly knocked her over with my tricycle she had remained expressionless.

"I'm sorry," I said, "I've kicked my ball over into your place by mistake."

"A ball?" she said. "By mistake?" she reiterated softly.

"Yes," I said.

"What colour is it?" she asked.

"Well it's black and white – almost like a proper one," I said.

"Wait there," she said as she shuffled back down her hallway. Then she stopped halfway into the darkness and turned back. I strained to see her. "You're the boy from The Corner House aren't you?" she asked.

I expected a long wait. I couldn't imagine I had propelled my ball particularly far but her garden did extend a long way. I also knew from peering through the iron fence that divided part of it from East Mill Lane that it was very overgrown.

My father's work colleague Derrick was looking out of the window of the electrical shop opposite. We waved at each other. I carried on waiting and tapped my foot. I looked back again at Derrick who now seemed even more inquisitive. Then just as I noticed people looking at me from Waite's little grocery store next-door to the electrical shop, I heard a door slam somewhere in the far reaches of Miss Carlisle's house. Sooner than I thought she came shuffling back up the hallway. It was not until she was framed in her doorway that I noticed her coat was covered in teasel heads, her hat was out of place and her hair quite dishevelled. There was one teasel head stuck conspicuously just above her left ear.

"There we are," she said softly, handing me my ball. I was surprised at Miss Carlisle – she was quite nice. Her pleasant attitude was probably influenced by the fact that Long Street corner had been free of my dangerous tricycle antics for a few years.

Tennis balls, model rockets and airplanes ended up in Miss Carlisle's garden over the years. Eventually she trusted me to go and hunt for them myself and she'd always wave at me whenever I saw her.

I was approaching the age when boys seek out dens to use privately as their very own. I had experienced Todd's allotment den and been very impressed with it. But it was Todd's own den really and I could only ever go there with him. Todd was kind and always made me feel part of his den and our wild mountain men game was fun; but I wanted a den of my own too.

At this stage in my life I was forbidden to go out very far alone, so during the summer holidays I would roam the house with Jill. Jill had become firmly established as my trusted companion and bogeymen were far less prevalent. However, quite often we would still sense a presence in the house when floorboards and purlins in the roof creaked. We'd hear definite scampering in the cubbyhole and would imagine someone or something around the next bend in the attic stairs or down in the out-of-bounds, locked passageway on the ground floor.

On one such day even Jill appeared apprehensive as we climbed the attic stairs. Behind the cubbyhole on the first floor landing, half way up the attic stairs – as they twist to the right – is another much smaller square cupboard door. Except there was no cupboard space behind it, just another tangled mass of cobwebs into a clutter of roof timbers.

Jill loved the excitement. I'm sure she was addicted to the adrenalin rush we both experienced upon exploring such places in The Corner House. The tiny door was difficult to open because there was no handle on it. For years I hadn't even realised that it was hinged because it looked like part of the fixed timber cladding. I clawed at it and we held our breath as I managed to prize it open. Wide-eyed and ears erect, Jill tiptoed to the edge of the one foot square aperture and peeped inside. She strained her neck stretching from the edge of a wide wedge of step for a better look. She almost barked but thought better of it at the last moment.

After a tentative inspection with the torch – red horn button at the ready – it became obvious that the dark cave formed the intermediate section of the complicated roof structure that connected the bogeymen's headquarters next to the landing, up to their playground that was hidden behind the wall in the attic. Jill at last felt able to breathe and she now panted – tongue flapping gently.

We had no idea at that time that Father – in a half-hearted attempt to survey the roof area for possible electrical rewiring – had battered a hole from the top attic room through the dividing wall into the secret void that we believed to be the bogeymen's playground. We crept further up the attic stairs and into the actual attic.

It was still officially an out of bounds area and Jill and I had only ever briefly gazed at the filthy window and chased butterflies around a tiny section of it before that day. In eerie silence we tiptoed over mountains of junk. Behind an old chest of drawers in an area we'd never ventured before, Mother's large old doll surprised us as it lay discarded staring wide-eyed at the ceiling. Jill was most concerned at this humanoid, lifeless form. She approached it very slowly her nose outstretched as far as she dared while she sniffed tiny exploratory samples of its scent.

"It's OK," I said as I knelt down and touched the doll's ice-cold china face. After perhaps decades of staring at the peeling, whitewashed, ceiling, one of its eyes – with real hair lashes attached – slowly closed on its own. I gently closed the other too as Jill – now more confident – approached with her tail frantically fanning the dust around. With its eyes closed Jill seemed to accept that the thing was either dead or had never been alive in the first place.

Next we struggled to step over a heavy stone washbasin stored on the floor. The great white lump was made to rest at an odd angle by the remains of the external pipe from its plughole. The lopsided world inside the sink and the dark plughole was home to one of many large black spiders who lived in the attic. The spider defiantly stood its ground in its safe plughole despite Jill's close inspection. A stack of books looked precariously near to toppling over. But then neither of us dared breathe as we spotted the sheet of hardboard that we somehow instinctively knew covered up a hole in the wall that led into the bogeymen's playground.

Adrenaline flowing, I eagerly removed the old casement clock that lay propped against the hardboard. Its innards broke the silence when its wavering hammer struck its rusty chime as if announcing – rather feebly – that another hour had past. It clattered more as I propped it in a new position and the hardboard fell away. Jill's fear of the falling hardboard was largely overcome by a shared and irresistible inquisitiveness. We scrambled over the hardboard and there revealed was a large dark cave of roof space.

Although fascinated Jill refused point blank to go in. I suppose that was just as well considering there was no flooring, just joists with weak lathes and plaster between them. I held the torch out in front of me – thumb ready over the red button – while remembering just where we were.

As I gazed into the darkness I became aware of them: One, two, three and four pairs of bright little eyes scattered haphazardly around the place. One or two fidgeted and my heart missed a beat as I shone my torch madly in all directions at them and pressed hard on the red horn button. The batteries in the torch were becoming exhausted which made the horn sound rather pathetic as its note wavered in a comical way, rather like a weak raspberry. Jill barked furiously and pranced around there at the edge of their territory. Despite the silly note the torch was making, I pointed it forcefully at the two nearest eyes like a gun. As I became accustomed to the lack of light I realised the two eyes were actually not eyes at all, but light entering through minuscule gaps between the roof tiles. I stopped pressing the horn and Jill howled for more. A starling rustled as it escaped the human intrusion through a larger gap to the outside world. I was so relieved when I realised that the other eyes were so obviously gaps in the roof tiles too and the fidgeting sounds could be explained. A pair of bats fluttered for a while and eventually settled, hanging high up out of reach.

I found I could see enough without the dwindling torchlight now and I ventured in, careful to only step on the joists. My eyes gradually became even more accustomed to the dimness and right across the middle of the space – hewn I like to think from a mighty galleon – was a massive oak rafter about the right height for a seat. I sat there and noticed more tiny cracks of light coming through the bare roof tiles.

"My den!" I whispered. Jill wagged her tail uncontrollably at my utterance but still refused to move any closer beyond the boundary of the safer attic room.

The bogeymen's den – all spirits exorcised – did indeed become my first private den. I even took a dustpan and brush and cleaned up the dirt on the rafter and tops of the joists. It didn't seem to bother me that there was still inches of dirt in between the joists or that I couldn't step on those areas; although after a while I did find a couple planks of wood from somewhere and made a walkway across to my private seat.

One day the soft pattering of rain again drew my attention to the roof tiles in my den. I discovered how they were slid together one over the other. At conveniently the right height for me in a standing position, I adapted one of the tiles to slide up and give me a little window on the outside world. When I opened my little glassless window fresh raindrops landed on centuries of dry dust to be instantly soaked up. Through the droplets I could see Castleton Church next to the railway line and somewhere in the far distance on a little mound, a solitary tree.

Over the years I espied that lonely tree in spring and summer bloom, in autumn with leafless spindly branches and in winter drooping with snow. If I adjusted my gaze and stance I often saw Mrs Fay or Mrs Beaton returning to Castleton Terrace opposite, laden with shopping, or Miss Molly hurriedly returning home to her reclusive sister up the road in Castleton. Occasionally lunchtime drinkers would stagger from the Black Horse. And I would be safe from the world in my own little den, bogeymen driven out and with Jill guarding the entrance.

9

Mischief, Frank's Place
And Teddy Roe's Band

Running a huge Ford Pilot car had become too costly for Father and customer numbers for his very personal and hence comparatively expensive taxi service had dwindled. Therefore the 'Pilot' was traded in for a little blue Standard 8. It was somewhat cramped compared to the luxury we were used to, but far more economical and highly reliable. Father proudly fixed his chrome and yellow Automobile Association badge to the bumper and AA officers on their motorcycle combinations saluted us everywhere we went.

For a year or two Father still occasionally transported a few loyal customers around. Despite not having the luxury of a large car any more, these people insisted that they would rather pay slightly more to employ a driver with a personal touch who they knew and trusted.

I became very interested in the blue Standard 8. Every weekend Father did his routine checks in strict order: Oil, water, battery, fan belt, brake fluid and tyre pressures. I became quite an expert and was even able to take tyre pressures myself.

Gradually I was officially allowed in Father's garage on my own, when no one else was around. In between admiring the gleaming Standard 8, I started to acquire practical skills, making things like a home for a newly arrived tortoise. I didn't exactly use fine dovetail joints and the rough planks of wood were belted together using nails that were far too big, but it worked for a year and stopped Joe the new tortoise from trying to bulldoze his way to freedom from the backyard.

Access to the garage also meant I was able to take on more responsibility for the one-eyed slowworm, which had been plucked from under a sheet of corrugated iron ages ago. I insisted on keeping the slowworm in captivity, but Mother refused to have him in the house so the nameless creature lived in a cardboard home on part of Father's workbench. I now regularly showed him the light of day, cleaned his box and fed him.

Jill was never able to travel well in cars as we found to our expense, but was perfectly happy to be left guarding the house and the backyard during our now more frequent motoring excursions on Sunday afternoons. Sometimes grandfather Frank would be encouraged to come with us and he obviously thoroughly enjoyed it. I would always sit in the front with the seat adjusted as far forward as it would go, to make as much room as possible for Frank's long, arthritic legs. Mother would sit beside Frank and direct most of the driving – much to Father's annoyance.

Typically, before a Sunday afternoon outing Mother would be left to get ready while Father and I drove up to Castleton to collect Frank. We'd then return to The Corner House to pick up Mother before setting off. Frank would take time to get ready and even longer to walk up the gravel path to the road.

One Sunday Father left me in the 'Standard' parked opposite the church while he helped Frank get ready. Father seemed longer than usual. Getting bored I climbed out of the car and had a good look around it. I had not seen Father do his car check that weekend, but the tyres looked OK, the windows were clean and the bodywork was gleaming with new polish. I looked in the boot and inspected the spare wheel. I thought about checking the tyre pressures. But then I noticed there beside the spare wheel was an aerosol can of 'instant puncture repair.' I had witnessed Father use one like it once before, when we got a puncture halfway around a busy roundabout. The hose on the top of the can attached to the tyre valve, then the pressure from the aerosol inflated the tyre to a reasonable pressure. At the same time the handy gadget would force in some sort of magic sealant that temporarily repaired the leak and hopefully got you to the nearest garage.

It was still and silent up at Castleton that day, apart from some rooks cawing as they circled around the old castle ruin. The congregation from the Sunday morning service had long departed and strangely there was no sign of Miss Molly – she was still finishing her Sunday lunch I thought. The sun was glinting off the rear bumper as I picked up the can nestling neatly beside a bag of tools. I inspected it meticulously. Deep in thought I looked down the end of the hose and wondered what the stuff looked like. Perhaps I should try a little bit on the kerbstone, just to see what it looked like. I could clean it up afterwards and no one would ever know.

I knelt down and aimed the end of the hose on to the kerb. The knob seemed to be stuck. I inadvertently moved my aim as I concentrated on releasing the jammed knob. But it wasn't jammed, it just required a definite jolt to set the apparatus in motion. Suddenly the knob released and the stuff spurted out like a garden hose but ten times more powerful. I was shocked as I tried in vain to turn the thing off. I had lost my grip on the hose and it was furiously waggling around spraying white frothy goo everywhere. As I wrestled with it I had no control over its unpredictable behaviour. I had already plastered part of the front door of nearby Lattice House. I had also made an abstract artwork all over the road and the solution was now dripping from the yew trees that overhung the churchyard wall. The last few moments of the hissing can I somehow managed to strangle in the gutter. The thing I didn't realise is that these 'get you home aerosols' are only intended to be used once, like a fire extinguisher. Once you start them you can't stop them and if the hose is not firmly connected to a deflated tyre the results, as I now knew, are catastrophic.

Father arrived. I kicked the can out of sight under the car – it tinkled conspicuously.

"What do you think you're up to?"

"Nothing," I said.

"What's he been doing then?" said Frank arriving near the pavement.

"I ain't done nothing," I said sneaking down the side of the car in a desperate attempt to hide the mess on the pavement. I then looked down at my feet. I realised the game was up when I noticed the stuff plastered on yet another new pair of sandals.

"He's been setting off my emergency puncture kit," said Father. I heard a door close and looked across at Middle House. Miss Molly had emerged, still eating and with a tea towel draped over her arm. I immediately looked to her for protection.

"What's he done?" asked Frank puzzled.

"Set off my emergency puncture thing – that's what he's done!" said Father losing patience, "they're twelve and sixpence you know."

"I'll put this stick about you – you young rascal," shouted Frank waving his walking stick around.

"I think he was experimenting at being a repair man!" said Miss Molly in her soft mechanical voice as she arrived next to me. Father, recognising that I was quite shaken and knowing I would have to suffer the wrath of Mother about ruining another pair of new sandals said,

"Well you'll know next time won't you – you messy pup."

Despite squirting Castleton with emergency puncture repair solution, it was eventually forgotten and I was gradually allowed out on my own more, not just to fetch cigarettes for Mother but also to do what I wanted to do – within reason. I often visited Castleton with Jill and became more aware of Frank's place.

One day the local newspaper came to interview Frank at Number 8 Castleton, they were gathering information for an article on ghosts and spirits. I was beside myself with excitement and couldn't stop fidgeting as I sunk deep into Grandma's old armchair.

"Bide still!" Frank said to me shaking his walking stick, "let the bloke speak!"

"When you were night watchman at the castle," said the interviewer rather seriously, "did you ever experience any ghostly activities?"

"Oh yes many times," replied Frank trying to disguise his broad Dorset accent. "I've often heard swords being removed from their scabbards of a night, and galloping horses hooves and men crying out."

"Were you never scared Mr Park?"

"No it never really bothered me."

"Do you recall ever *seeing* any ghostly activities?" asked the reporter, "as opposed to just hearing things?"

"Nope – I never saw anything at all."

"Why do you think it was that you never actually saw anything?" Frank thought for a while.

"Well," said Frank, "it was too dark!"

The Harts – who lived next-door to Grandfather – seemed to share the same back garden; apart that is, from an area at the farthest end, reserved and fenced off by Frank for his rabbits, which he bred for meat and he also kept chickens in there too. Jill was always rather wary of Frank – I think she had an inkling about Frank's activities. Few rabbits would escape the handle end of Frank's walking stick, which he would use to catch them. Then a quick jerk and a twist and a rabbit would be ready for skinning. A similar fate awaited hens that would no longer lay. I remember seeing this first hand, along with the chicken plucking and rabbit skinning, but I was too young to realise exactly what was happening. In any case Frank's attitude to these things and his skill and speed meant it all seemed rather unimportant and commonplace. It had only been a few years since Frank and his family would regularly raise and fatten a pig, then kill it themselves. In later years Father had told me many times how it used to be his job to stir the pig's blood as it spurted from its slit throat.

Visits to Number 8 Castleton were further encouraged by more hard-boiled sweets from Mrs Hart next-door. She seemed to have an endless supply and whenever I met her she would offer me a selection. I met her husband Len who was equally as kind and trustworthy. He was a carpenter in the estate woodyard and often meticulously and lovingly sharpened both Frank's and Father's wood saws, chisels and knives by hand. Len had a small, very tidy little workshop adjoining Number 7 and would love me to sit and watch him at work. I would be amazed at his skill and concentration setting and filing each single saw tooth in turn. Collections of workmen's chisels would be lovingly honed to razor sharp perfection on a large velvety oilstone. Len said they were almost as sharp as Frank's cut-throat razor.

The estate woodyard is situated around New Road before the slopes and opposite Purley's 'under water' trees. It is behind a high wall and there are several vehicular entrances through large doorways. However, every working day Len trod a shortcut to work across the field behind and to the south of the two cottages. His only obstacle on his route that took him in the backdoor of the woodyard was the river Yeo. Len overcame this many years ago by building and maintaining a wooden footbridge across the river. The bridge was just upstream from a waterfall, near where I was to have my first tree camp. Len's daily footsteps ensured a prominently worn pathway always existed through the grass from the garden gate of the cottages to his place of work; the bridge and pathway both symbols of his pride and dedication to his job and way of life.

Further down the very bottom of the garden just beyond Frank's rabbits and chickens there was another garden gate that led out into the adjoining field. Well it wasn't really a gate, it was an old shed door half covered in ivy with a latch. During Father's youth, it was there just inside this doorway that many a fattened pig had met their end, on a large oblong flagstone laid in the grass.

Across the field from this slaughter area in a south easterly direction towards the lake was what Frank called the 'hatches.' These were the sluice gates that controlled the flow of water from Sherborne lake into the river Yeo. Although geographically close by, the 'hatches' were always accessed via Raleigh Lodge back up in the centre of Castleton. Apparently there was a meticulously kept record book noting by how far the gates were opened or closed at any particular time.

Close by to the west of Number 8 and Number 7 Castleton – a little nearer the railway line – stood a tumble-down shed. It was Frank's sort of workshop-cum-storeroom and it was also just big enough for a car. Not that Frank ever owned a car, but one or two family members did from time to time and vehicular access into the area was possible, at a squeeze.

Frank seemed quite secretive about his shed and I had only ever had fleeting glimpses of the dark interior when the door was half opened on brief supervised occasions. I was fascinated by it and was itching to see inside properly.

Along with the slaughter of rabbits and chickens, another aspect that had seemed unimportant and commonplace when I had heard it spoken about, were Frank's grisly gin traps, which he often set in the shed to kill rats. I had seen mouse traps set in The Corner House and I imagined gin traps to be much the same.

One day after spending the afternoon with Frank, he continued to be totally engrossed in repairing his rabbit pen at the very bottom of the garden and I was bored. There was no one else around so Jill and I sneaked back up near the house to explore that old tumble-down shed.

I carefully removed the contorted nail that held the hasp and staple together on the double doors. The right door fell open a little way and I heaved it up to support its weight and opened it more, just enough to squeeze inside. Thankfully Jill seemed to sense danger and refused point blank to enter the shed. She stood patiently with her head just poking in. Light from two small windows made the interior just about visible. There was a massive iron vice – exactly like the one in The Corner House garage – some old pots and pans and a battered watering can on the bench. As I entered my eyes began adjusting to the dimness and I could see sacks of meal or grain stacked up on the far end of the bench. I was fascinated by the old bits of bicycle and an old motorcar magneto on a shelf to the right. There were also shelves above the sacks of food on the left and I was itching to see what was up there.

With its seat shoved halfway under the bench there was an old captain's chair that had been partly repaired, but its legs were quite sturdy. I stopped and listened intently to make sure that Frank wasn't returning from the bottom of the garden yet and Jill sniffed the air outside as if checking too. When I had convinced myself that I could not hear Frank's shuffling steps or the creak of the garden gate, I dragged out the chair and climbed up on to it. As my eyes levelled with the top of a sack of grain I drew breath sharply as I noticed something metal and gruesome. There nestling on the top of the sack was a cold, mechanical gin trap; set, primed and waiting for its victim – any victim. Although I had never seen one before I somehow instinctively knew what it was – thank God –

with its ominous gaping jaws, rows of arrowhead teeth and ticklish pressure plate there in the middle of things.

I forgot completely about exploring the top shelf and withdrew back down to the ground. A little further beyond the last sack and near the end of the bench was another carefully laid gin trap, its chain secured firmly to the bench with a six inch nail hammered part way into the timber and bent over. As I inquisitively edged my way closer to it, an old saucepan fell against the watering can and made me jump – Jill ran away. I turned instantly and another saucepan lower in the pile tinkled slightly. I told myself it was the wind and stubbornly refused to acknowledge the fact that there was none.

As I was inching my way back toward the door something moved and caught my eye just below the window on the bench. At first I thought it was a massive worm or a small snake, but as it disappeared behind the saucepans a head and whiskers appeared between the watering can and the sack of food, thus confirming that what I had first seen was a rat's tail and I was now staring at its head. It turned and looked straight at me sniffing the air with its whiskers quivering. The other window reflected in its little bright eyes forming catch-lights. We just stared at each other for what felt like ages. Then it seems we both made decisions to carry on about our business at precisely the same moment and I noticed Jill had reappeared motionless at the door with baited breath. The rat disappeared behind the sacks and I made for the door while listening for Frank. Jill was now very inquisitive and I had to physically push her away in her mesmerised state. It seemed the whole shed was liable to collapse as I forced the door shut and reinserted the twisted nail, like a Chinese puzzle.

As we crept away we heard the jangly clank of a gin trap's jaws bite shut, propelled into mid-air by its own force. With it there was a plaintive squeal. Then instantly the chain jangled again as the iron thumped back down on to the bench. Two more weak squeaks, then nothing – just the ten past five train charging under Castleton Bridge, summoning us to The Corner House for tea.

When we returned to The Corner House we found Father huffing and puffing as he lifted a new heavy television set on to the sideboard. The cabinet was massive and crammed full of rows of valves, capacitors and cumbersome electronics. But the screen, sunk deep behind thick glass was tiny, almost oval and a sort of greyish green in colour.

The previous weekend Father had been erecting a huge multi-element aerial on the middle room chimney helped by Derrick from the electrical shop so as to enable us to receive the new ITV channel. Now the round coaxial cable that led from it was trailing untidily into the room through a hole in the frame of the window.

"Your tea's getting cold!" said Mother watching in anticipation.

"I'll just connect it up first," said Father, "they take a little while to warm up."

Jill inspected every inch of the cable and even appeared to strain to look up at the back of the set, high on the sideboard.

"There," said Father, "that should do it."

"And what about the cable?" said Mother, "we can't have that tangled mess of wire trailing across the floor like that, someone'll trip over it."

"It'll do just to try it," said Father sipping his tea. He eased the thing back into place and plugged it in.

"Ready?" He sort of ducked a little as he threw the switch, as if he thought it was going to explode or something. We sipped our tea and waited.

"I don't think it's going to work!" said Mother chuckling slightly. Then there was a slight hissing noise. Father leaped up and started adjusting the knobs; on the front, on the side and some around the back. Jill stood transfixed, eager to help Father wrestling with this big heavy intruder. Then a simple but catchy tune faintly fizzled through. As it grew louder we were all startled by people singing about a particular brand of toothpaste. It faded back out then in again, roughly in time to the reflex action of Jill's ears.

As she twisted her head to sample the sound from a different angle, a very fuzzy picture of the head and shoulders of a man appeared, revolving hesitantly top to bottom of the tiny screen. Jill was at first fascinated but then seemed to quickly accept it. It was as if she had reached her own conclusion and was saying to herself: 'It's not real – I don't know how they do it but it's not real – it doesn't smell like it's alive so it can't be a threat.' She chose to try and ignore it in preference to studying the flickering flames of the open fire. It was as if she remained totally puzzled – deep in thought over just how such a thing could ever happen.

Eventually Father tuned in a reasonable picture and we all became consumed by the marvel of independent commercial television and its adverts, so much so that I really didn't want to go to bed. In the end I was bribed. Father told me that if I went to bed on time every night for the remainder of that week, then as a special treat I could stay up and watch the real live Teddy Roe's Band on Sunday night.

I'd heard of Teddy Roe's Band, indeed at one time I thought Teddy Roe was a modern day living person who ran some crazy band that paraded around the town each year. In actual fact the assumption I had formed in my mind from listening to snippets of other people's conversations was partly true – except for the fact that Teddy Roe was no longer alive and had in fact died centuries ago.

The annual parade, procession or march – call it what you will – goes back so far into history that there are many theories as to its origin. But by far the most popular belief among Sherborne folk is that Teddy Roe was the foreman in charge of the workmen building Sherborne Abbey. When the Abbey was at last completed on a Monday in the year 1275 the workmen were invited to 'pack' up their tools and celebrate. That day is still celebrated on the first Monday after the 10th October, and has become known as Pack Monday Fair. The start of the fair is heralded – on the stroke of the preceding midnight – by what has become a raucous, noisy procession known as Teddy Roe's Band. No one knows what instruments were used to make a noise all those centuries ago. But in more modern times, anything from real musical instruments to hunting horns and dustbin lids are utilised and the idea is to make the loudest racket possible which need not necessarily be musical.

Over the years the actual fair has evolved from a simple sheep sale to include a boisterous market with many visiting street traders and a traditional fairground. There is much merriment and consumption of alcohol.

The following Sunday at about eight o'clock in the evening, I fell asleep in a chair in the middle room with Jill curled up at my feet. I was awoken by Mother insisting to Father that the TV should be turned on. Father always preferred radio and was tuned to The BBC Home Service on his pride and joy – a large wooden radio with a yellow lit dial. Mother apparently didn't have a clue what was scheduled for broadcast on TV that night – she just wanted it turned on.

"Why don't you look in the paper and choose a programme that you're interested in," said Father, "that's how you should use a television anyway, you shouldn't turn it on just in case." Mother didn't answer. Sensing an argument I yawned loudly and stretched, this woke Jill up.

"I should go to bed for a while," suggested Mother, "we'll wake you up before midnight." Jill got up and shook herself and strolled across to gaze into the glowing embers of the fire. I knelt down and hugged Jill goodnight, she turned towards me from the mesmerising fire and licked my ear.

"Promise you'll wake me up," I said to Father yawning again.

"Yes we'll wake you up, you needn't worry about that."

I didn't sleep much. I probably drifted in and out of consciousness a couple of times. Each time I awoke I managed to enlarge existing finger holes in the wallpaper next to my bed. I really didn't know what to expect of Teddy Roe's Band.

It wasn't long after being awoken by a train that I heard the familiar screech of the makeshift curtain track above the middle room door and Father climbing the stairs, closely followed by Jill – who wasn't usually allowed upstairs at night. I leapt out of bed and down the corridor. With no need to restrict my steps to the more solid, quite areas of floor, the floorboards creaked loudly in a wide variety of tones.

"Oh you don't need waking up then!" remarked Father. Jill wagged her tail sensing late night shenanigans. "The front door's locked isn't it?" Father asked Mother who was just climbing the stairs with a tray of hot drinks.

"All the bolts are on!" shouted Mother.

Soon we were all assembled in my parents' bedroom and Jill seemed to know what was happening. Despite the fact that she didn't usually like being picked up Jill begged to be lifted up on to the seat that was built into the window that overlooked Black Horse Corner. I think she could easily have jumped up herself were it not for the fact that the seat was quite narrow; and the inevitable momentum of her leap would have surely meant her colliding with solid wall.

We opened the window to the cool night air and Jill stretched up with paws resting on the sill and sniffed hard. I knelt in the window seat beside Jill. Little did my parents know that I had done this a few times before when surreptitiously experiencing rock 'n' roll from the public bar across the road. Tonight the pub seemed black and empty.

As I sipped my hot drink I heard the din of the band as it echoed on its way around the streets in the distance. There was shouting, whooping and screaming, the jarring single note of a brass instrument, the furious banging of dustbin lids and somewhere intermingled a clang of a solitary bell. As it seemed to round another corner and get a little closer, there were whistles too and football rattles just discernible.

Then Jill suddenly started barking furiously. Mother had a fit and shouted at her. Father said not to worry because there'd be enough noise shortly anyway. But I was curious as to what she was really barking at. The band had been audible for a while and Jill had better hearing than any of us. So why had it suddenly started to bother her? She was also transfixed by the wrought iron gateway that led into the garden of the house that formed the corner of Newland and Long Street. I put my arm around Jill and her barking became less urgent, she seemed to roll around her milder oral protests with her tongue, like she was trying to speak.

Then I noticed a glint of a streetlight reflected in something in the shadows near the gate. My brain suddenly picked out the human form of a policeman, well camouflaged in the gateway. The streetlamp was reflecting momentarily in his helmet badge as he moved slightly. He stepped out of the shadows for a moment to reveal himself fully, he looked up and smiled. This seemed to confirm to Jill that he was a friend and she settled down.

Soon the first people came striding purposefully – although a little unsteadily – down Newland. These first ones had no instruments and relied entirely on their voices to make a din. There was a cacophony of different songs, the words being shouted at the top of their voices. Jill started to whine, then couldn't resist a little playful bark at the first few dustbin lids. This made one of the vocalists stop suddenly and look up at us. Although his feet stopped dead, his head carried on a little way and he nearly fell over. After recovering his balance he gesticulated wildly and shouted – even louder – unintelligible gibberish up at us.

"I don't know why they need to get so drunk!" whispered Mother. The man stopped shouting and flung his arms around wildly again, as if expecting an answer. People behind him with whistles and rattles started bumping into him. He nearly fell over again, then shrugged his shoulders and took off around the corner into Long Street.

A man constantly playing the same single note on an old bugle came marching down the middle of the road. He seemed totally sober and closed his eyes as he blew for all he was worth. Another man carried a large piece of iron suspended with a chain, as he walked his mate clobbered the metal with a large stick whenever he could manage it, the result was a deep reverberating clang every so often.

My parents remained quite serious until a man with an old car horn came staggering along. It was the very earliest type of horn, operated by a large squeezable rubber bulb. He would charge forward as if frantically trying to keep up with his out of control feet. It was only when his head appeared to miraculously synchronise with his feet – or one of his spurts of energy was inevitably cut short with a collision with someone or something – that he blew his horn. If it was a collision the horn was squeezed short, sharp and angrily; if a ponderous stationary attempt at composure, then a wimpish little raspberry was squeezed out of it. The comical timing was brilliant and the tone of the horn well suited to his clown-like antics.

Apart from the yet unnoticed policemen well hidden in the garden and the occasional slight movement in the bottom corner of curtains in a window opposite, we seemed the only spectators. The chap with the solitary hand bell had ceased ringing it and ran hurriedly by to catch up. Then came the stragglers; a scattered crowd of people who just wanted to complete the course. Following up the rear trying to hurry-on the last diehards, were a dozen or more policemen. Their deep voices echoed slightly as they exchanged notes with the policeman in the garden. A combination of cool air and cigarette smoke made Jill sneeze loudly. Just as all the policemen turned to look up I instinctively ducked back inside. That night I dreamed of wildly caricatured bandsmen trampling through my mind, warding off anything evil at the expense of an unbearable din.

10

Acquiring An Air Pistol

It became a regular thing to visit Todd and Flo in their new flat in Newland. I would spout forth to them my dreams and wishes in great detail and far more often than I ever did to Mother or Father.

Aunt Flo spoilt me wicked; one day when visiting Flo while Todd was at work, I expressed my curiosity about a tobacco pipe that I'd found in some of Father's junk in the attic; I was itching to try it out. Flo was almost as mischievous and reckless as me; she found some of Todd's Navy Cut cigarettes and broke one open into the pipe bowl. It was fun for a while mimicking Popeye The Sailor Man and sucking in real tobacco smoke, but then I was quite ill and didn't smoke again for years.

I think Aunt Flo was the only person I had told of my yearning to own a particular air pistol. She seemed to understand that it would feel more real than a plastic cap gun during my Wild West fantasies. I was far too young to be able to buy the weapon myself, but I continued scraping together every penny in anticipation.

In the far corner of my attic den, which I shared with starlings and bats, in-between the joists covered in dust that had been shut away from the light of day for a hundred years, I hid my stash of cash. It was kept in a large old leather wallet I'd found amongst Father's junk there in the main attic. Largely helped by birthday donations and Aunt Flo, after counting it twice a week for over a year, I eventually discovered I had in my possession six whole pounds.

At the far end of Long Street near the centre of Sherborne stood Harry Hunt's Pushbike Shop that I had first encountered on Sunday morning walks with Father. The 'boys' wonderland' figured prominently within the hearts of every Sherborne boy and no one's more than mine. Harry sold much more than pushbikes. He sold everything a boy could ever want; from joke black face soap, life-like plastic flies that floated in drinks and stink bombs, dartboards, knives and of course air guns. Father had told me it was the only place in the world he could find a replacement spanner to fit a Spitfire aeroplane radiator cap during the war.

Harry, his brother David and Mr Roberts who worked there were also very kind, understanding and trusting. Apparently when my mother first moved to Sherborne from South Petherton, a complete stranger, she couldn't afford the bicycle she desperately needed. Harry let her have it 'on tick' – no paperwork involved just verbal trust.

It was indeed on Sunday morning walks with Father when I'd first set eyes upon that particular air pistol on display in Harry's crammed shop window. At first I just admired it, the thought of actually owning it never really entered my head. But as a year or two passed by my attention was drawn more and more towards it. Once I had noticed a neat circular area on its wooden stock that remained a slightly darker colour than the rest of it. I realised that the pistol had been in the window for so long that a pocket compass had protected that small area from the bleaching effect of sunlight, until that particular compass had been plucked from the window for a customer. Presumably the pistol had been kept in the window specifically for display purposes and purchasers of that model would be given one in an unopened box produced from the secretive rear of Harry's shop.

The five pounds fifteen and eleven pence price tag gradually sounded less of a fortune as my cash steadily accumulated. Harry never seemed to update his prices, so it evolved that the age barrier was the only thing that prevented me from getting my hands on it.

The pavement outside of the shop was a popular gathering place for boys on Saturdays as they stared lovingly at the collections of lead soldiers, model steam engines and of course the bicycles. The shop front was adorned with hanging items like watering cans, buckets, spades and bicycle tyres.

One particular Saturday, numb with excitement and with my fingers grasping as tight as I could the paper money in my pocket, I arrived at Harry's shop. The pistol was still there nestling in the window between a set of screwdrivers and some pocket knives. I had not realised how difficult it would be to ask someone to buy it for me. I must have aroused some suspicion loitering there looking at each customer entering the shop. I stared at each one to see if I knew them at all, or to test if I could pluck up enough courage to ask them.

Most of the morning passed until a much older boy I vaguely knew came along. Well I didn't really know him; in fact I didn't even know his name. I had only ever nodded to him occasionally when he'd ridden his bike down Castleton Road and past The Corner House. He lived somewhere up Pinford Lane and his father worked for the estate.

He parked his bicycle with a pedal propping it against the kerb of the pavement. I surprised even myself by blurting out,

"Will you buy that gun for me?" I pointing vaguely at the pistol and thrust the money at him. To my amazement he calmly confirmed which one and took my money. The thought crossed my mind that maybe he wouldn't buy it at all and he'd ride off with my cash. What would I do then? As luck would have it he appeared an honest chap and entered the shop. Then to my surprise he came straight back out again.

"Shall I buy some pellets?" he asked. The way he whispered the question softly while cautiously looking up and down the street confirmed that he knew he shouldn't be doing it. I'd completely forgotten about ammunition and wasn't sure if my money would cover it. But I said yes anyway and he strolled back in.

I tried my best to look inconspicuous and innocent by turning away from the shop, but realised I was stretching my trouser pockets to their limits with fidgety fingers and I was biting my lip hard until it hurt. Then suddenly I remembered it was possible that Father might pass by in the electrical company van – he often delivered things out in the town on Saturday mornings. The thought made me grimace and I turned back from the street. I pretended to look intensely at something in the window as other people – I hadn't dared to look who – came and stood beside me. I breathed deeply and went to the other window. From there I could see Harry in his typical pose with an ear cocked towards the boy and listening intently. Unusually the boy was the only person in the shop; so it shouldn't take long I thought. I was sure Harry had already seen me hanging around outside, but I didn't want to chance him noticing me again; so without thinking, I returned to the other window where the gun was. But then Harry appeared before me behind the glass, between two racing bikes and waist deep in paraphernalia. When he reached out for the gun I realised I was being bought the actual gun I had admired so often – presumably he had no more left out the back. I pretended I had dropped something on the pavement, then turned and walked up the street a little way. I folded my arms then unfolded them.

A few minutes later the metallic clonk of a little hammer on to a tired bell that had lost its ding decades ago, signalled the shop door had opened again. The boy came out and unceremoniously handed me the heavy parcel. I was so excited I dropped all the change he gave me and it rolled down the gutter. I wasn't sure if I'd picked it all up but didn't care. I ran all the way home feeling the weight of this boxed weapon inside my coat.

I actually burned the cardboard box it came in and dug the ashes into the neglected flowerbed next to the animal graves in the backyard. The thought briefly entered my head about God's reaction at finding the ashes when looking for more deceased creatures to take to heaven. I chuckled to myself when I realised that I was unsure if I believed that nonsense anymore.

I fondled the cold metal and smelled the oily newness. I obviously wanted to use the gun straight away but my parents were due home at any moment. So I wrapped it in a soft rag and hid it under my bed for the time being.

Father was noticeably suspicious of my willingness to go to bed that night. I hardly slept a wink, but it wasn't the rock 'n' roll drifting across from The Black Horse that kept me awake, it was the excitement of owning the pistol. I sat up alone most of the night and gazed lovingly at it in the moonlight.

The backyard became a secret shooting gallery when there was no school and parents were not around. I'm sure that the people next-door heard me firing the gun and the ping of pellets knocking over tin cans, but they never seemed to complain. Surprisingly Jill began to thoroughly enjoy it. She would wait in anticipation for the firing of a pellet. Unlike the football, when tin cans were knocked over she would pick one up and rush back to me with it while shaking it violently, as if finishing off one of the enemy for me.

Then one Saturday a few weeks later, Father was at work in the electrical shop across the road in Long Street and Mother was shopping with Aunt Flo – Jill and I were alone. I had not seen my gun for a whole day. I raced upstairs, the protective rag dropped unnoticed to the floor as I caressed my pistol. It was a real weapon, not the light plastic imitation cap-firing revolver I had been used to before. I tried various stances aiming at imaginary enemies. I carefully climbed the creaking attic stairs pretending to be The Man From Uncle cautiously peering around each bend in the stairs before peppering the area with imaginary bullets. Jill was very concerned and waited on the landing while I acted out my fantasy.

Reaching the top I became Billy The Kid and dived on to the floor. I twisted my body at the last moment, landed on my back, grasped the gun with both hands and pretended to fire at the no-good, double-crossing varmints behind the chest of drawers. I got 'em! I got 'em good!

Similar to a real Western movie a light breeze caressed the filthy lace curtains in the attic window. A stronger wind through a broken pane moved the thick black cobwebs. I even imagined the clang of Castleton Sunday church bell – but it was a Saturday. My mimicking of every single imaginary bullet's ricochet had ceased as I stopped for another feel of the pleasure of the pistol there in my little hand. No bogeymen now! I was soon fumbling for real ammo. I placed the pellet there in the breech and managed to cock the weapon.

Now tentatively – knowing the gun was loaded – I approached the other grubby window halfway down the attic stairs that looked out over ours and next-door's backyard. Jill stared at me from down on the first floor landing as if she thought I had lost my mind. I intended to really put the pistol sights to the test and try and hit a tin can still left perched in the make-shift shooting gallery below. But on top of the far high wall that divided next-door from

Miss Carlisle's wilderness, singing its heart out stood a bright-eyed, plump-breasted song thrush.

The hinges of the old iron window creaked as I pushed it open. I placed my elbows on the wide sill and gazed down the top of the barrel. My heart was pounding fast, I didn't really think about it as I held my breath. I gently squeezed the trigger. I had forgotten how sensitive the trigger mechanism was. I remember hearing the slight whistle and soft thump, almost in slow-motion. The thrush still stood there motionless. The abbey clock started striking in the far distance.

"Missed," I muttered.

But no! Upon gazing up from fumbling for more ammo I witnessed the bird slowly lurch forward. It toppled and rolled down the tin roof of next-door's garden shed. Its beak and claws could be heard scraping the metal as it tumbled over and over. It plummeted from the roof to land a lifeless bundle on the hard concrete path, its supple neck bent back double and a single claw protruding awkwardly. I was transfixed and awestruck.

When next-door's cat approached, it was only fear of being caught that prevented me from shouting aloud to shoo it away. Then I experienced the welling up inside me of the sickening realisation that – yes it was dead – so it didn't matter anyway. It was no more. It was just the physical remains of its former self. So it wouldn't hurt anymore. Life was extinct. I had killed it. Dead!

Father had been right! The only advantage of a predetermined grave is as a memorial to a previously living thing. But they aren't really there in the grave. Their spirits leave them instantly when they die. It doesn't matter where they die or even how they die as long as it's quick. Grandma Eliza comfortable in warm hospital sheets or icy naked lying in the snow in Parson's Field? Joey the budgerigar tucked in earth or chucked on the fire? The anonymous wood pigeon hit by a car safe in my flowerbed or dumped in the clump of stinging nettles? A peaceful exit like Timmy the tortoise – never woke up from hibernation? The friendly rat in Grandpa's shed – life bitten out of it by the lightening jaws of a gin trap? My pellet penetrating deep into the heart of this innocent songbird? None of them knew anything about it – so everything was all right. But I and I alone had chosen to end this particular bird's life and for no reason – apart from my own entertainment.

Mrs Field from next-door disturbed my thoughts by shooing her cat away and mumbling something unintelligible as she swept the remains of the thrush into a dustpan. My mesmerised state had turned to contemplation cut short by unresolved confusion, as sounds of the dustpan being struck on the side of the metal dustbin echoed around the yard and the abbey clock finished striking. I looked down at Jill there waiting on the landing as the doorbell rang. Usually Jill would race down to the front door and bark when the door bell rang, but she must have sensed my growing anxiety and we both stayed quiet and motionless like startled wildlife.

The doorbell rang again and I was convinced that the police had come to arrest me. Jill and I both crept and tiptoed silently back across the landing and into my bedroom. I hid the gun under my bed. I dragged my bedside chair to the window, climbed on it and peered out in time to see Mrs Fay walking away from our front door. She'd obviously wanted to speak to Mother about something. She caught me out again and quickly turned and looked up at my window. Through the old wavy and reflective glass panes I must have looked rather ghostly again; she turned and almost ran back to her house in Castleton Terrace.

I knew that the next-door neighbours would probably now complain to my parents. Unless they assumed that it was some rare act of the almighty that had struck this garden bird stone-dead before them. So I decided to hide my gun properly. The obvious place was in my attic den, now devoid of bogeymen and containing all my little treasured possessions. But I was sure Father now knew that I regularly used it. I didn't mind him finding my money or indeed any of the other things that were already there; most things had my name and address emblazoned across them anyway and I knew Father would just leave them there and smile to himself. But I was certain he'd blow his top if he found an air pistol.

In the front room of The Corner House there stood the old pianola. Until recently it was only ever used when Aunt Emily – Father's sister – forced piano lessons upon me. But a few weeks ago I had discovered how to load its paper rolls and pedal it into life with strange tunes like tinkly ragtime or grand waltzes. I hid my gun deep inside its workings wrapped in its oily rag and I only viewed it occasionally when I was sure that no one else was around. I was questioned many times about the shooting of the thrush but always denied all knowledge.

Decades later in 1999, shortly before my father died at the age of 96, I was talking to him about all sorts of crazy things when he confirmed that he had indeed known all about my den. I also cautiously confessed to him that I had hidden an air weapon in his pianola all those years ago.

"Oh yes," he said straight away – smiling broadly, "I knew all about that – but I never told your mother."

My pet slowworm with only one eye – that I had plucked from under a sheet of corrugated metal in the estate woodyard when visiting Mr Hart's workplace with Father one day – still led a rather miserable existence in a cardboard box down in the garage. I knew in my heart of hearts it was wrong to keep a wild animal penned up, but at the same time I felt I was protecting him from the cruel, outside world. Jill was fascinated by him and would prance around and whine whenever I showed him to her, perhaps with a hint of jealousy.

One Saturday morning the festering bitterness about the shooting of the thrush escalated into a full-scale argument. Mother flew into a rage about it and any other little flaw concerning me that she could trawl up. She marched around the kitchen exaggerating and dramatising her actions. She threw cutlery into the sink and shouted at Jill in-between a constant stream of abuse and accusations levelled at me and Father too.

After complaining bitterly about the antique boiler balanced on scaffold planks on the end of the bath, she mentioned my Portland Bill escapade, the disaster with the puncture repair aerosol at Castleton and then the welfare of my slowworm. Each thing she remembered seemed to perpetuate her hysterical state.

"He isn't kept under control!" she shouted to Father, "you should make him do what he's told ………. and get to the bottom of this airgun thing. Mrs Field is at her wits end! How would you like it if someone shot a lovely bird in your garden? Tis obviously he who did it! Who else could it be?" Mother never called me by my name, nearly always 'he' as if I wasn't there.

There was deathly silence for a while – Jill crept under the table for fear of another onslaught. Then she started again.

"He ain't got no decent footwear to his name! A brand new pair of sandals ruined up on Portland and another pair t'other day when he were mucking about with that stuff in your car! Well money just don't grow on trees do it Vic?" Father opened his mouth to reply but was interrupted.

"And thik poor snake thing down in the garage ………. Well if the RSPCA got to know about it then you'd be in trouble! Keepin' a wild animal cooped up like that – you should make him get rid of it."

"I'm certainly not going to get rid of it!" I said, "but I might set it free."

"That's the best thing to do son!" Father said, "you know he'd be far happier."

I knew Father was right and unlike my mother he definitely had the slowworm's well-being at heart. Fuelled partly by a desperate need to get away from my mother and partly knowing that setting the creature free was the right thing to do anyway, I ran from the house and slammed the backdoor.

Whenever these arguments climaxed – usually with me leaving home as fast as I could – Mother would bleat for me to come back. It was a sort of emotional blackmail that I had become used to. In fact I had on occasions turned the tables and played her at her own game. I would insist that I was definitely leaving home forever and stride dramatically out of the house. I knew full well that I was just going for a walk and would be back within the hour. Secretly I think Father always knew this too.

While opening the pedestrian door into the garage at the end of the backyard, I could still hear Mother's muffled shouting.

"Thik bloody boiler's donkey's years old – he's gonna blow us all up one day………"

This eventually ended as it usually did, with Father's short, sharp last word. Mother would always push Father to this very precise final point as if she needed some sort of confirmation or acknowledgment of her grievances. Like clockwork after an exact amount of time Father's patience would run out. There were no grey areas with Father, just tolerant or intolerant. When he shouted his final word everyone knew – including Jill – that the end of the matter had occurred. If you still felt upset your only comfort would be the steady tick-tock of the mantle clock in the middle room.

Everyone then knew better than to utter another sound of any sort on the subject.

The movement of the slowworm resonated slightly in his acoustic, cardboard home as I approached. He was extremely tame and never seemed to want to get away, but I kept the box closed for now, I didn't want to prolong any emotional trauma; I just wanted to get it over with. I picked up the box and hugged it to my chest.

The main garage door into the road was in three hinged sections that slid completely out of the way to get the car out. Or the first section would swing open inwardly and independently to allow pedestrian only access. I squeezed past Father's car and fumbled to open the Yale type latch. This door was really designed to be closed from the inside and for years Father had meant to fix some sort of handle on the outside of the door to enable easy closing from the outside. However, if one timed it just right it was possible when outside in the street, to grasp the door by its edge and pull it quickly shut. The trick was to tug it fast enough for the force to operate the latch and click the door shut; but the faster one tugged on it, the quicker one's hand had to be withdrawn from between the concrete wall and the door edge. Timing was crucial.

When outside I placed the box down on the pavement. I must have been angry, sad and fed up all at the same time. I yanked the stupid door hard and withdrew my hand as quickly as I could. But there was no slamming of the lock just a soft thud as the edge of the closing door trapped my fingers against the rough concrete blocks of the garage wall. In the split second it took for the pain to start I realised that I would have to endure further pain to release my fingers, and the quicker I could do it the better. I closed my eyes and booted the door hard. I didn't give a damn about the door swinging in and hitting Father's car as I retrieved my fingers and nursed them tightly between my legs.

My fingers were grazed and bruised quite badly, so I wrapped my handkerchief around them and secured it with an elastic band. Although throbbing with pain I somehow managed to tie a piece of binder twine around the inside lock handle of the door. I yanked it shut with every ounce of my body weight and the twine was left trapped there, dangling.

I ran around New Road clutching the box, through the swirling steam of a passing locomotive as I crossed over the railway bridge. The road on the other side of the bridge curves gently to the right, where the field on the left slopes down to where the stickleback brook trickles into the river Yeo. Beyond that Mr Hart's well-worn footpath was prominent, all the way from the back gardens of 7 and 8 Castleton to his wooden footbridge over the river. I briefly thought about leaving my slowworm in there, overlooked by the old castle ruin. But I realised that considering my injured fingers, trying to climb the prefabricated concrete fence that formed an effective barrier from the road, would hinder things and prolong the heartbreak.

On the right of New Road at this point is a small triangular field called Little Purley. It is shaped in that way by the river, the railway line and of course the road. It was divided from the road by a fence that formed an effective barrier to horses and cattle, but not so much to boys. It consisted of concrete posts with hollow iron pipes running through them. This fence extended about a hundred yards to the river bridge at the start of the trees that often reminded me of being under water.

On happier, more mischievous days I would sometimes wait for someone to walk past the far end of the fence near the river bridge and then blow a raspberry down one of the pipes. I had laughed until my stomach ached as poor unsuspecting victims looked around for the source of the rude noise.

On this sad day, eager to get it over with quickly I decided to kneel near the first few feet of the pipe fence and set him free there. I turned the box on its side allowing my slowworm freedom into Little Purley. I told him to make himself a good home in amongst the dock leaves and stinging nettles. I assured him that the field was never mown or cultivated because of its awkward terrain; sloping down sharply as it did from the road embankment. I reminded him as he eventually poked his head out not to go near the railway line. I couldn't see properly as tears trickled down my cheeks. My companion slithered hesitantly half out of the box, then someone behind me asked,

"What are you doing?" It was the unmistakable voice of my headmaster. I turned briefly to see the black figures of him and his wife towering over me. I turned back just in time to see my slowworm ease his way out through a large tuft of grass into his new home.

"Nothing sir," I said. I was livid that the headmaster of all people had interrupted this private moment and made me miss the very final goodbye.

"This is Park," said the headmaster to his wife, "the little urchin I was telling you about."

"It is ..... was my slowworm sir..... I've set him free," I said between sniffles.

I ran away as fast as I could, not able to stop thinking about my slowworm fending for himself in a huge new world. I wondered if he would think I was still there waiting for him by the fence and return to the spot sometime later; maybe he liked his cardboard home. I told myself he definitely didn't and hated captivity and would now be extremely happy in the relatively vast expanse of Little Purley. Stupid adult voices continued as I ran down over the river bridge and scrambled through the rusty fence into Purley.

"A slowworm – how ghastly!" remarked the headmaster's wife.

"Little pest!" echoed the headmaster, "God help any other creature or person you come into contact with."

I was fascinated with animals. If they were wild I might want to satisfy a sort of morbid curiosity and shoot them or cut their heads off, although this urge was diminishing after the shock of killing the thrush. Yet if they became pets I would want to protect them at all costs from anything and anybody. I could never define what qualified an animal to become a pet. I know the gamekeeper's son found a whole family of slowworms near where I had found mine in the estate woodyard. He and a gang of older boys had first tried to shoot them with air rifles. When this didn't work because they kept missing the wriggling targets, they beheaded all of them with a machete. I suppose I could just as easily have done the same to my slowworm or the mouse I'd caught near Todd's allotment. For some reason, unlike the thrush in next-door's backyard, they instantly appealed to my protective instinct and relationships grew.

11

A Bigger Bicycle
And My First Friend

My parents and our next-door neighbours eventually forgot about the shooting of the thrush. But the image of that songbird slowly falling forwards, stone dead into next-door's garden will remain with me for the rest of my life.

As the months passed I was gradually allowed out even more on my own and my energies began to concentrate on longer exploratory pushbike rides. But as I explained in great detail to Uncle Todd one Saturday morning at their place, I was fast outgrowing my small machine and longed for a bigger bike with gears. Uncle Todd seldom, if ever worked on weekends and usually enjoyed a fried breakfast on Saturday mornings.

"So what's so special about having gears?" asked Todd.

"Well when you get to a hill," I said, "you can change down so it ain't so hard to pedal – it makes it easier." Todd tossed his head back and drank the remaining drop of tea from his special big mug.

"And you've got a lot bigger an' thik liddle bike is same size innit!" exclaimed Aunt Flo as she picked up Todd's dirty plate and took it through to the kitchen.

"I speck your knees do come up to yer chin when you'm riding it now!" she shouted back from the kitchen. Todd got up and stretched as he gazed out across Newland from their first floor balcony window.

"And I spose you'd wanna go faster too?" he remarked while continuing to yawn.

"Yeah 'cause when you'm on the flat or going down hill …. When you got gears you can change up, an your legs ain't going so fast."

"Ah you wanna be careful mind – and look out for cars!" Todd turned to look at me as he readjusted his wide leather belt. "Have you read yer Highway Code?" I answered,

"Yeah," knowing full well that I hadn't read it, not properly anyway.

"I'm going downstairs!" Todd shouted through to the kitchen where Flo was washing up. "Rabbit's said he'll help me clear out the shed." Todd sometimes called me 'Rabbit' and I never really knew why.

"Alright!" replied Flo in a high-pitched singing voice she often used.

My heart sank as I had not agreed to help Todd and I had other things planned for my Saturday morning. Todd put on his sports coat and a slight smile appeared on his face. I followed him down to their lock-up storeroom on the ground floor of Newland flats.

Todd always called it his second shed. But it was a small concrete cupboard near the coal bunker. The little room crammed bursting full with Todd's tools. There, poking through the bottom of an old raincoat was the rear mudguard of his large, heavy bicycle. All the tools were dragged out into the stairwell. Todd muttered about needing to throw out some items as he wheeled the Rudge Whitworth with flat tyres out into the light of day.

"You can have it if you want!" exclaimed Todd out of the blue. I was totally stunned and dumbfounded.

"What take it as my own?" I asked.

"Yes, I've bought a little car now and I never use the bike any more. So Flo and I thought you might like it."

I scrambled onboard, toes just about reaching the ground. The next few minutes blurred into hysteria. The pump didn't work so Todd hurriedly found another one under some old newspapers. His enthusiasm seemed to equal mine as we prepared the machine for its first outing in years.

The next thing I knew I was waving goodbye to Todd and pedalling with ease up Newland to the top of Cheap Street. The bike had one of those three speed gear mechanisms in the hub of the back wheel that emitted a steady tick tick tick in varying frequency and tone, depending which gear had been selected and of course how fast the bike was travelling.

From the top of Newland I turned left down the busy main street and freewheeled. It was so much higher than my old little bike and felt wonderful, until I applied the brakes. I clasped both brake levers on the handlebars as hard as I could. My heart sank as their looseness revealed no tension in the brake linkage. The bike was gathering speed. The car in front was slowing. I was getting closer.

I ruined yet another pair of shoes as I instinctively sat on the crossbar and scraped the tarmac with my toes. The sole of my right shoe came away from the upper part as the front wheel of the bike hit the rear bumper of the car. I slid down the boot of the car and landed on the hard tarmac. I was OK but the bike looked damaged. I later discovered it was only the handlebars twisted in their stem. I never rode a bicycle again without first checking the brakes.

The machine received a general overhaul in Harry Hunt's pushbike shop and I paid for it a little each week from my pocket money – unbeknown to my parents. Despite the fact that it was too big for me and I still felt that I was just looking after it for Todd, I cycled every street of Sherborne on the rather stately Rudge Whitworth.

It was probably the first day of the summer holiday, riding up The Avenue when I first encountered Kim. I think she was with some other girls in the driveway of her house. I rather self consciously cycled by and one of them called,

"Hiya!" Surprised, I turned too sharply and fell off the Rudge Whitworth there in the middle of the road. Kim's mother made sure I was OK and put some ointment on my knee while I insisted time and time again that it was the bike at fault and definitely not me.

My relationship with Kim grew and she became my introduction to the curious pleasure of girl companionship, which hitherto I didn't know existed. The very thought of girl company had typically been classified in my mind years ago as sissified and wimpish. But without a second thought I started visiting her nearly every day. Kim and I were far too young for anything other than innocent friendship; she was indeed my first true friend who just happened to be a girl.

One hot summer day I was off to see Kim for the umpteenth time. Jill the dog was quite content sprawled out in the backyard of The Corner House with Mother hanging out the washing.

"Where you going?" asked Mother sensing that I was about to leave the house.

"Out!" I said. This single syllable response had evolved to be the norm when Mother enquired about such things. I suppose it was my way of dealing with my inability to articulate such intricacies of my boyhood world. Not that Mother would have understood anyway.

Kim lived in the first of the comparatively smaller houses up The Avenue on the right a little way before the gangway that goes through to the A30. After I had ridden the Rudge Whitworth around the corner of Newland and into The Avenue I made straight for a familiar gate that led into the grounds of one of the larger properties halfway up the hill. Placed on a low wall by a carved wooden sign, which read 'Applegarth,' was an old tea tray laden with large red, windfall-apples. Scrawled in large spidery handwriting on a tatty piece of hardboard propped close by was the message 'Please Help Yourself.' I had never seen anyone at the property but apples were often left there – free for the taking. I carefully chose two, popped one in my pocket and started to eat the other.

I pushed my bike with my elbows leaning on the handlebars. I munched the delicious fruit savouring each bite as juice trickled down my cheek. As I was finishing the apple my mind confirmed the fact that apples could taste quite nice. My young brain ticked rapidly from one thought to the next and for one fleeting moment I experienced a sinking feeling when I remembered that my pocket money had run out, drained by the commitment to maintaining the Rudge Whitworth, but it was worth it. Then in the blink of an eye, all these thoughts were forgotten when I noticed Kim in the distance sitting on the wall outside her parents' house.

Visiting Kim had now become my favourite activity above all others during this one particular summer. Her parents' property backed on to the playing fields of Foster's Grammar School. We would play in there, often rolling down the grass slopes from the raised tennis courts or playing hide and seek. Sometimes quite serious tennis matches were staged with old rackets rescued from the school dustbin.

The allotments adjoined the playing fields nearby and I once took her to visit Todd's patch there. I shared with her my fascination of the old bath, told her about Todd's magazine of bathing beauties and how I had rescued a mouse from drowning. She giggled a lot. Maybe, if the mood struck us we would just sit and wonder what we might be when we grew up. If we stayed near the house and the weather was hot, Kim's mother would give us fresh, iced orange juice served from a heavy glass jug. Very occasionally other children joined us, but they always seemed an interruption to our magic world. We just seemed to 'click' and had grown to adore each other's company.

Kim squinted in the bright sunlight as I approached and kicked her heals against the stone wall smiling.

"Can you play today?" I asked as I propped my bike against the wall and handed her a large red apple.

"Yes I expect so," she said. She jumped down from the wall and opened the wooden gate into their driveway.

"Come on," she said, "I'll race you to the tennis courts!" Just as the gate closed the family's boxer dog came bounding down the drive. He was quite friendly but very boisterous. He snorted loudly and made disgusting noises with his flabby lips as he jumped up at me time and time again; he probably smelled Jill's scent on me. Finally, after satisfying his need to greet me Barnaby the boxer dog galloped off up the driveway out of sight, only to return a minute later with his old deflated football, which he tossed into the air inviting us to play. As we approached the side doorway of the house trying not to step on the dog prancing in front of us, Kim's mother shouted.

"Who is it dear?" and then popped her head around the doorway. "Oh it's the boy from The Corner House," she continued, "be careful if you're going to play in the school grounds and be sure not to annoy the Mr Smith." Mr Smith was the groundsman who hated too many children around the school during the holidays but tolerated Kim and me.

We raced each other over to the wicket gate that led out into the school playing fields. Our frantic need to run was interrupted as we made sure the gate was securely closed – dogs were not allowed in there except on a lead. The boxer dog watched in dismay through the chain-link mesh of the gate as we raced off across the grass. After a while the dog's jaw dropped subconsciously and the old ball fell unnoticed on to the ground.

We forgot about the tennis courts for the time being and Kim led the way over to the old wooden cricket pavilion. As we arrived both panting, we could hear Mr Smith on his ride-on mower. We peered around the corner of the building and could see him down the far end of the grounds perched on the metal sprung seat and being jostled by the trundling machine. Mr Smith would go crazy sometimes waving his hands frantically if we didn't keep to the perimeter of the grounds.

We sat on the steps of the veranda fronted pavilion dreaming that we were sitting on the steps of our own homestead in the wildest outback of Australia. The building did rather resemble a log cabin somewhere on a lonely prairie. The pavilion was just about visible from the house and I'm sure Kim's mother sometimes pondered at the antics of us two youngsters. The minutes would dissolve into hours with ease as we scribbled and doodled on the first scrap page of each other's innocent minds.

At that moment our private world was rudely interrupted by the sound of other children from the north side of town. They invaded the playing fields from time to time breaking through the dividing hedge near the allotments. Kim got up and crept to the corner of the building. She carefully surveyed the situation and glanced at me as I stood near her. I strained over her shoulder for a look.

"It's Steve Mitchell and Gary White's lot," she said quite annoyed. Everyone knew that a game of cowboys and Indians would ensue.

"Come out with your hands up!" shouted one of the gang as they rapidly approached down across the 'prairie.'

"Let's make a dash for it," I said. "Come on! If we hurry we should make the groundsman's hut over there." We both ran for all we were worth down to the small hut some seventy-five yards away. As our small feet skidded around the corner of the hut Steve Mitchell's gang, all five of them, came bounding down the same route whooping and screaming like the wild Red Indians I had learnt to mimic at infant school. Mr Smith who was now approaching the long jump pits a hundred and fifty yards away, nearly fell off his machine; gesticulating frantically, his faint shouts were just discernible in the afternoon breeze. We ran on again both knowing that the little hut hid our line of escape from the eyes of the marauding scalpers. A few more seconds and we were out of sight behind the red brick walls of the school buildings.

Panting heavily we surveyed the confusion of our pursuers back at the groundsman's hut. Kim bent over with hands on her knees.

"If we double back up the other side of the school we should be able to ambush them," she managed to utter, totally out of breath. With the sound of Mr Smith still shouting in the distance, we ran out into Tinneys Lane by the main entrance of the school. We surprised a man loading a lorry at a frozen food depot on the other side of the lane. He glanced up.

"Hello there!" he said, slightly concerned at our apparent distress.

"Hello," we replied in unison while trying to hide any signs of our pumping adrenaline. We walked quickly towards the second school entrance trying not to run for fear of attracting any further attention from the man. As soon as we were back in the school grounds and out of the man's sight we ran up the other side of the school. We heard things being moved inside the building like tables being dragged across the floor.

"It must be the holiday cleaners," I whispered. I stretched up to peer just above the sill into the classroom and there was Aunt Flo mopping the floor. I instantly crouched down. We scurried up the tarmac pathway, again crouching low at each of the other windows. Then just past the tin bike shed Kim tripped over a concrete kerb and grazed her knee.

I was still quite shy of other children but found myself kneeling down beside her. I hesitantly placed an arm on her shoulder. She looked up at me just about managing to hold back a tear. I guess I instinctively recognised this look and gently massaged the area around the injury.

"My dad taught me to do that!" I remarked. She managed a smile.

Kim was a bit of a tomboy and she was soon on her feet and hand in hand we walked straight into Steve Mitchell's ambush.

"Bang you're dead!" shouted Steve Mitchell as he mimicked bullets ricocheting off every available wall. I dramatically held my chest and took ages to drop to the floor with a series of prolonged grunts and groans.

As I lay on the ground squinting at the blue sky and specks of swallows gathering insects, I heard the rest whispering. Apparently they were going to capture Kim and tie her to a tree like true Red Indians do on the TV. So I slowly inched my fingers over the neat cropped grass to my imaginary six-shooter. My hand pretended to grasp the weapon and I suddenly jumped up.

"OK hands up!" I shouted in an awful American accent, "I'm taking you in."

"But you're dead," said Gary White.

"Yeah," agreed Steve Mitchell and a young Indian squaw by his side.

"It was only a flesh wound and I've just come round," I explained as I stood there, my right hand now pointing an index finger like a gun and my left clutching my shoulder to where the wound had now miraculously moved. Kim moved over to my side and announced that I was indeed the county Sheriff and why didn't everyone know. Together we took our prisoners in to the county law office where Kim's mother supervised; administering more ointment, serving orange juice and listening to the charges.

The following day at half past ten in the morning Kim was just about managing to walk down the driveway of her parents' house wearing her mother's huge stiletto-heeled shoes while sucking an ice-lolly. The shoes were many sizes too big and she struggled to stay upright.

"No Barnaby!" she shouted to the boxer dog as he followed her closely with pleading eyes, believing that Kim was eating something that dogs liked.

"You always spit it out when you're given ice lolly!" she mumbled to the dog as she placed her elbows on the top of the front gate and finished the remainder of the lolly. Then, climbing on to the bottom rung she gazed up at the blue sky and cotton wool clouds passing by. The new record Good Golly Miss Molly was pumping out loudly from the Light Programme of next-door's radio. Kim looked down at the high-heeled shoes she was wearing and pointed her toes skywards wondering when she would be old enough to have her own fancy pair of shoes.

It was then that I arrived. I remarked jokingly that I knew who Little Richard was singing about on the radio. Kim didn't seem very interested. Nonetheless, I mumbled that the record was about a little old lady I knew who lived down in Castleton. Kim smiled slightly but was strangely quiet as she unlatched the gate. She kept one foot on the gate and propelled it open with the other. High-heeled shoes discarded for the time being, we strolled over towards our favourite spot – the cricket pavilion.

We both lay on the well-worn veranda examining the embossed grain of the timber and listening to the song of a far-away skylark. The lyrics of the record we had just heard were still floating around in my head. I imagined in semi-slumber the Miss Molly I knew in fancy hat mechanically 'dancin' in a house of blue light,' or was it 'moonlight.'

The timber was warm on our backs and waxy soft to the touch. The structure clicked and moaned a little as it adjusted to the heat of the late morning sun.

"Hello there!" We were suddenly aware of Mr Smith the groundsman standing right there in front of us.

"Hello Mr Smith," said Kim sitting bolt upright, shocked, "you don't mind us being here do you?" He smiled slightly and squinted in the sunlight.

"No I don't mind you two being here as long as you behave yourselves, but if you see any of those others who were here yesterday, you let me know – all right!"

"Yes Mr Smith," we chanted almost together.

"They trampled right through my flowerbeds out the front yesterday...........they'll have something to answer for if I catch 'em.....I shall have to get the police up here I reckon." After straining to peep in through one of the pavilion windows, Mr Smith made his way back down towards the school. He walked in a peculiar sort of way and his braces appeared to hold up his wide trousers far too high. We tried to suppress our giggles until Mr Smith had completely disappeared from view.

"What you gonna be when you grow up?" asked Kim. I thought for a moment.

"Cowboy," I said, "Or a pop star."

"A cowboy …. in real life?" Kim remarked tauntingly, "there's no jobs around here for cowboys!"

"I don't have to stay around here," I said, "I could go to Australia." There was a long silence.

"Anyway you can't ride a horse," said Kim eventually, dozing in the heat. "Or sing." she continued.

"It's easy enough to learn," I said, "you can do anything if you really want to – that's what my father says." Kim started chuckling.

"What you laughing at!"

"I can't imagine you singing a pop song," she managed to say, now laughing heartily.

"I can sing Rock Around The Clock," I said, knowing full well that I'd never attempted it without Aunt Flo's accompaniment and I certainly didn't know all the right words. Fearing she was going to ask me to prove my singing ability I hastily asked,

"So what are you gonna be when you grow up?"

"A sheep farmer."

"What in Wales?" I asked.

"Nope… anyway bet you can't find me!" said Kim hastily changing the subject. She composed herself and stood up.

"But you must count to fifty SLOWLY with your eyes CLOSED!" she continued.

"OK," I said starting to count. Kim made off up across the open expanse of playing field behind the pavilion. I could not resist opening one eye slightly but Kim was nowhere to be seen. In my anticipation I had forgotten just how far I had counted so I waited for as long as I could bear.

"She must have gone somewhere up the top of the grounds," I muttered, "near the allotments." I wondered briefly if she had in fact gone into the allotments, but I came to the conclusion that she'd never leave the confines of the school grounds on her own without telling her mother.

I crept up the side of the pavilion and peered carefully around the corner. I couldn't see her but some way away near the hedge that divided the playing fields from the allotments, there was a tall, slightly curved brick structure used to play some sort of ball game. Kim was in fact hiding there but she had seen me approaching as she lay flat-out partly hidden by the structure and partly by a convenient tuft of long grass. So as I reached the structure Kim – as skilfully as any soldier – carefully chose the precise second to make her break down towards the school while I innocently continued on around the rear of the structure. Finding no one there I ran right around it just in time to see Kim in the distance back down by the school disappearing around the corner of the main building.

"Right," I muttered biting my lip, "this so called game of hide and seek has turned into a game of cat and mouse."

The late morning sun was getting hotter and I could hear a dog barking in the distance somewhere. As I squinted down towards the school a few of the open windows reflected brightly.

"No point in running," I whispered under my breath. With my hands in pockets I eventually reached the corner of the school building where I had seen Kim disappear. Half-heartedly I peered around the edge of the brickwork. Kim was nowhere to be seen. Casually I strolled out into the lane where I heard the faint hum of the deep freeze units opposite the school entrance. I looked both ways and turned right, past a double lockup garage where Mr Parsons repaired motorcars in his trilby hat and a long khaki work coat.

As I walked towards the field next-door where two horses lived, I heard a car start up and a bonnet slam shut. I reached the field gate and the grey mare ambled up closely followed by a small white pony. I used to feed them Cow Parsley which grew in great abundance just there by the wall, but the lady who owned them had reprimanded me the week before, she said it made them ill.

Just then I heard a shoe scuff on the tarmac, I spun around to see Kim creeping up. She stopped about five feet away with hands on hips.

"Careful they don't bite you," she quipped.

"I'm certainly not scared of horses," I replied immediately.

"You're moody and sulking!" she continued.

"I am not moody," I said turning back to the horses.

"Yes you are," she sang, "just because you couldn't find me."

"Yes I did find you," I said, "but you ran off, you're not allowed to change your hiding place."

"Well you didn't count to fifty so there."

"I don't want to play any more anyway," I said.

"Nah nah na nah nah.........can't catch me, can't catch me, can't catch me for a toffee fee!" I was furious. I spun around and lunged forward but Kim was too quick. She took off across the lane, up the side of the school, past the bike shed – I was in hot pursuit. We reached the school tennis courts between the science block and the pavilion before I caught her. Kim fumbled to open the chain link gate to shut herself inside the courts and I grabbed her just before the latch gave way. We both toppled over and rolled down the grassy bank shrieking and giggling together. Horizons of roofs and chimney pots, sky and the sweet grass tumbled higgledy-piggledy, topsy-turvy past our senses.

"Don't you hurt me or I'll tell my mum!" Kim shouted breathless. But we both knew we could never willingly harm each other.

Our giggles were interrupted by an almighty crash of thunder. One of those low, loud crashes that make you realise just how powerful the forces of nature can be. We stopped dead and noticed the sky had quickly turned inky black above us. A sizzling spurt of angry fork lightning appeared to actually touch the allotments. Then the heavens opened.

"I don't like thunder!" said Kim, her voice drowned out by the next rolling clap.

"Come on!" I shouted, "lets shelter in the pavilion veranda, it's the nearest place."

"We can't go in there," said Kim, "lightning could strike it."

"Don't be daft," I said, "It would strike those trees over there first."

I had never seen Kim look so frightened. I took her hand and we ran, heavy drops hurting our heads and drenched to the skin, over to the veranda of the cricket pavilion. Lightning was shooting through the skies all around us, the next rumble made the pavilion windows shake as we arrived. I felt the hairs on the back of my neck stand on end. Unlike years before I now knew that lightning did indeed strike things in this country. I was therefore a little scared but fought not to show it. My father's words echoed through my head: 'What ever will be will be…. And you wouldn't know much about it anyway.'

The water drops pelting down were so huge and had such velocity that it seemed they were setting off little explosions in the grass just in front of the veranda. Torrents of water gushed off the simple roof and the increasingly angry wind blew it in over us.

"I'm going home!" announced Kim, "Mum will be worried."

"Not yet," I said, "we'll get soaked even more."

"Well we're wet enough already."

"I know but you're asking for…….." I was interrupted by the loudest clap yet, we both instinctively ducked our heads. Kim hugged me.

"We'd be asking for trouble," I continued, "to go out across the open playing fields in this." I turned and tried the door of the pavilion, to my amazement it opened. We shot inside and slammed the door against the storm. Lightning sent shafts of light through the pavilion's tiny windows to emphasize our misty puffs of anxious breath. The little structure shook as another roll of thunder circled overhead.

"It's gonna strike us!" said Kim biting her lip and staring at the vibrating ceiling.

"Don't be daft," I said, "we're safe as anything in our pavilion – safe as anything."

After that thunderstorm had passed and left us unscathed, there was just one more full summer day we spent together rehearsing for future roles and growing even fonder of each other's company. Then all too soon, the carefree school holidays came to an end – much to the relief of many parents.

My journey to school took me right past Kim's house every morning and if I was early enough I would catch a glimpse of her in her smart uniform being driven to convent school by her mum.

Then one particular morning about a week after term started, I was as usual riding to school on my Rudge Whitworth. It was an uphill struggle going to school but well worth it for the fantastic freewheel home. I rounded the corner from Newland into The

Avenue whistling the Z Cars theme tune from the television. Once on the straight I rose from the saddle and stood on each pedal in turn to conquer the hill.

As I was passing Kim's house I nearly fell off my bicycle – like I had done when I first met her. Because when I looked up the driveway there was Kim hiding from her family by the garden wall, crouched low on the gravel beckoning wildly. I doubled back and propped my bike on the kerb of the pavement. I ran over and stood in front of her. Before I could say anything she jumped up and with a hand on my shoulder, pulled me down to her crouching position. Reminiscent of Sandra a few years before, she handed me a brown envelope and as a grinning postman cycled past she kissed me squarely on the lips. I hadn't time to realise what had happened before Kim ran back into the house. I never saw her again.

Puzzled, I raced to school as quickly as I could. The route took me along the walled passageway between houses that came out on the busy A30 where the old crossing patrol man supervised children across the road. That morning I didn't notice the pain of being clasped by the ear as I pondered over the package that I didn't have time to open. For once the old man spoke to me.

"What you got there then?" he asked.

"It's from my girlfriend," I said without really thinking.

"You ain't got no girlfriend have you?" he replied teasingly.

"I have!" I said as he released his grip.

"We're going to Australia when we're old enough!" I shouted back as I pedalled frantically away.

"Australia?" he repeated, scratching his head.

I managed to get to school with only seconds to spare and in assembly that morning I stood in the back row near all the awards and trophies. After the Lord's Prayer had been said and with the headmaster lecturing, I pulled out the package and tore it open. There inside was a magnificent Swiss Army penknife and a packet of chewing gum along with a hand-written note that simply read 'To dearest Colin - All my love forever Kim XXX.' Suddenly the headmaster stormed.

"What have you got there boy!?" I looked up sharply, confirming my worst nightmare. The headmaster was shouting at me. I looked around nervously in a last desperate attempt to see if by any chance the headmaster was referring to someone else. But no, anyone who dared was looking at me, some sympathetically but at the same time thankful it was not them who had attracted the headmaster's attention.

"Bring it here boy!" blared the headmaster with bulging eyes. I slowly walked out in front of the whole school and handed over the penknife to be confiscated. As I did so the note fluttered to the floor.

"Pick it up boy!" shouted the headmaster. As I bent down to pick it up the chewing gum fell out on to the floor.

"Pick it up boy!" repeated the headmaster, "pick it all up!" I handed the headmaster the chewing gum. "And the piece of paper," demanded the headmaster.

"It's umm private," I stammered.

"Private!" roared the headmaster, "I'll tell you what's private in my assembly laddie – I'll ask you one more time, give me the piece of paper boy." He snatched it from my hand. There was silence as he read the note to himself.

"Now," he began, looking over his spectacles at the rest of the school. "Let this be a lesson to you all, this pest has had the audacity to bring two banned items into my assembly. You all know knives are not allowed and chewing gum – well it's just about your level isn't it, chewing gum." He hit me hard across the top of the head and I nearly lost my balance. He held the note up in front of himself again.

"All my love – with kisses." he said mockingly. "Well maybe we should have you kiss all the girls in the school?" He was right in assuming that such a threat held deep terror to a young boy. He ripped the note apart in front of me as he muttered further through clenched teeth. I felt like kicking him in the crutch.

"Get out of my sight!" he bellowed at the top of his voice as he hit me even harder across the back of the head. Before I could recover my balance the deputy head sprang out in delight and shoved me down the corridor, barging into me every time I tried to compose myself or recover my balance. There was deathly silence. Everyone knew the fate that awaited anyone who interrupted morning assembly.

It was a day I will remember for the rest of my life. Firstly I had yet another beating watched by the old man in the headmaster's study. Then later when cycling home past Kim's place I noticed the house looked empty – really empty. I doubled back for a second look. The place was completely deserted. There was a 'For Sale' sign newly erected in the front garden and the rooms were bare to the floorboards. I couldn't understand it.

It was some weeks later that I heard through the Sherborne grapevine that the family had emigrated to Australia. My Kim had gone in search of her dreamland. Despite being the rough and tumble tomboy who'd fight any boy, I guess she just couldn't bring herself to tell me of her family's plans. For the rest of my schooldays I carried around a map of Australia sketched on my satchel in marker pen. I vowed to emigrate there myself just as soon as I was old enough.

It was far more difficult to visit Foster's Playing Fields now both physically and mentally. No longer able to gain access through Kim's old place meant the more conspicuous main entrance was my only option. But I did visit one rainy Saturday in October. I wasn't sure if anyone had noticed me but the building and grounds seemed totally deserted. I sat with my arms folded on the very edge of the pavilion veranda. Sheets of fine rain floated randomly across the green expanse like the contents of a giant watering can being sprinkled over the area. Football goal nets gently moved in the breeze of a grey, cold day. Water drenched me as it trickled down my cheeks and made my hair curl as it stuck to my forehead. I was not aware of my sopping clothes. I felt nothing but the gentle rain on my face. Later in the lane I jumped repeatedly into rain-filled potholes savouring each brief thrill of the explosion of displaced water.

I told my tale to the two horses by the gate. They both stood there motionless except for the occasional blink of their eyes as rain ran down their faces too. Although they appeared totally fed up wishing the rain would stop, their ears and eyes focused on me sometimes and they seemed to understand as I gently stroked their noses.

When not being comforted by the ever faithful Jill, my favourite place in the whole world became the highest point within the branches of a Scots pine tree, down by the river and waterfall near Len Hart's wooden footbridge. It had become my exterior den. I began to spend more and more of my time up in this tree gently swaying in the breeze. There were wonderful views of the estate woodyard immediately to the south, the river snaking its way across Purley after passing by from the lake and the bright, gently curving railway lines to and from London and Exeter. Just across the field were 7 and 8 Castleton where Frank Park lived and the church beyond with its little belfry poking through the yews. Sometimes a magpie, crow or wood pigeon would land there beside me, they never seemed to realise there was a human nestling in their branches. Above the constant rushing sound of the waterfall little steam trains could be heard chugging along or the urgent Doppler shift affected whistle of a non-stop express locomotive.

It was very pleasant. And in the evenings dearest Jill was ever sympathetic. But I was beginning to realise just what Kim had meant to me. I tried to imagine what she was up to, maybe on a sheep farm with thousands of miles around her – a new life, a new country. I often wondered if she thought of me. I never really worked out what sort of relationship we had. We were so young, but we just fitted neatly into place with each other. Despite our tender age the experience had brought with it all the typical bickering, playfulness and love of a genuine human relationship. Losing her left a cruel taste of what it was like to have a sister or a brother.

My parents didn't even know about her. We never really discussed my friends or school. Father or Uncle Todd would still occasionally, jokingly ask if I'd had the slipper recently or if I'd found a girlfriend. I would always say no to save any further inquisition. My naïve thoughts about being a cowboy or indeed a pop star had diminished, the harsh reality of life had started to kick in. The branches rustled, time passed in my tree.

12

Potting Shed Gang, Records
And A Tape Recorder

Jill was not exactly a young dog anymore – she was probably middle aged when we got her. She didn't enjoy such long walks now and was perfectly content to relax in The Corner House during the day while looking forward to my return with tales of my ever-expanding experiences in the outside world.

During my daytime activities I very gradually developed other acquaintances. I feel that in some ways I had grown up before most of my peers in the sense that I had gone some way to fathom and quell on my own, the irresistible urges that boys seem to have to experience what it's like to carry out gruesome and cruel acts. I suppose this was at least partly due to my shock realisation that I had wantonly destroyed life to satisfy some twisted pleasure when I had shot that song thrush.

In my solitary ponderings I had questioned my motives. Were it not for the fact that I seemed to be held in high esteem by other boys when I recounted the act, I may well have come to the conclusion that I needed some kind of psychiatric help. Other boys were definitely continuing more horrific acts to 'see what it is like,' and to prove macho one-upmanship. I guess this is some sort of instinctive, primitive way of establishing or confirming a boyhood hierarchy system.

I had recently been told of a gang who had shot starlings and then – before life was completely extinct from their little bodies – had doused them in methylated spirit or lighter fluid and set them alight. Also I had witnessed older boys – from high in my very private tree-perch above the waterfall – wait patiently next to the river where the bank was highest and the water shallowest for wildlife of any kind to wander by. When something appeared like a water vole or moorhen, they would drop massive boulders on to the unsuspecting creatures and eagerly inspect the resulting squashed mess. Further musing and comparisons confirmed that I was just a typical boy and I was fairly normal and sane. However, I still remained a little gullible as far as social interactions were concerned.

I became associated with a gang of three other boys who had two comparatively sophisticated dens. The father of one of them ran a petrol station and garage towards the far end of Newland, which also incorporated a coach and taxi service. It was almost opposite what was then Lord Digby's School for Girls. The large garage premises stretched from Newland down to the edge of Hound Street car park where sheep were sold on market days. There were three or four long abandoned motor coaches half-hidden in tumble-down shelters deep in undergrowth at the rear of the premises. One of these coaches had been cannibalised for spare parts and hardly had any seats left in it. It had an old cylindrical paraffin stove inside, carpets that had been discarded from parents' living quarters and filthy curtains had been hung at the windows with binder twine.

I was never really a true member of this gang, but once found myself at one of their gatherings. Sausages were placed two at a time in direct contact with the top of the lit stove. Although somewhat sooty they eventually cooked – almost. Having passed the initiation ceremony of eating half-cooked, paraffin tainted sausages from the top of the stove, I was one day invited to their second den.

One of the other boys lived in a house with quite a large garden. The entrance was exactly opposite the petrol station and next to Lord Digby's School. In the garden of this boy's house, which extended up behind the high brick walls of the girls' school, there was a semi-derelict potting shed. It had been turned into their second den with the addition of an old sofa and a mattress. The floor was largely mud and it smelled like Todd's allotment shed.

It was here where I first experienced a transistor radio. It was hung in the den on a nail and tuned to the Light Programme. I was quite used to the common radio interference Father called 'motor boating' but I had only ever heard it produced via the glass valve innards of big radios, which produced deep bass tones. I had recently begun to understand that this 'motor boating' phenomenon was caused specifically by electrical interference from the high tension spark of unsuppressed engines and the sound produced through the radio's speaker had nothing to do with the actual sound that a particular engine made. This knowledge which I had gained by constantly questioning Father, had now been proven a few times on my sixpenny radio when it had given me prior warning of the midday two-stroke motorcycle approaching The Corner House long before I could actually hear the machine itself. This snippet of scientific knowledge did not quell my imagination lying in bed late at night. In my semi-conscious state my sixpenny radio's 'motor boating' fading in and out and changing tone represented weird and wonderful machines that zoomed and chugged around my world.

Therefore I was curious and fascinated how Alan's tiny Japanese radio still occasionally made these familiar noises, but very scratchy and tinny like a telephone. Transistorised interference reminded me of insects or model aircraft rather than big real vehicles.

John suggested that we play 'surprises' and I was to go first. Apparently anyone entering the den had to participate in 'surprises' as a second initiation ceremony. To go first meant to lie on the mattress; eyes closed and wait for the surprise. In retrospect I cannot believe my naivety. I waited eyes closed. Suddenly – it seemed in perfect synchronisation – the contents of three bladders came gushing over my face. The urine trickled and into my eyes and mouth. I frantically wiped my eyes to see three stumpy, adolescent penises dangling and dripping below laughing faces. I spat, cleared my throat and spat again. I was stunned at what had happened. One boy at least was apologetic and even appeared frightened by me shouting at them. I was furious, not only at them but myself for being so stupid and trusting. I suppose it wasn't any worse than any barrack room horseplay that probably happens every day and I'm sure I wasn't the only one.

My old sixpenny radio with its deep 'motor boating' continued to be my best companion – apart from Jill. I learnt to connect headphones and unbeknown to Father I would listen late into the night. The dial fascinated me; there were places mentioned like Athlone, Warsaw and Droitwich, but scanning the needle over these destinations often produced more 'motor boating' and a wide variety of whistling.

Although it constantly faded in and out and became distorted, there was always Radio Luxembourg 'The Station Of The Stars' on 208 metres. Despite its broadcasts being annoyingly punctuated with boring adverts, Luxembourg constantly pumped out pop songs.

There was one advert in particular that was sprinkled in more merciless repetition than any others across the broadcasts. From it I learnt how to spell Keynsham perfectly and the name of Horace Bachelor lodged in my mind forever. Apparently Horace Bachelor held the secret of being able to win large amounts of money playing the football pools and he would share this knowledge if you sent him money. Listeners were instructed to send postal orders or cheques to a PO box number in Keynsham and Keynsham was always spelled out a letter at a time.

Then one night my radio sounded grossly distorted – so much so that the pop songs were barely recognisable. My radio had broken. I took the back off to reveal the dusty, smelly innards. Stupidly, I actually turned it on with the back removed and tapped things with a lollipop stick to no avail.

In the electrical shop across the road it was Derrick who was the wireless and television repairman. Whereas Father's forte – even though he worked in the shop most Saturdays – remained house-wiring and perhaps the occasional repair of domestic appliances like irons and kettles. Secretly, while home from school one lunchtime, I went to see Derrick in the shop.

"It's totally distorted," I said, "you can't make anything out at all."

"Have a look in the back," said Derrick. "After you've turned it on and given it plenty of time to warm up, if you can see a glass valve that's lit up purple then that's what it is – I wouldn't mind betting it's the rectifier valve."

"I'll go and have a look," I said running from the shop.

"Don't go operating it with the back off!" shouted Derrick, "you should be able to see all the valves through the ventilation grill at the back!" I was oblivious to Derrick's warning as I ran back across the road to The Corner House.

The school lunch hour would go by very quickly so I raced upstairs and turned the set on. Against Derrick's advice the back of the set remained removed. I peered carefully over the transformers and capacitors. Sure enough there was one valve glowing bright purple as the electronics warmed up. I switched the set off immediately and grasped the offending valve yanking it from its seat.

Back at the shop Derrick put his glasses on and peered at it.

"Yes it's a PEN A4," he said, "we've got these in stock." He disappeared out the back and almost instantly returned with a brand new one on a box.

"They're nine and sixpence," he said. My heart dropped. I had no idea they would be that expensive – I only had about two shillings.

I quickly resigned myself to the fact that I would have to save up to repair my radio. I had recently paid off the repair of the Rudge Whitworth bicycle but money was still very tight. I was even racking my brain as I stood there for things that I could possibly sell.

"How much you got then?" asked Derrick.

"Two shillings," I said.

"Well that's not enough is it?"

"Nope."

"But it's enough for a deposit though."

"What and then I pay you a bit each week?" I said excitedly.

"Yeah why not – we know where to come if you don't pay."

"Aw thanks Derrick," I said. I ran forward and hugged him.

"Steady," said Derrick, "we don't want to drop it." I thrust the two shillings in Derrick's hand and ran for the door with my prize.

"Hey!" said Derrick making me pause in the doorway, "I bet your old man's gonna be pleased." I raced directly back to school and spent the whole afternoon surreptitiously nursing my new rectifier valve. I skilfully kept it hidden from everyone, ensuring it was not confiscated.

By this time I had become aware of 45rpm records. Some shops had installed individual booths for listening to a particular record before you bought it. However, the chap in our local music shop soon got wise to the fact that I couldn't afford to buy any records; he therefore refused to let me hear any – not that I had any way of playing records anyway. It was often the wavering tones emanating from The Black Horse jukebox intermingled with chatter and laughter that gave me my first taste of a new record. But it was so frustrating lying in bed straining to hear it again should someone choose to select it; or waiting and waiting for a DJ to play it on Radio Luxembourg. I yearned for a record player.

They started trying to teach us 'Country Dancing' at school. For us boys it always remained a girly thing, galloping in circles holding hands and then weaving around each other while skipping along like a fairy. But what I wouldn't have given for a record player system like the one they used to play the country dancing records. I think the turntable was the sort that the BBC used and the speaker was housed in a massive wooden cabinet that resonated the bass notes perfectly.

I actually suggested to the friendly teacher who looked like Roy Orbison one day that maybe we could play some more up-to-date music like the Beatles. I didn't realise the deputy head was standing nearby. He said the Beatles and the like were utter rubbish. He actually bet us all a shilling each that the new group called The Beatles would not last longer than a year.

Then one day while on a visit to Aunt Dorothy with my parents, I must have expressed my wish to acquire a record player or gramophone. At this time I thought of them as being pretty much the same thing. To my great delight Aunt Dorothy – who was Father's sister – said she had a record player that she and her husband Horace did not want any more. It was upstairs in their bedroom and we could take it home there and then if we wanted it.

Unfortunately it wasn't exactly what I expected. It was an old-fashioned, wind-up gramophone specifically designed for playing only 78rpm records and it was massive. The piece of polished furniture resembled a cupboard on legs. It had a heavy lid on the top that lifted to reveal the brass arm that took the sound through an acoustic box and out through a large horn below. Simply opening or closing doors on the front of the cabinet was the only way of controlling the volume.

I had spilled over with excitement when Aunt Dorothy confirmed that I could definitely have the item. But that was before I'd actually seen the thing. Now here we were standing in Dorothy's bedroom doorway gawping at the monstrosity. But I didn't want to hurt my aunt's feelings.

"It's very nice," I mumbled, as Father – more or less assuming a decision had been made – considered how to get the thing home.

Neither my parents nor my aunt seemed to recognise my disappointment and lack of enthusiasm now that I'd seen it. I tried to smile as I wondered if it was actually worth all the effort of manoeuvring it down the awkward, narrow stairway. But Father fetched a tape measure, measured it up and tried to get an idea of its weight by heaving on one corner a little.

"It might just fit!" muttered Father as he raced back down the stairs to check the dimensions of the car's boot.

"Are you sure about this?" said Mother. For a moment I thought my mother was asking me, but before I could answer, Aunt Dorothy replied,

"Oh yes definitely – I've not used it for years." She quickly wiped dust from its waxed top with her fingers as she spoke.

"Tis a nice thing!" remarked Mother stepping back and admiring it.

Another uncle and two cousins were called upon, and they and Father took an hour to grunt and groan and struggle with it down the stairs to the front door. We drove the ten miles home with it poking precariously from the rear of the car, covered in an old blanket.

I so wanted an electric record player, most other children had one and played loud, pounding pop songs in their bedrooms whenever they wanted. I later discovered that Aunt Dorothy – bless her heart – didn't even know modern electric record players existed. Because of this I had now ended up with an ancient clockwork contraption. But at least my parents seemed to like it.

After it had been positioned in the corner of the front room Jill gave it a full inspection. The cabinet doors just above its spindly legs were opened and she paid particular attention to the dark cave formed by the huge horn inside.

Father fetched a 78rpm record from his bureau. I had no idea Father owned a record. It was called Who's Afraid Of The Big Bad Wolf. Father lifted the heavy lid and wound the cranked handle on the side until it would wind no more. Amid the crackles an old woman sang over and over again of the big bad wolf, occasionally intermingled with a 'Tra La La La Lah.'

The woman's voice reminded me of an old white witch Father had told me about from his youth called Old Mother Hearne. Apparently she had totally cured Father's friend from stuttering by unexpectedly throwing a bucket of water over him. I thought for a while if a similar act might cure my stuttering. Eventually the repetitive lyrics became monotonous. It was nothing like the Black Horse jukebox or Radio Luxembourg. Even Jill the dog turned her back and went to gaze upon the flickering embers of the open fire. The awkward great thing was forgotten for a few weeks and I grew more envious of other children and their stories of bedroom discotheques.

One evening near Christmas my parents, Jill the dog and I sat huddled around the open fire in the front room.

"I've found some more 78s!" said Father, "shall I try one?" Neither Mother nor I answered him. The mantle clock continued its steady tick-tock, a log fizzled and spat sparks as it burned, and

Jill was briefly startled. Then eventually, typical of an arrogant youngster, I muttered,

"Yeah I spose."

There followed the familiar crackle through the open doors of the gramophone cabinet. The dog turned her back on the machine, Mother put another log on the fire and I concentrated on the new flames licking up the back of the hearth. The flames flickered yellow, blue and red. The simple yet heart-rending notes of a violin wafted from the gramophone. Then a man's voice sang 'Oh play for me gypsy – under the moonlight.' Bathed in moonbeams I dreamed: Imaginary wind rustled the make-believe trees nearby and the real fire was warm against the 'airy wild outdoors.' The gypsy came and played more and the man sang of being her vagabond – just for that night. Jill flung her head back and howled at the stars in sympathy like a little wolf. In my childhood world The Lone Ranger, Tonto and Davy Crockett joined us there while Champion The Wonder Horse stood guard for varmints, critters and no-good cattle rustlers.

I stubbornly refused to acknowledge – or maybe I didn't even realise at the time – the fact that I quite enjoyed the experience brought about by this ancient fuddy-duddy music.

My mother's sister Maud and her husband Frank ran a farm about twelve miles away in Somerset with their daughter Jean. They were jolly down-to-earth country people and we visited them from time to time. Uncle Frank would always call me 'Sonny Jim' and just like Uncle Todd he always took great delight in asking me when I'd last had the slipper at school and if I'd found a girlfriend yet. Todd and Farmer Frank always made and encouraged such a big fuss about such things. Typically a room full of relatives would wait with baited breath for my reaction, often erupting into uncontrollable laughter when I uttered any sort of response. I daren't ever tell them the truth or mention my all-to-brief encounter with Kim because to me the humiliation of beatings with the slipper and the experience of finding and losing true friendship wasn't funny.

Through listening to pop songs and singing along with them I rekindled my naïve thoughts about one day taking to the stage with a microphone. So when relatives went on to ask what I was going to be when I grew up my answer became very predictable: "Pop star."

I stayed on the farm once for a week and spent a lot of the time sitting on the doorstep whittling a stick – trying to make a penny whistle like Father had once shown me. The rest of the time I tried my utmost not to appear scared when going to round up the massive, lumbering cows for milking.

Towards the end of the week Aunt Maud said that if I wanted to be a pop star I would have to give a performance for my parents when they returned. I assumed they were joking but on the day when my parents were due to pick me up I discovered a large farm cart had appeared in the yard parked in front of the high red brick garden wall. It formed an ideal stage.

My so-called performance was the first few lines of Rock Around The Clock that I had picked up from Aunt Flo when she and Todd had stayed at The Corner House. Of course like Aunt Flo, the words were all wrong and I finished abruptly with a 'Cha Cha Cha' and quickly clambered down the side of the cart. I made my excuses and said that I needed more practice but didn't have any appropriate records to help, which of course was perfectly true. Aunt Maud asked what sort of records I needed. At the time I thought 45s not only referred to the speed of modern records, but was also a generic term for rock 'n' roll or at least 'pop,' so I mumbled,

"45s." She thought for a while then whispered in Jean's ear. Before we left that day Jean gave me a 45rpm record she didn't want anymore. It had Toy Balloons on one side and Side Saddle on the other; interesting piano instrumentals by Russ Conway but disappointingly not the rock 'n' roll I craved.

For the past fortnight or more the front room in The Corner House had been locked up and out of bounds. This sometimes happened during the winter months after Christmas to economise on coal and firewood thus leaving the room freezing and icebound. But for some reason this regime had recently been enforced at the start of spring. I briefly wondered if it was anything to do with someone finding my air pistol in the pianola. Perhaps Mother had contacted the police I thought and then they had advised that the area be cordoned off while they made investigations. But I needn't have worried; my secret was still safe. Apparently Mother was going through a short-lived phase when she believed that the front room should be reserved strictly for visitors only. This idea had now been abandoned because it was realised that visitors to The Corner House – apart from being extremely few and far between – were always out-of-the-blue hence the front room was never prepared for them anyway.

Having endured a period shut out of the front room and unable to use the gramophone meant Jill's curiosity and fascination with the machine had been revived. She sniffed every inch of the monstrosity with renewed enthusiasm as if she'd never encountered it before, especially up the horn behind the doors. In fact if Jill had been a little smaller and black and white, she'd have been a perfect double for the dog on His Master's Voice record labels.

I knew the gramophone wasn't designed for it, but I tried playing my Russ Conway 45 record on it. Conway's tinkling piano was just about discernible at nearly twice its normal speed. But only for a few short seconds as the heavy brass arm with its sharp thick needle, dug deep into the soft, modern vinyl and ruined the record forever. Jill annoyingly looked at me with her 'I told you so' face.

But I still hadn't learnt my lesson. A few weeks later I spent all my saved-up pocket money on a new 45 rock 'n' roll record and I just couldn't resist trying to play it. I had fixed up a simple make-shift device on the gramophone that partly suspended the heavy pick-up arm so it wouldn't dig into the record. It consisted of a short strip of thin metal attached to the rear of the arm with an elastic band. From the end of the metal strip through another elastic band hung the head of the pick-up arm. The needle still touched the turntable but most of the weight of the arm was taken up by the loop of elastic and I felt sure I could slow down the turntable to a more acceptable speed with my finger.

As gently as I possibly could I placed the heavy brass pick-up arm in its make-shift sling on to the microscopic grooves of my new record. For a little while my pop idol sounded like a trembling girl soprano. Then before I had time to think about slowing the record, the sound deteriorated rapidly as the elastic band broke and the sharp, crude needle dug mercilessly into the soft material. This time the arm scraped right across the whole record in a neat sweeping ark, leaving an ugly gouge carved forever into my precious disc. How I despised that ugly great thing.

My den in the top-most part of the roof of the house – through the hole in the lathe and plaster wall – remained my personal space. However, as well as the resident villains and no-good horse thieves, the top floor and the actual attic room still contained a few surprises amongst all the junk. Father would go to auctions trying to obtain cheap fittings and furniture in readiness for future renovation of the house. Typical of house clearance auctions he would often have to buy a 'job lot' to get the one item he wanted.

One day, I was on yet another ramble around some of the attic's unexplored wild territory with Jill. Behind the small chest of drawers amongst the plumbing bits, the upturned bathroom sink and Mother's old doll, I found a 78rpm record without its cover. The artiste was Buddy Holly, on the 'A' side was Peggy Sue and on the other was Everyday. I was sure that Father had never even known of its existence behind the chest of drawers, if he had he would have probably destroyed it. Any sort of pop music annoyed Father intensely and he often remarked that the creators of such noise should be 'put out of their misery.'

I raced down to the front room with the record. After ripping off my unsuccessful Heath Robinson cradle device from the gramophone's pick-up arm, I wound the large cranked handle on the side of the cabinet. I climbed on a chair, set the record on the turntable, released the brake and placed the heavy arm on the record. Crackle crackle crackle. Then suddenly the gentle pitter-patter beat of the introduction to Everyday by Buddy Holly started up. Jill howled gently – almost in tune – and peered further inside the horn as if searching for the true magical source of the sentimental lyrics and what I thought at the time was a glockenspiel.

I loved it so much I played it again and again until Father came home from work. Then Mother joined us with a tea towel draped over her arm as I set it playing yet again. Mother and Father stood there waiting for an assault on their ears but they were soon nodding their heads and tapping their feet to the beat and they didn't even realise it. Everyday by Buddy Holly was the only song that my parents and I ever mutually loved.

I wound it again and put the other side on, Peggy Sue did not go down so well. In retrospect I can imagine my father thinking of Peggy Sue as some big-eyed floozy out to sabotage men's hearts. Mother echoed this when she said half way through the record.

"I think you should turn it off now, that's enough for today."

Soon they got an oldies section on The Black Horse jukebox and occasionally I witnessed Buddy Holly's Everyday sooth and inspire Elvis look-alikes and pony-tailed girls into close, private smooches that often resulted in long snogging sessions against the wall outside the bar.

There were two things in life I wanted, a tape recorder and an electric record player and I couldn't decide which was the most important. I wanted a tape recorder because despite my awful performance on the back of the farm cart, Buddy Holly and his song Everyday had convinced me it would be pretty damned easy to record myself singing and become a pop star. I wanted an electric record player to of course play the latest records without having to rely on the distant sound of the Black Horse juke box or the whim of a DJ late at night on Radio Luxembourg.

The next Christmas I knew Father had bought me one or the other but I had no idea which. It was probably Christmas 1963 that the parcel was presented to me early in the morning in my parents' bedroom. It was a 'Defiant' tape recorder purchased from the Co-op and I remember it to this day. It cost twenty-one guineas, probably about two weeks wages for my father at that time.

After the excitement had died down and I had ceased recording every single thing that made a sound, I tried my first singing experiment. It must have been the tail end of the Christmas holidays; Father had returned to work and Mother was out doing her morning cleaning. Jill the dog was now definitely showing her age, she found it a bit of a struggle to climb the steep stairs. However, she still liked nothing more than an exploratory ramble around the house with me.

She struggled up the stairs ahead of me – she knew I was going to the spare room at the end of the corridor. It had been cleaned up for Uncle Todd and Aunt Flo to use as a bedroom and since they'd left it had become my unofficial playroom. A neat hand written notice in red and yellow crayon on a piece of cardboard attached to the top of the door frame with drawing pins now proclaimed the spare room as 'The Fab Club.' Heavily influenced by pop stars of the day, posters adorned the walls. I had created 'The Fab Club' in direct competition with the filthy scoundrels in the abandoned coach and potting shed, but no other children had ever visited or seen my 'club.'

Jill was no doubt expecting one of our chase-me games. I would pretend to attack her and she would race down the corridor to my parents' bedroom and hide under the bed or she'd struggle up the attic stairs and hide behind the junk until I found her. I would always approach slowly to add to the tension. Then sometimes she'd make a break for it back past me. It would usually finish with some gentle rough and tumble.

Today Jill looked bemused, almost fed up as she watched me set up the tape machine. I thrust an old broom handle into a cardboard box to support it upright and used some of Father's insulation tape to fix the microphone to it. I felt that by using a microphone stand I could concentrate on giving full feeling to my performance with bodily movements – like I'd seen pop stars do on the TV.

I switched the tape recorder into record mode and following the words from the song that had been published in an old magazine I had found in the attic I 'sang' Everyday by Buddy Holly. Jill couldn't stand it. She squat on the bare floorboards and threw her head back as far as she could and did her wolf-howling act. I was utterly horrified with the result when I played it back. Not only was Jill's howling the prominent feature, but my so-called singing was just awful and I erased it immediately.

This put paid to any further thoughts of being a pop star and for many years after that I was mindful not to record myself in any way, shape or form. But I did acquire a reputation for surreptitiously recording other family members and usually when they least expected it.

I think my father secretly fancied experimenting with singing. The only time my parents and I ever went to the cinema was to see a film starring Tommy Steele. It included a song called The Dream Maker and my parents were smitten. When playing with my tape recorder one day I was astonished when Father agreed to my suggestion that he and Mother should be recorded singing this song. Disappointed and mildly objecting, Jill was shut in the kitchen for fear of howling. It was hilarious. My parents were hesitant, out of tune and awful. But Father didn't care and found it as I did, most amusing. Mother was more embarrassed and insisted that I 'rub it out' but thankfully I never did and still have the recording today.

Recording Castleton Church bell also fascinated me. The less than perfect tape transport system of my Defiant tape recorder made the tone of the clanging chimes waver slightly, giving them a strange haunting charm. A microphone hung from my bedroom or 'The Fab Club' window on many a Saturday or Sunday morning and as well as capturing the bell on tape, new families of sparrows in the cherry trees were often prominent on recordings too.

One Saturday prepared well in advance with a microphone held carefully at the open 'Fab Club' window, I managed to record the midday two-stroke motorcycle. I waited patiently with Jill poking her nose out of the window beside me for the very first distant approach of the loud machine. It didn't come every Saturday and I hoped and prayed it would arrive that day, now that we were all set up and ready. I guess it would have been somewhere around West Bridge or Dancing Hill when we first heard it. I had become quite adept at successfully recording things – apart from my own voice – and I turned the recording gain up full and listened carefully through headphones. Between the close-by chirps of the sparrows and occasional mechanical clicks and whirs of starlings perched up on the roof, the sound of the bike drifted closer. It stopped somewhere, its idling two-stroke engine popping and spluttering.

Then it accelerated up through the gears closer and closer. I turned the gain down as it came over the railway bridge by Little Purley. When it arrived outside The Corner House popping and spluttering by the halt sign and brakes squeaking, Jill almost barked but realised she shouldn't at the last moment.

I had never really studied the rider before. His slight unsteadiness as he wrestled with the handlebars and his hesitance as he placed a foot on the ground to coincide with the bike coming to a gentle halt, suggested that he was an older man. As he turned his head to look for traffic approaching up Long Street I caught a very brief glimpse of an old man's face partly hidden behind a wide strap that held his white peaked helmet in place.

I was very familiar with the actual sound of this part of the performance, I had pondered over it countless times from my bed. The machine stayed ticking over while the rider carefully looked for any traffic approaching from the other direction. Then the engine, as if caught by surprise and with a certain reluctance, was given plenty of throttle and the machine took off gradually gathering speed until it reached the start of the incline up Newland. Then the little engine's tone slowed as if wailing a protest at having to propel the full-grown man up the hill. The changing tone of the machine faded in and out and echoed around various streets until it could be heard no more.

Father had now bought a Bedford Workabus in place of the Standard 8 car and it was manufactured before car radios were common. Indeed I think with its engine positioned as it was – half inside the cab – the vehicle was far too noisy when in motion to be able to listen to the radio properly. However, Father invested in a rather cumbersome large transistor radio for use when the vehicle was stationary. He used to balance it on the dashboard or in the glove compartment to listen to the news or the weather when parked up. The 'Workabus' was far more spacious and comfortable for staying inside when parked up. That's what we did most Sundays, drive to the coast, park up and watch the sea for what seemed like hours on end to me.

Often Mother would fall asleep only to wake herself up with her own snoring. I would plead with Father to let me listen to pop music on the radio. Sometimes he would give in and my parents would probably endure about two records at extremely low volume. Neither of them could bear more than that. I often wished I could have taken Jill to explore more coastal destinations but as we found to our expense on our Portland holiday, she just couldn't travel in a car; after a couple of miles she was always sick. She was left at home with the whole of The Corner House and the backyard to wander around in.

If Bowleaze Cove was chosen for a Sunday outing then things were different. I often had trouble controlling my excitement. I would urge Father to drive faster on the way there, because at Bowleaze there was a tumble-down wooden café with a jukebox. It was best in the winter when the only customers were local teenagers. Similar if not identical to customers in The Black Horse bar, each boy sported an Elvis quiff and the girls wore pleated skirts and kept their hair in ponytails. Occasionally they danced rock 'n' roll there on the creaky floorboards, skirts a swirl, ponytails swinging and quiffs being constantly adjusted. I yearned to rock 'n' roll like them.

The jukebox was large and shiny with a good selection of music from the fifties and right up to what was then the present time of the mid 1960s. The windows of the fragile looking little building would vibrate to Frank Ifield, Jim Reeves and of course Buddy Holly. I was utterly fascinated by the chromium plated and brightly lit Wurlitzer there in the corner pumping music out across the rocky shore. The gang of boys posing to the girls would drink frothy coffee and usually keep the music flowing. However, if there came a quiet moment I would oblige if I could. My pocket money would soon be spent and I would beg for more sixpences. If Grandfather Frank was with us and I had not misbehaved he would give me some sixpences to ensure a peaceful snooze back in the front passenger seat of the 'Workabus.'

In summer the amusement arcade was open nearby and attracted gangs on motorcycles. Grandfather often said they should bring back national service to sort them out, Mother always agreed, but it was only their appearance that they hated so much. I once commented to Mother that she didn't know them, so how could she pass judgement. This erupted into one almighty argument and I jumped out of the back of the 'Workabus' and slammed the door. Father who had been half asleep shouted after me.

"I'll knock you into next week if you behave like that!" I knew I had just blown any chance of listening to the top twenty.

I once won a miniature plastic guitar in the arcade, but was very dismayed when the strings wouldn't stay taut – let alone in tune. In the summer if the coffee bar was uncomfortably crowded or if I had no money and had exhausted all the adult's finances, I would inspect the rock pools around the little cove. I once collected three crabs in a plastic bucket. Without waking anyone I covered the bucket and wedged it between the seats in the back of the 'Workabus.' When we got home, to Mother's horror and Father's frustration they were still alive but moving very slowly. I assembled them on the ground in the backyard intending to build a pond or something. Then suddenly, all together they darted off behind the immoveable homemade, bursting coalbunker never to be seen again.

Worse for my parents were pop programmes that had started to appear on the TV. Anything more outrageous than The Beverly Sisters or Peter, Paul and Mary would cause excruciating, displeasure. As he yanked the plug from the wall, Father would typically mutter,

"I'll soon put those buggers out of their misery!" Life would fizzle out of the TV, my excitement would be cut short, Jill would sigh and The Corner House would again return to the dull, steady tick-tock of the mantle clock.

Father eventually built basic bunk beds into the back of the 'Workabus' with rough sawn timber. But he often wished he hadn't. He had bought the 'Workabus' as a commercial vehicle and therefore had not paid Purchase Tax on it. He had not realised that putting bunk beds in the back would be deemed a conversion to a domestic vehicle requiring Custom & Excise Purchase Tax to be paid. For many years I would judge how expensive something was by comparing the price to the cost of my tape recorder. It was a total shock when Father received a demand for twenty eight pounds – five pounds more than my beloved recorder cost and well over two weeks wages for him then. Somebody had reported him to the authorities.

We spent a week exploring London always returning to a car park in Richmond to sleep. The car park had a toilet block that was opened at 8am every morning. The attendant was very kind and didn't mind us washing there. This was the only time we ever used the bunk beds.

13

Tragedy In Bristol Road

I failed the 'eleven plus' exam – I treated it as a joke. I remember consciously writing down any old nonsense for answers and the idea that it actually held any sort of significance never entered my head. I just wanted to escape from the confines of the classroom and the possibility of further humiliation from beatings with that awful plimsoll.

The headmaster told my father that not only had I failed the examination miserably, but also that my answers indicated a rather concerning lack of sanity. I think it was the first time I'd heard the expression 'skin of (his) teeth.' I guess I took it to mean I was immeasurably close to being categorised as 'not all there.' The headmaster's new name for me of 'imbecile' exacerbated further my lack of self-esteem.

Father sometimes remarked that I should try hard at school, but I detected more than a hint of cynicism in his voice. Both my parents had been expected, and encouraged, to get their schooling over with quickly in order to contribute to the running of the family household as soon as possible. That philosophy had stuck with them and it obviously rubbed off on me. My mother had my future mapped out for me: I would leave school sooner rather than later and get a job in the local helicopter factory with Uncle Todd. I think everyone and especially Todd, assumed that is what I would be doing just as soon as I was able to walk out of the school gates for the last time. They seemed to forget I was only eleven going on twelve.

At primary school we had been separated from the successful pupils for whom grammar school awaited. Then came our crude preparation for our start at St Aldhelm's Secondary Modern School. We were told to draw our impressions of the main buildings after they had been described to us. Although teachers made it appear light-hearted, the process seemed very suspicious with an underlying seriousness and intensity. I felt as though we were being psychoanalysed for any signs of unusual skills, mental illness or other irregularities. The pictures we drew were all pinned on the wall and we were told that we were entering a more responsible time in our lives. We were warned that if we misbehaved teachers at the new school wouldn't think twice about sending pupils for the cane – not just the soft slipper anymore.

The PE teacher told us boys that we were no longer allowed to substitute proper sportswear with everyday underwear when participating in PE. It was imperative that our parents now invested in proper sports shorts with adequate lining, because we were now almost young men.

I don't remember feeling particularly scared as I cycled up the main driveway to St Aldhelm's School. A temporary hand written notice directed me to the cycle shed where I found other boys loitering around, I didn't know them and we didn't speak.

There was one thing I had underestimated and that was the sheer number of busses – they were everywhere. I remembered the ancient solitary dark green bus used for transporting infants to Simons Road School, which still passed right by The Corner House every day of term. I had gotten used to this bus and the friendly driver would wave at me standing in the doorway of The Corner House as he waited at the junction. The poor man always seemed rather guilty because he was prohibited from giving me a lift because I lived just a fraction inside the one mile perimeter limit from school. He did chance giving me a lift once – many years ago before I got my first pushbike – but was apparently threatened with the sack for his trouble.

At St Aldhelm's there were dozens of anonymous, comparatively recent busses. They were more rounded than the old green bus with chromium plated radiator grills, bumpers and decorative strips down their sides. Although more modern and fairly grand compared to the basic infant bus, most were actually obsolete models. Retired from long-haul excursions these streamlined coaches were now only utilised twice a day for the short but often riotous transportation of children. There was a constant stream of these vehicles that were once considered luxurious, arriving and depositing masses of maroon uniformed children from the farthest reaches of Sherborne and the outlying villages.

There were lost, frightened new children immaculately groomed and well behaved, and untidy returning pupils who were far more relaxed and engrossed in chasing each other and hurling satchels and duffle bags around. Standing out from the crowd – conspicuous in a drab grey, ill-fitting dress instead of a uniform – was the infamous Miranda. Miranda was a violent, vulgar girl with ice-blue piercing eyes. She was a familiar figure in the town, usually to be seen frantically pedalling an extremely small bicycle around the streets. I had never actually spoken to her before – just espied her from afar. She stared straight at me and I was astonished to detect a slight smile on her lips.

Us boys were herded into the large courtyard at the rear, away from any vehicles and girls. We milled around in a homogenous mass until one or two fights broke out. Then concentrations of pupils formed circles around the brawls chanting and gesticulating. One such fight spilled up the grass bank and on to the playing fields. Two or three innocent boys who would become notorious loners stood apart from any of the commotion, one of which was a small boy called Timothy. Three or four boys with prefect badges consulted each other and hesitantly approached the more serious looking fight. These prefects were soon joined by large bellowing male teachers who – after separating the more determined aggressors – signalled towards the headmaster's office like policemen on point duty. The offenders were herded away in that direction.

Order was eventually restored and somehow we were assembled in rows relevant to our 'form.' One form at a time we were then led into our corresponding classrooms. After a brief induction the school's electric bell system echoed around the buildings summoning us to the first of many morning assemblies.

It seemed to take ages for everyone to file into the assembly hall. It was massive compared to what I was used to. There was row upon row of chairs and, a stepped choir stall to the left of the stage and a piano nearby. The creaky sounds of the tubular steel chairs seemed to echo around the place. Random, nervous coughing ensued and we waited.

The last few coaches drove away after the drivers had chatted and had a cigarette together. The electric wall clock's longer hand mechanically clicked over the next segment of its dial confirming the passing of another minute. Then we all stood up – almost together – as the headmaster entered taut lipped and frowning heavily. He completely ignored the assembled pupils as he climbed the few steps to join his colleagues who had now entered the stage from behind. He placed his paperwork on the lectern and focusing on an area high up in the ceiling he launched into his presentation.

We were told to sit down to listen, after a while we stood up again to have a go at singing. Eventually we bowed our heads for the Lord's Prayer. Then we were told to relax for a more informal, sort of 'noticeboard' session. Through one of the windows that stretched from floor to ceiling I was watching the groundsman trundling a wheelbarrow across the car park. I mused over the notion that apparently all school groundsmen seemed to walk in the same peculiar manner. I remembered Mr Smith the groundsman at Fosters School and I briefly thought of Kim.

"Cycling Proficiency Test!" I was aware of the headmaster saying. I looked up to the stage. It was the first and probably only time that I detected a slight smile on the headmaster's face. In the midst of his next sentence I thought I picked out my name. Everyone started clapping. He repeated my name and looked around at everyone, searching for the boy. It suddenly hit me that I was the boy in question, I was being awarded something and I was expected to receive it on stage. As I squeezed past other pupils I remembered that months ago I had performed a practical cycle handling test and a road sense exam at primary school. I had forgotten all about it and had no idea I had earned my little badge.

I had only been at the school for a few days when I met happy-go-lucky comedian Frankie. Frankie was a fellow pupil of the same age as me but I'd never met him before St Aldhelm's. I think he had attended the other primary school in Sherborne known as the Abbey School. Frankie seemed to take everything in his stride; he was always smiling and easily won the hearts of bullies, loners, no-hopers and teachers alike. He always talked fast and was sometimes quite cheeky – in the nicest possible way. He reminded me of a stand-up comedian able to communicate with all classes of people from all walks of life.

After meeting Frankie and memorising most of the room numbers and corridors it actually seemed better than I had expected. But I couldn't help but notice the constant harassment poor little loner Timothy endured nearly every day. He dreaded any of the common loutish onslaughts and he became famous early on for hurling his duffle bag in circles round and round his head to keep the bastards at bay. Of course any sort of unusual behaviour like that only served to attract more attention and pushed to the limits, he would remove one of his shoes and use it like a hammer. Timothy appeared less than agile and rather clumsy, but – always after several warnings – he wouldn't think twice about lashing out at people. Sadly he would often still get goaded to breaking point with a swarm of boys after him chanting cruel jibes. Driven this far almost weekly, Timothy would often dash, tearful, to the toilets and lock himself in. The only people who seemed to actually talk to Timothy were Frankie and myself.

Other older boys – usually bigger than most – would be hero worshiped in the playground. Typically a trail of hangers-on eagerly followed, copying and chipping in thereby confirming support for their superior's actions and unwittingly displaying publicly their willing acceptance of the hierarchy system. A hierarchy system that most pupils were unaware existed but automatically reacted to. Reacted to by submitting to a miserable life constantly fending off attackers, or to the other extreme enjoying a life of superior luxury extorting dinner money and only occasionally defending their status with a serious fight.

But these big lads were often brought down a peg or two by aggressive male teachers who formed the core of the corporal punishment regime. These ultimate showdowns when the cane had proved ineffective were often carried out in public, usually in the main foyer by the snack machines at midday. This area was the busiest crossroads of the school where boys and girls were allowed to mix at break time. I occasionally caught a glimpse of Miranda there, stony faced with that piercing stare.

To me this heart of the building was like the village green of a strange community. Both teachers and pupils going about their business had no choice but to pass through it. Others lounged around in the area eating snacks, waiting for the next batch of people to be called into the canteen for lunch or perhaps reading the notice board.

Two or three of the older boys would be lined up against the wall and guarded by a teacher and prefects for ages. When the chief interrogator was ready – usually after he'd had lunch and in the busiest period when he could expect more spectators – he would appear in front of the gang leaders and shout the odds.

It was within the first week while passing through the foyer that I witnessed a boy I'd seen previously confidently leading a gang in the playground, reduced to a quivering wreck. His mate was in a similar state beside him. As I walked past they knew they were going to be hit hard; they had floods of tears streaming down their cheeks and were very jumpy.

"Don't do it again boy!" bellowed the towering, menacing teacher. Then there was silence as the boys fidgeted around avoiding the man's stare.

"Stand still!" shouted the teacher at the top of his voice. "Stand Still!" he repeated even louder, hanging on to each syllable. Both boys stood as still as they could, not knowing whether to look at the floor or ceiling. Then the man struck out like lightning. The boys had obviously been through it before and it was not exactly unexpected. The man caught one boy a clout on the side of the head and the lad's reflexes meant he nearly hit his head on the notice board behind him. The other boy cowered almost pleading, knowing he would be hit next. The girlfriend of one of the boys stood biting her lip nearby. I scurried past, I didn't know what they had done wrong.

Then came a subject called 'current affairs' none of us knew what to expect in the first lesson. We found the room eventually and piled in. There, studying her hands as if unsure about her choice of nail varnish was the woman teacher. She was sitting cross-legged on top of one of the tables. She wore a fluffy fur coat and a fairly short skirt but to me she seemed instantly unattractive and suspicious.

When we had all shuffled in and found a chair she lounged on the table and asked where we had been. Assuming she was trying to tell us we were late, someone said that we had trouble finding the right classroom.

"How long have you had to find the classroom?" she asked. Nobody dared answer having realised her attitude. "It's been on the notice board for the past two weeks!" she continued. "I am not accustomed to be kept waiting by a bunch of snivelling first years." There was silence. "When you are unsure of the classroom you jolly well find out." As she continued to make it quite clear that she thought first years were not worth bothering with, I noticed she had chewing gum in her mouth. I briefly thought of my previous headmaster's attitude to finding chewing gum about my person – and that innocent present from Kim wasn't even inside my mouth at the time! Then she got up and strolled casually around the room, occasionally looking out of the window while hurling more abuse. We never learned anything in her lesson and we found it miserable and depressing.

Despite successful completion of the Cycling Proficiency Test by most cyclists and the constant warnings from teachers, Bristol Road, which led down into Sherborne from the school became a mad racetrack at four o'clock each weekday. Sherborne children riding bicycles found themselves showing off to friends and gesturing to enemies who were being carried home in modern-day charabancs. Frankie was the worst. He would steer his bike with no hands, make faces and obscene hand signals; he rode so close to the rear of coaches that he had no hope of stopping should the vehicle suddenly brake.

I had become just as bad. One day after leaving school we were keeping up with a brown Bedford Duple coach racing down the hill towards the junction with the main A30. On the rear seat of the coach, in a row making faces with their noses pressed hard up against the glass, were three village girls from our form. They were occasionally joined by boys at the window who constantly made V signs or showed clenched fists. Sometimes it appeared it would be easy to overtake the coach as it slowed to negotiate a gap in parked cars, but in reality it was far too dangerous.

Our front wheels actually skimmed the rear bumper of the coach, it then accelerated away and we pedalled frantically to keep up with it, egged on by rivals and a machismo nurtured by female eyes. Then the coach actually stopped by a notorious chicane to give way to an approaching car. Frankie and I both pretended to adjust the satchels on our backs and looked around the edge of the coach. We assumed the girls, still peering out from the rear window were now taking advantage of a less frantic, perhaps more in-depth study of us and we were momentarily too shy to acknowledge them. We skilfully remained balanced on our bikes despite being virtually stationary. Eventually we just couldn't resist looking up at the window. One girl blew a kiss while another poked her tongue out. A boy's hand appeared above the seat mimicking masturbation.

"You bastard!" murmured Frankie. The coach edged forwards a little and then seemed to stop again, even though there was no car approaching from the other direction. In a split second I decided to overtake on the outside. At that point Frankie disappeared down the nearside of the coach. I flew past the vehicle despite the fact that it had now started to move again. I expected the coach to catch up with me but it didn't. I turned in time to see the handlebars of Frankie's bike touch the wall of a building where the chicane started. As if in slow motion he lost his balance and went under the busload of juveniles. My bike stopped with my head stuck in a rear looking position in the middle of the road. The coach stopped too with an awful crunch and squeal of brakes. But it was too late. I was frozen in the middle of the road with my bike at my feet. A teacher and soon a policeman arrived. The bulk of Frankie's body still moved a little between the coach and the wall, but it was the last jolts of his nervous system. Frankie was dead, with a bunch of wiser, wide-eyed children looking on. For years I experienced gruesome, surreal dreams about the awful incident and I guess it kick started a more mature, responsible attitude towards using the roads.

I think it was an attempt by Uncle Todd to show me how much other people liked working at the helicopter factory that made him invite me to their works Christmas party – well I didn't have much choice really. Todd assumed I would be ecstatic at the chance and Mother said I had to go anyway.

Mother would never offer discussion or put forward proper reasons, like perhaps: Colin I think you should go because.... She'd just say, 'You are going and that's the end of it.' She would then mutter under her breath, ranting and raving about how kind Todd had been to think of me. Father seemed to stay out of this one.

So a few days before Christmas with my obligatory knife, fork and spoon the coach picked us up at Newland flats. Todd giggled and joked with fellow workmates in-between whispering to me that he could 'get me in' the factory easily enough when I left school.

I now realised just how naïve my aspirations to become a pop star had been. But despite Todd ignoring everything on the subject of my future except for trying to encourage a non-existent interest in obtaining a steady job with him, the dream of emigrating and becoming a cowboy was still alive within me. Todd didn't seem to pick up from my reactions that being shut up in a noisy factory all day was the last thing I wanted to do and that the very thought of it I found nightmarish.

All the way to the party crude jokes were told and just about all the adults smoked cigarettes and their raucous banter was an indication of what the evening ahead held. I guess it was all organised by the workers themselves who probably saved in a Christmas party fund for all the preceding year. In the town of Yeovil five miles away and where the helicopter factory is, they had hired a school assembly hall. There were balloons all over the place stuck to the high ceiling, rolling around on the tables and gently bouncing around the floor. Up on the stage there were reserve supplies behind a stack of chairs. An inadequate little record player echoed out pop songs lost in the corner and drowned out amongst laughter and raised voices.

The tables were arranged roughly in rows, I think we were suppose to have a meal first but not many people seemed to want to sit down.

"Look after my mate will you?" said Todd to two older girls who were the first ones to grab a place at one of the tables. Todd went off, probably in search of a drink. I sat down next to the two girls. They stared at me intensely and then started whispering to each other. There was noisy chaos around me but I was oblivious for a while as all my concentration was funnelled into deciding whether I should ask the girls who they were with or something. I plucked up enough courage and opened my mouth,

"Are you...." I started. But I was immediately drowned out by the loud high-pitched feedback from the PA system up on stage. The girls collapsed into hysterical laughter.

"OK!" said the man on stage just about managing to control the feedback. "OK... thank you.... Please... thank you very much. Thank you all for coming again this year. Can you all please find a seat at the tables for the meal?"

The meal was OK, loads of jelly and ice cream afterwards. Todd came back a couple times but insisted on sitting some way away with his mates where he could tell and be told dirty jokes. I never made conversation with anyone and stood lolling with my back against the wall as they cleared the tables away.

Amid much whooping, screaming and whistling some of Todd's mates appeared on stage in drag. Todd stood up quite drunk, fag in the corner of his mouth and shouted smut as a balloon used to represent a mammary gland on one of the men burst. I was bored.

As well as parent problems I had the senseless policies and regimes of secondary school to contend with. Pupils were being made an example of for the most trivial of things and sometimes through an innocent occurrence or genuine misunderstanding. There was always confusion at the start of term with class timetables etc. Not only between pupils but staff too.

We were told we had metalwork on a Wednesday afternoon, so after break on the first Wednesday of a new term we strolled leisurely down to the prefabricated workshops at the eastern edge of the playing fields. We found the buildings locked and we hung around outside for ages. I knew the teacher carried out his own practical projects in his free time, one of which was making a miniature cannon on one of the lathes. Twenty minutes after the lesson should have started there was one almighty explosion in the metalwork shop. We all stood on tiptoe in the flowerbeds at the foot of the workshop wall and peered in through the metal framed windows. There was the metalwork teacher kneeling on the floor having just fired his cannon down through the walkway between the benches at a concrete target at the far end of the room. He was obviously not expecting us and appeared startled at all our faces gawping in at him. He was very angry at being disturbed from an activity probably disallowed in his teaching contract.

"What are you lot doing down here?" he asked when he eventually came to the door. Everyone recognised his unpredictable state and did not reply. "Where were you told to go this afternoon?" he continued. A small Dorset born and bred boy in hand-me-down trousers many sizes too big and very long socks shouted innocently:

"Down yer!"

"Who said that?" shouted the man, his words just recognisable in a blind rage. I think the boy thought he might be praised for being the first one forthcoming with information. So he confidently walked out and put his hand up. I think the man knew full well who had said it without the need to ask. The teacher lunged forward and hit the boy hard across the top of his head sending him flying backwards into the flowerbeds.

"Speak properly when you talk to me boy!" he shouted at the top of his voice. A boy had been knocked senseless for speaking in his native Dorset dialect. We spent the whole lesson just standing in silence by our benches occasionally sneezing in the stench of smoke and gunpowder.

My big radio, covered in wrinkly black vinyl was still going strong, it was the best sixpence I had ever spent and the nine shillings and sixpence for its new rectifier valve was by far my best investment. Apart from Jill it continued to be my true and trusted companion, especially at night.

I would often wake up to the faint hiss and crackle of the old tattered Bakelite headphones nearby on my pillow. They were connected to the radio with cotton covered twisted flex, joined in many places. Having fallen asleep with comforting patterns of the radio's rear ventilation holes projected on my bedroom wall, Radio Luxembourg had closed down while I slumbered.

One warm Sunday morning I awoke earlier than usual. Instead of clicking off the dusty glow of my radio I placed the rather uncomfortable headphones back on my head and moved the radio's tuning dial. The clamp effect of hard Bakelite on my ears was instantly forgotten as a strange ding of a bell came through, twice in quick succession. It promptly faded almost completely away and then back again. It was Radio Caroline.

14

Jimmy

At St Aldhelm's School I eventually established another friendship with a boy called Jimmy. He was younger than me and therefore a year or two below me. I suppose it was rare to establish a friendship across different year groups at that age. There was usually great rivalry, fear or resentment between different years – depending if the others were older or younger than 'your lot.'

Jimmy had attended a different infant school than me in Yeovil. Therefore despite him living quite near The Corner House at the Long Street end of East Mill Lane, I had never actually spoken to him before I attended St Aldhelm's. He had 45rpm records, an electric record player to play them on and a superb red ten-speed racing bike. His bike was so fantastic it was probably the best in the school, which created more than a little jealousy amongst the cycling fraternity.

It was near Christmas time and I was off school recovering from a particularly bad cold. Late in the afternoon I was allowed out of bed for a while and I was huddled up in an armchair in front of the fire in the middle room. Aunt Flo and Mother were there deep in discussion about how much 'divvy' they should be getting from the Co-op. They were so engrossed in conversation they didn't realise I had set up my tape recorder in record mode behind the armchair. The microphone poked out on the floor near one of the chair legs. Jill had sniffed it a couple of times and had given a few of her tiny sneezes, which sounded like chuckles as if she knew exactly what was going on. But Mother and Flo were completely oblivious.

"I love thik there yellow plant of yours!" remarked Flo after a short silence. The two women turned to study Mother's houseplants arranged on the sideboard.

"I must gee they a droppa water in a minute," said Mother sighing, but more interested in the one remaining ice bun left there on the coffee table. Mother took a sip of tea and thought better of eating the bun for the moment. She pondered over the fact that the frost had damaged all the 'sturshions' in the garden of the big house where she cleaned and therefore she couldn't pick any for herself.

"Ah the frost 'av had all yours out backyard ain't it?" remarked Flo.

"Vic said the Fuchsias should grow again."

"Ah you should put 'em in somewhere."

"Well Vic's gonna put 'em up the back passage – Colin stop sniggering!"

Recently at school I had heard the term 'back passage' used to refer to a person's bottom. My uncontrollable giggles quickly turned into a hearty laugh and Mother's increased anger seemed to embarrass Flo.

Eventually Mother sighed and remarked that she had a headache. Flo eagerly started a conversation about which brand of

239

headache tablets were the best. Then the front doorbell rang. Jill barked casually but loudly as if she knew it was a friend at the door but thought she ought to bark anyway. Mother panicked a little knowing the front room was not prepared for visitors. The doorbell rang again, this time for longer as if the caller was impatient.

"Thas a nice liddle bell ain't it!" remarked Aunt Flo.

"Ah I'm gonna get a ding-dong," muttered Mother as she hurriedly glanced in the mirror and shoved a hairgrip in her hair. The middle room door closed and we recognised the familiar sound of the heavy front door's groaning hinges and then voices. It was impossible to hear exactly what they were saying, let alone who the caller was through the solid middle room door and the thick, substantial curtain that hung from it. But I detected a very concerned tone in Mother's muffled voice.

Jill buried her head under the bottom of the curtain and placed her nose level with the slight gap under the door. She started her fire-bellows breathing technique. She would carefully inhale to maximum capacity every three or four seconds, then rapidly expel each sample after detecting any unfamiliar smells. It was like having a living air analyser, if she could have spoken she would not only have been able to tell you who was at the door, but when they had last changed their socks; and she sometimes sounded like a champion wrestler psyching themselves up before a fight.

I had to giggle again and Aunt Flo found this rather puzzling, but I couldn't tell her that Jill's behaviour also reminded me of her husband Todd's occasional cold remedy of inhaling steam from a bowl of boiling water with a wet towel draped over his head.

Jill occasionally took a short break from sniffing and whined a little. I was then able to recognise Jimmy's voice at the door, but he didn't sound at all happy. It seemed he had been attacked and beaten up or something, he was almost in tears. I wanted to invite him in but I knew better than to suggest such a thing – nobody except family or the doctor were ever allowed anywhere in the house except the front room, and that had been abandoned for a month and was cold and dirty. I listened intently.

"I think it's Jimmy and he's been beaten up!" I said, "I ought to go and say hello."

"Don't you dare," said Flo, "your mother will have a fit if you go to the front door in your dressing gown."

We waited and waited and the doorstep conversation went on and on. It was so frustrating only being able to catch the odd word here and there and his tone of voice now sounded desperate. I thought about suggesting that we set up an electric fire in the front room, I was sure Jimmy wouldn't mind the lack of dusting – he must have thought us very rude.

Jill had the skill of predicting when the middle room door was about to open down to a fine art. She was always sniffing at the door so this was quite important if she was not to get clobbered by the door flying open. This particular time she left it to the very final second for one last sniff. Then she flew back out of the way as Mother flung the door open into the middle room accompanied by the screech of the curtain rail.

"Ain't they some bad buggers!" Mother exclaimed as she used her foot to prevent Jill from pursuing a final scrap of evidence.

"Why?" I asked.

"They've beat his bike up, up school and he's broken hearted – a new bike!" I couldn't prevent myself from chuckling out loud. It wasn't the fact that Jimmy's bike had been sabotaged that I found funny but Mother's choice of words. To 'beat up' meant nothing other than to rough a person up to me. 'Tough nuts' could be heard every day in the school playground claiming that they had 'beat some kid up.' The thought of an inanimate object like a bicycle being beaten up for some reason I found hilarious.

"Colin stop sniggering!" shouted Mother.

"Oooohwah!" exclaimed Flo fully intending to further express her dismay. But Mother interjected.

"They've cut the straps off of his bag thing at the back!" Flo tried more noises to further express her shock and sympathy.

"And his wheel's like that," continued Mother hastily outlining a misshapen bicycle wheel in the air with her forefinger. "An' he's afraid of his life to go home to his mother."

"Is he?" I questioned - although it wasn't really a question more an exclamation of my sympathy for Jimmy.

"Well 'course he is Colin," retorted Mother, "all that money!"

"It just don't grow on trees do it!" agreed Flo.

"I think tha's a cruel, wicked thing and Mr Barnett if he don't do something about that then I think tha's awful."

"They'll do it again…" remarked Flo trying to get a word in.

"I will I'll run 'im down to the ground to everybody, I think thas awful – thik kid his heart's up in his mouth."

"I heard he were talking pretty sad!" said Flo. Mother was in such a state she could hardly get her words out and she recounted Mr Barnett's reaction as if she'd actually been there when Jimmy was showing him the damaged machine.

"I think tis terrible they've cut the …. they've had ……. you can see. Mr Barnett said I don't know about the front wheel but we may be able to do something about the bag 'cause he said they've had a knife and cut that – there tis you can see….. An' that were a new bag on the back of thik kid's bike … an' his front wheel, his front wheel's like that."

"They want the police up there," said Flo as we both stared at another hasty mid-air diagram of a damaged bicycle wheel.

"He gotta walk to school tomorrow!" Mother continued as she disappeared out into the kitchen where scraps from the butcher were being boiled up for Jill. She ranted and raved as she checked the saucepan simmering on the stove. Her voice echoed around the thick walls and flagstone kitchen floor.

Pondering over the predicament and trying not to sound like I was assuming I'd have another day off school tomorrow, I thought out loud that Jimmy could borrow my bike.

"They'd do the same to yours," said Flo, "'cause they'd know it was yours an' you wouldn't be there."

I'd almost forgotten about the school Christmas play. Not that I was involved in it but Jimmy, at the same time as unloading his grief about his bike had also delivered tickets for it. It was after Mother had studied the tickets and while eating that single remaining ice bun that she noticed the microphone poking out from under the armchair. I was instantly told to,

"Turn thik bloody thing off and rub it out!" But I've still got the recording today.

Jimmy's bike was no longer the best in the school. But it didn't really matter because Jimmy and I soon preferred dirt track bikes rather than racing bikes. We became quite good bike mechanics and Father's garage would become cluttered and strewn with bike bits and tools. Father – bless his heart – would often shunt the 'Workabus' on to the drive outside to accommodate us. A more modern Trent Sports touring bicycle I acquired in place of the Rudge Whitworth was stripped down to the bare minimum and endowed with cow horn handlebars and fat, dirt-track tyres from Harry Hunt's shop.

Jimmy's mother was horrified when he ventured home with what used to be a racing bike, now sporting huge high handlebars and knobbly tyres; the brand new bike had been a prized birthday present not so long ago. But there was no stopping the dirt-track champions and our mean machines.

I also developed a daring circus act, which I carried out in the deserted Culverhayes car park down in the town early on Sunday mornings. It all started by seeing how far I could freewheel across the flat expanse of tarmac having gathered as much speed and momentum as possible. Then one morning I experimented by taking my feet completely off the pedals and resting them up in the frame of the bike. This evolved into clambering up on to the crossbar and into a crouching position each time. Eventually one day I took it a stage further and actually stood upright on the crossbar of the moving bike. After a few weeks I was making regular Sunday morning freewheels across the car park while balancing precariously on the crossbar like a tightrope walker.

Occasionally Miranda would appear on her minute, decrepit machine and silently stare at my antics. Her pink bike was so small that when sitting stationary astride it, her knees almost reached her upper arms.

A little way around New Road from the Corner House, immediately past the slopes and opposite the top of Gashouse Hill, is a track that actually used to be the main road to Dorchester. It climbs steadily cutting through the end of the slopes and eventually past the Terrace Playing Fields to its right. It ascends up to an area known as Gallows Plot and emerges near the modern day road to Dorchester at the top of Sherborne Hill.

As you enter this track from New Road, on its right the terrain is much like the slopes – steep and ridged. In fact it is easy to see that before the track was cut in, the slopes continued unhindered into this heavily wooded area. There are pathways winding through the trees which all lead up to the Terrace Playing Fields. Jimmy and I would tear through this area on our adapted dirt bikes with knobbly tyres churning the earth and the massive handlebars made us feel like we were battling with mad bucking broncos.

One day during a wet autumn, eager for the ultimate adrenaline buzz, we fought our way through thick undergrowth up to the highest accessible ridge. Up on the mini plateau sitting astride our bikes we contemplated the steep woodland below with front wheels just inches from the edge. We dared each other who would go even closer to the brink with our mean machines. Jumpy with nerves but bravado hiding most of our fear, we both teetered precariously.

For some reason and out-of-the-blue, Jimmy asked me how many girls I'd kissed. Partly in surprise and partly in anticipation of answering, I momentarily lost my concentration. As I turned to him my left foot, which at that point was bearing all my weight, slipped on the wet leaves. My crutch hit the crossbar, the bike lurched forward and I instinctively applied the brakes. Unlike my first ride on my Rudge Whitworth the brakes on this machine instantly locked both the front and rear wheels but it was too late, I was over the edge and gravity rapidly took over. Applying the brakes had no effect on slowing the bike, let alone stopping it. Despite Harry Hunt's knobbly dirt-track tyres there was no grip and I tore down the steep hill gathering speed with every second, sliding and slithering on the well lubricated ground.

The thought of probable death briefly entered my head but this was soon taken over by my concentrating on steering frantically through spaces in the woodland, desperately trying to avoid the big trees. Within a few seconds the bike had picked up enough speed to tear straight through a bramble bush that I thought would save me. I think I may have shouted as I raced over a ridged gravel path and took off to land with a crash on a clearer section of the steep carpet of mushy leaves. Miraculously I stayed upright, but the bike was now travelling at breakneck speed. In a nanosecond I was aware of the next gravel path. The angle of this path launched my bike into the air again, but this time I landed in the middle of a massive clump of stinging nettles. Twigs snapped and a hawthorn bush tore at my flesh before I realised in a hazy mishmash of green, that I was still upright and whistling through the undergrowth. I squinted for fear of spiky thorns or brambles entering my eyes but daren't let go of the handlebars. I glimpsed the rusty iron fence ahead that divided the area from New Road. My legs were being battered by thick shrubbery as were the wheels and pedals of my bike. Before I realised that this had slowed me somewhat the front wheel hit the metal fence and I was tossed over it. I lay crumpled in a heap by the roadside. Luckily no vehicles were passing at the time.

Jimmy arrived at first concerned, but when I got up with no broken bones, he laughed uncontrollably at my shocked state. Despite the stings, cuts and bruises, it wasn't long before I was fully recovered and accepting acknowledgement of my brave feat from other children. Miraculously, after an afternoon in Father's garage my bike was fixed up too.

It evolved that Jimmy was the only friend to be allowed inside The Corner House. But strictly only ever in the front room where the pianola and the monstrous gramophone were still housed. We still didn't think much of girls, but even at that age I think we subconsciously recognised the charm of my beloved Buddy Holly record; even though it was a while before I discovered what a roller coaster was and indeed many years before I truly appreciated the metaphorical representations of it in Holly's lyrics.

One summer holiday Jimmy and I were miming along to a newly acquired 78 rock 'n' roll record – probably another one I had rescued from the depths of the attic. I remember being unsure of why a man would call his girl a 'baby' or how a girl could 'shake your nerves' or 'rattle your brain.' Nonetheless, we were making grossly exaggerated movements and facial expressions – totally in a world of our own. We imagined we were playing to the packed throng of The Six Five Special on TV. We must have looked truly ridiculous there in the front room of The Corner House, the old gramophone with doors wide open full blast and Jill occasionally howling gently. I think over the years Jill's howling actually got better and sometimes she seemed to be almost in tune.

Then came the squeal of tyres and a loud bang outside. We instantly ran to the front room window that looked out over the staggered crossroads in front of The Black Horse Hotel. The front room of The Corner House is partly subterranean; this and the fact that the wide pavement is banked slightly up to the higher road, meant that when we managed to climb up on to the window seat, our gaze was almost level with the road surface. There on the tarmac just outside the main entrance of the hotel was a crumpled heap and a man hysterically beckoning another man. Mother came bolting up from the kitchen and ran out of the front door. We promptly followed her. Jill stood obedient as ever on the front door step. The woman's leg was facing the wrong way and bent where it shouldn't be. I will always remember her desperate cries of pain and our first witnessing of adults in panic.

My mother threw her cardigan over the woman and turned and shooed us boys back in the house. We looked back over our shoulders and Mother momentarily stood on the edge of the road and pointed a finger at us.

"Stay in the house!" she said before moving back to the poor woman. I'd never seen my mother so stern. We scampered back inside the house like frightened rabbits and watched saucer-eyed through the window again as the gramophone slowed to a stop after repetitively playing the click of the inside groove. Jill hid behind the sofa.

In the hazy mixture of shock and distress an ambulance bell came echoing nearer down Newland and the woman lifted her head briefly and shouted in the air. She then turned her head as if looking straight at us both gawping at her out of the window, her teeth were clenched tightly. A police car arrived and blocked our view. Jimmy and I had grown a little closer. It was later that I discovered the woman who got knocked over was apparently my great aunt – Frank Park's late brother's wife.

A day or two later, still a little shocked from the accident outside The Corner House, I was riding my bike down the narrow, quiet East Mill Lane past Miss Carlisle's wilderness on the right. I was heading to Jimmy's place, which was almost next-door to a large veterinary practice at the far end of the lane where it joins Long Street.

East Mill Lane isn't a short cut to anywhere and it would have probably been quicker to take the Long Street route to Jimmy's place. But I enjoyed the quietude and passing Miss Carlisle's dark, intriguing and overgrown wilderness; knowing I could escape quickly on my super-fast bike should anything nasty emerge through the wrought iron fence.

Further on past a gravel yard with half a dozen lock-up garages, there was a mini dirt track we had created along the top of an earth bank that started just where the lane begins to veer right, away from the railway and back towards Long Street.

Ahead of me that day there was a blackbird rummaging through the tufts of grass on the trail of a worm, or perhaps nest building material; it reminded me of an old woman frantically sorting through clothes at a jumble sale. The bird had obviously seen me approaching but didn't seem too bothered. Then suddenly a chap in an Austin Westminster came tearing up from Long Street. There was a tremendous dust cloud swirling up, around and behind the speeding vehicle. The breeze blew some of the dust towards me. I squinted and managed to glimpse the blackbird take off back across the lane. Before I knew it the car was level with me. The blackbird, not used to vehicles travelling at such speed, completely misjudged things and flew straight into the car's path.

I fell off my bike while at the same time I turned to see the car disappearing rapidly towards The Corner House. A ball of feathers was rolling down the gutter. I ran to the bird's side and it seemed to recover slightly. But although the right way up, its breast was touching the tarmac as if its legs were not strong enough to support it. It was still definitely alive, its eyes blinked from time to time. It made no attempt to move away. I knelt down and cupped it in my hands. I had never held a bird before. It didn't seem to mind at all. I thought about taking it home. I thought about feeding it an aspirin – just until it recovered – then I'd set it free.

I suddenly remembered that there was a veterinary practice nearby. I forgot completely about my bike and walked quickly to the vets carefully nursing the patient. It was quite a large veterinary practice with a yard and a tiled vehicular entrance for horse boxes and the like to unload larger animals. The tiled area had only recently been hosed down and it smelled strongly of disinfectant. I think they were closed but I rang the bell anyway. A man arrived with half rimmed spectacles on the end of his nose. He peered hard over the top of them at me.

"What have we here then?" he asked.

"This blackbird's been knocked over," I said.

"What was it a car then? he enquired. He didn't wait for an answer. "Better come this way then." He gestured for me to follow him and led the way into a rear treatment room.

"Now what do you want me to do Hmm?" He held out his hands to take the bird, "I think we should do the right thing don't you – and put him to sleep." I was rather shocked. He hadn't even looked at the animal yet and he was talking about putting it down.

As I handed it over I noticed there were two beads of blood on the bird's plumage and some more smeared on my fingers. The man didn't even look at the blackbird but calmly walked over to a glass chamber and placed the bird inside and closed it.

It seemed to sort of settle down in there as if it was content to make the warm box its home. It looked at me and blinked, but it didn't seem distressed or anything. Then I realised that the man was turning on the gas. It suddenly dawned on me that the fate of this little bird could be influenced by me stopping the vet's action, but I didn't.

It toppled over on to its side. Again it just looked like it was nestling down – getting comfortable – it probably was. Its head went down, its beak opened wide. Its breast heaved once, twice. Its last breath was like a massive sigh. Then it just lay there relaxed, limp and supple but for one last claw at the air. Probably nerves I thought – or its spirit attaching itself to some ideal perch in birdie heaven.

"Well that's your good deed done for the day eh?" said the vet as he scooped the body out of the box. I must have looked a little despondent. "Don't worry," said the vet, "we'll bury it properly." I muttered a thank you and ambled around to Jimmy's house.

As I knocked on his door I felt I should have taken the bird home and buried it in the flowerbed under the stone wall in the backyard. I briefly remembered Mrs Field not so long ago, sweeping the thrush I'd shot into her dustpan. Then Jimmy opened the door.

After I had discovered that Jimmy was at home alone that day, right out of the blue, he suggested that we go to bed together. In those days 'going to bed' with someone – at least to me – meant just that. I was not conscious of any sexual connotations. My father was one of seven children in a tiny two-bedroom house. He had often told me stories about having to squeeze three or four in a bed – to sleep. Therefore I was not particularly shocked. But I suppose Jimmy and I had begun to feel a little curious about sex or at least human bodies and presumably it was this curiosity that influenced Jimmy to ask me how many girls I'd kissed the other day.

Jimmy's bedroom was far more cosy and conventional than mine. I suppose because he had three sisters all older than him, he purposely made it very macho. There were posters and shelves with toys on them covering all the walls and aeroplanes hung from the ceiling with fishing line. His bed cover had a motif of a sports car emblazoned on it and the carpet was deep pile. In the corner was a Dansette Party Time electric record player.

Jimmy was very eager but I was more apprehensive when it came to it. It turned into a sort of dare thing more than anything else. Jimmy closed his curtains, quickly stripped and got into bed first. He peeped at me from under his deep inviting covers.

"Come on then!" he laughed. I got undressed slowly while Jimmy started a fit of the giggles. By the time I had slipped under the covers Jimmy's giggling was uncontrollable. There was much fidgeting and more laughing at the thought of our bodies actually touching. Eventually they did touch thigh to thigh and that's all that really happened. I think more than anything else we just wanted to experience lying beside someone – anyone – and to see if the other would chicken out. I think when we both got over the initial novelty we found it quite unremarkable, but the bed was warm and cosy.

We lay there for a while talking about pushbikes. Then I recalled in great detail the fate of the blackbird a little earlier. After deep silent thoughts about if songbirds went to heaven, Jimmy eventually confessed how he felt strange sometimes being the only male in his household. It seemed his bedroom had become a male sanctuary in the midst of a female run domain. Apparently his father had died when he was a baby and there was his mother and two much older sisters left living in the house.

Talking about his siblings made Jimmy suddenly remember that one of his sisters was due home at any moment. We leaped from the bed and rushed to put our clothes on getting various items mixed up. I was pulling my trousers up when Jimmy let out a high-pitched scream.

"Shit shit shit shit shit – oh fuckin' shit," he whispered.

"What?" I asked, "what's up?" As I was finishing getting dressed, Jimmy was bent double over his bed.

"What?" I repeated, "what's the matter?" He turned towards me. His flies were still open and there was lots of blood.

"I've trapped my fuckin' willy," he whispered with a deep grimace.

"Lets have a look," I said. Jimmy took his hands away. Unable to look at the injury himself, he looked me in the face as I surveyed the damage. It was just the very tip of his penis – a tiny flap of foreskin caught fast in the metal zip. However, it must have been excruciatingly painful.

"It's a bit like tearing a plaster off," I said – remembering when I'd trapped my fingers in our garage door. Jimmy fluctuated quickly between laughing and crying.

"Jimmy!" I shouted. He looked me straight in the face again. "I'm gonna yank the zip down hard to free you," I said.

"Yeap do it," whispered Jimmy, tears trickling down his cheek. I held the top of the zip firmly and yanked hard on the fastener. Jimmy yelled and his penis fell free as his elder sister shouted up the stairs.

"What are you up to Jimmy?"

"Nothing," shouted Jimmy whilst packing his penis in a handkerchief and very carefully doing up his flies.

"Well it doesn't sound like nothing," came the reply.

"We're rehearsing for the school play," Jimmy shouted back seriously. He then collapsed into fits of uncontrollable giggles at the hilarity of what he had just said, and the relief of realising that his injury although painful, was only slight.

Jimmy at that time was far more confident and forthright than I. So when a mutual friend of ours who happened to be a girl and also older than us came to visit at his house, he asked her outright to show us her body. I was fairly shocked when she showed us every crack, hump and crevice of herself. I guess we were too young to experience any serious sexual feelings and I was far too embarrassed to do anything other than stare in pure curiosity. Any hint of sexual interest was soon taken over by the hilarity of lighting her farts in Jimmy's blacked out bedroom.

This phase of new-found fun and games and dirt-track pushbikes was interrupted when my grandfather Frank became ill. The silent solemnity created in The Corner House at the time affected me and I somehow knew the slightly feared, but much loved Frank had not long to live. Father visited him up the road at Number 8 Castleton every evening.

Then late one night I was in bed and heard voices and a commotion downstairs. I heard Father mutter something before leaving the house in a hurry. I kept my bedroom light off but stayed fully awake sitting upright for hours. I heard logs spit on the fire downstairs and Mother letting Jill out into the backyard.

Then eventually the outside silence was broken by heavy footsteps. I heard the curtain rail screech on top of the middle room door downstairs. I crept out of bed and down the passageway, my feet only stepping on familiar silent floorboards. I crouched near the top of the stairs and peeped around the corner just in time to glimpse my father enter the house; my mother met him there just inside the front door. My father simply said,

"He's gone!" and sank into my mother's arms. It was the first time I had seen my father cry.

I remember the funeral service in Castleton Church where Frank had served as sexton and verger for so many years. I wish I had taken my tape machine and recorded the angelic children's voices emanating from the choir stalls that day. In the middle of a hymn – occasionally mouthing the words and conscious of Father's deep tones – I acknowledged a slight smile from the doctor's daughter as she sang. In retrospect I guess I was suddenly and unexpectedly struck by her beauty and missed the end of the hymn – I nearly forgot to sit down.

The clanging shut of the big iron churchyard gates that day summoned the end of an era and 'verdicts' at Number 8 Castleton. I missed Frank's towering frame with his long black coat, collarless shirts and mirror bright boots. I learnt years later that he died seconds after singing Psalm 23 (The Lord Is My Shepherd) and just before he slipped away he mentioned that he was entering a beautiful garden.

15

Tolerating Acquaintances
And First Fag

The notion of Grandfather Frank exiting this world and entering his 'beautiful garden' stayed with me. I thought about it a lot in my private Scots Pine tree camp high above the river. Len Hart's well-trodden footpath often led my gaze across the field to 7 and 8 Castleton, the church and Frank's final unmarked resting place amongst the deep green ivy and yew trees.

Sometimes the peace and my contemplation of human mortality were disturbed. Below me the small but deep section of river just after the waterfall was brimming full of dozy, slimy tench. Dangle a hook caked in bread paste in the water and within minutes another tench could be yet again easily hooked. They spent most of their lives on a continuous cycle of being hooked, dragged out and thrown back in again by serious coarse fisherman.

But occasionally older boys high on pretend SAS survival techniques, wild cowboy routines or just sheer devilment invaded the area. As well as watching them drop boulders on unsuspecting creatures, from my secret vantage point I witnessed them effortlessly haul tench out of the water too. The lucky fish sometimes had their heads chopped off; collections of heads and bodies would be left strewn around the place. The unlucky ones were left intact and alive but speared through the tail and left hanging up in bushes to pump their gills in desperate gaping heaves to flap their life away for hours.

Maybe it was because I felt I had been too sentimental about losing Kim – and now Grandfather. Maybe I had to regain my machismo by proving I was tough enough to carry out 'manly' acts; or maybe I needed a diversion from the grief and doldrums I was experiencing. Whatever the reason, I copied older boys and briefly reverted to unwarranted acts of killing again.

One day there on the riverbank one of my solitary fantasies resulted in me pretending to be a wild mountain man desperate for food. But of course I wasn't really desperate for food – the slimy tench no doubt tasted foul anyway; I wasn't desperate to kill either, but desperate to prove to myself I could actually do it without wincing or signs of weakness. I wanted to prove I was a fearless young man.

The freshly caught twelve-inch tench lay flapping half-heartedly on the bank as if it was fed up with being constantly yanked out of the water day after day. I took my newly honed bowie knife and effortlessly sliced its head off. It cut so quickly I was left holding the body as the head rolled down the steep dusty bank. I remember my mood changing and I became so concerned at how dirt had stuck to its eyeballs. I was oblivious to the still flinching body in my hands as the head plopped back into the river. I leant out over the river in time to see the bright clear waters cleanse the eyes again as the head gently sank to the depths – mouth still moving.

My wincing had gone unnoticed, my thoughts taken up by wonderment.

One day I heard men's voices and undergrowth rustling below my heavenly retreat. They were getting closer and closer. I strained to take a peek through the thick branches and a dead branch snapped.

"What's that?" I heard one say.

"Lets find out!" said another. In that split second I realised someone was going to shoot at me with a shotgun, but it was too late. A shot rang out. Luckily the aim was too low and the thick, coniferous foliage protected me anyway. Amid little pellets hitting branches just below me I shouted,

"Hey don't shoot!........Don't shoot!" I repeated, scrambling down the tree. I fell down the last few feet of the trunk and lost my balance on the ground, nearly falling in the deepest part of the river. A massive hand grasped my shoulder tearing part of my shirt.

"What the hell do you think you're doing?" shouted one.

"This is private property!" screamed the other, "you could have been killed." They never gave me a chance to speak, just booted me up the backside in the direction of the stepping-stones back across the river. I composed myself, clambered over the prefabricated concrete fence, crossed New Road into the public Purley and ran along the riverbank.

I soon found another tree hideaway further downstream and sandwiched in the narrow strip of wild land I called 'no-man's-land' between the railway line and the river. The trains were much closer here and the tree shook whenever they passed by. Unfortunately Castleton and the church were not visible from this tree. But from time to time when on my solitary rambles I took time to gaze across in that direction from New Road railway bridge. This scene of Castleton remains a picture-record of men like Frank and Len, where they lived, worked and died.

Despite now having one or two friends and acquaintances, I chose to spend a lot of time on my own. It seemed perfectly natural and I only tolerated other children in small doses. When not in my new secret tree I occasionally met up with Jimmy or on rare occasions, the potting shed gang. Things had mellowed between the potting shed trio and me, but unlike Jimmy I still looked upon them as acquaintances rather than friends.

Then one day I was invited to the long abandoned, tumble-down buildings behind the petrol station in Newland again. Their den had spilled out from the old motor coach into quite a large expanse of semi-derelict workshop area. Paul, John and Alan had arranged four old, large, wooden radios evenly on the floor space and one of them was working and tuned to the Light Programme. In the middle of the menagerie sat John amid a pile of stout cardboard boxes. He threw his head back and forth to the beat and tapped two or three of the box tops with bits of stick. Paul grabbed a broom handle as did Alan. While doing so they gestured in the direction of another length of wood that roughly resembled a guitar. As I picked it up I realised that each 'guitar' had a piece of old electrical flex attached in a vain attempt at authenticity. First Paul then Alan thrust the other ends of their flex into make believe sockets in their respective 'amplifiers.' I followed suit forcing the flex into a ventilation hole in the side of the nearest old wooden wireless set. At first I thought it was a little silly and felt very self-conscious. Then as The Swinging Blues Jeans belted out The Hippy Hippy Shakes I thought what the hell and started gyrating around like a lunatic with the others. Then I realised why the others were taking the pantomime so seriously, we were performing to Miranda.

Miranda had grown so big for her tiny pushbike that she now found it difficult to even sit on it, let alone ride it. But she still occasionally managed to do rear wheel skids on the fine gravel that had accumulated there on the old workshop floor. Then she'd stop and stare at us before repeating the act. Astride the little bike, with her feet firmly on the ground, her knees now seemed to be almost level with her chin. She smoked a cigarette and sometimes spat with perfectly rounded lips in our vague direction. She had short boyish hair and wore tight turquoise shorts and a fluffy pink top.

I was sure none of us had ever spoken to Miranda – I knew I hadn't. She just whizzed around the town on her minuscule bike popping up all over the place when least expected. She was becoming more noticeable to us boys with her bare legs and piercing blue-eyed stare. Then after the gig was shut down by John's fuming father, Miranda typically disappeared and us boys went for a walk around New Road to cool off.

We met Jimmy at the end of Newland just by The Corner House, he was just about to call for me. We didn't know where we were going and no one seemed to care. We strolled around New Road under the 'under water' trees. There were cows in Purley, some right next to the rusty iron fence and the tarmac path. Paul made faces at them then John pretended to charge them. The cows stampeded out across Purley and John threw a large stick after them. Miranda reappeared and buzzed back and forth past us standing up and pumping the little bike for all she was worth. Then she came charging back along the pavement straight at us.

"Look out!" shouted Jimmy as we all dived out of the way.

"Fuck off!" shouted Miranda. Her voice echoed barely decipherable comments off the high walls of the estate woodyard as she tore off around New Road.

Someone mentioned Kevin the gamekeeper's son who used to live in the estate woodyard cottage and how he had beheaded six slowworms with his father's machete. Alan said he had heard that I once had a slowworm as a pet.

"Did you?" asked Paul.

"Yeah but I set it free ages ago."

"What did you do that for?" asked John.

"'Cause it's cruel to keep a wild animal."

"Pity you 'ain't still got it – 'cause we could have shot the bastard."

"You bloody wouldn't," I said. John just chuckled and walked on ahead, hands in pockets. Jimmy and I looked at each other.

We reached the old kissing gate in the wall by the entrance to the new castle. It groaned loudly as we all piled through and up the sharp incline that led to another much taller gate at the entrance to Sherborne Park. I anticipated there was something I and Jimmy didn't know about as we lingered there by the gate with John whacking dock leaves with a supple stick he'd found. Then Alan said,

"Wanna fag?" He held the pack of ten Guards out towards me. I had never really thought that much about smoking before. I had bought Woodbines for Mother many times without thinking. I had once, out of pure curiosity, taken a few puffs of a pipe at Aunt Flo's house a few years ago and had been very sick. But without question and so as not to appear wimpish, I plucked one of the cigarettes from the packet.

It was all very serious as we stood in a line backs leaning against the high iron fence that divided the park from the slopes. Alan had the matches too and he skilfully shielded the flame from the breeze with his hands as he offered each of us a light in turn. He had obviously done this before.

"Don't you inhale?" asked Alan after a while.

"Yeah," I said as my lips popped open to urgently expel smoke from my mouth.

We watched each other's cigarette smoking techniques and ash flicking skills; then tried to perfect our own whilst hoping we looked like we had been doing it for years. I took a drag and cautiously inhaled. I exhaled straight away and nearly burst a blood vessel trying to cover up my urgent need to cough. I became more confident and inhaled quite deeply. I felt quite light-headed as I realised none of us had spoken for ages.

After a while I was aware of a prominent hissing sound coming from a large bramble bush over near the gate into the park. I walked across. I thought I was handling my cigarette quite well now and casually flicked ash. Then as I took another drag I began to recognise the shape of a loosely coiled and well-camouflaged adder.

"What is it?" shouted John arriving with his stick and ready to poke it.

"Don't touch it!" I shouted as the rest arrived, "it's an adder, look at the V on its head and the zigzag pattern down its back."

"Kill the bastard!" shouted Paul, "they're poisonous."

"No!" I said, "what's it done to you."

"You're just a chicken!" shouted John, "what you gonna take it home to mummy as a pet?"

"Yeah," agreed Alan, "like that other one you had."

"Quiet!" I said, "you're frightening it."

"Cut the fucker's head off!" shouted John barging through with his penknife open.

"No!" I said.

"What, you gonna stop me?" I took a swing at John and it landed squarely on his nose. He stood there in total disbelief, wide-eyed and checking the trickle of blood on his upper lip with his forefinger. Wary of so many stupid humans the snake rapidly slid away into the undergrowth of the bramble bush. I suddenly became aware of what I had done and the fact that I was outnumbered. Then John turned, almost crying and ran away, his knife still hanging limply in his hand.

"You'll regret that," he bawled back at me.

"What you going home to tell Mummy?" I yelled after him, "by the way that was for pissing on me too."

"Come on lets go home," said Jimmy.

I still occasionally thought of Kim, especially in the summer or when it thundered. When not in my new tree camp next to the railway line in Purley, my favourite pastime became stalking people around the wooded area below the Terrace Playing Fields; near where I had hurtled down through the undergrowth on my out of control bike two years previously.

To a boy approaching early teens who delighted in watching cowboy series on TV like Wagon Train, Gunsmoke and Davy Crockett the cutting opposite the top of Gashouse Hill that use to be the main road to Dorchester could appear like a massive canyon within a pretend wild-west landscape. I guess I was a sort of cowboy on some strange misunderstood mission. I often 'cut them off at the pass.' 'Them' being any unsuspecting walkers I came across strolling up the track. I would watch them undetected in the undergrowth high above at the top of the steep bank on the 'slopes' side of the track. I would wait to see if they turned right on to the lower pathway or carried on up the track. Either way they usually ended up emerging on the Terrace Playing Fields and either way I knew how to get there first. Of course I would never reveal to my pretend quarry that I'd been watching them; just surreptitiously confirm to myself that they were definitely the same people I'd seen earlier and had I been the local sheriff and they dangerous outlaws, I could have ambushed them and taken them in.

Ambushes were usually carried out anonymously with no exchange of words and on people who didn't know me. It was the thought of inevitable complicated interactions and boring dialogue that curtailed my ambushing of familiar people – especially Miranda.

Miranda now found it physically impossible to ride that bike of hers and had to walk everywhere swishing a supple withy stick at everything and everybody as she went. If Miranda walked through the bottom of the canyon I'd watch her pass by with baited breath. She was never aware of my presence and could sometimes be heard mumbling curses as she swung her stick violently.

Just at the foot of the last tree high on the top of the 'slopes,' just a little way back from the steep edge of the 'canyon,' is a small, fairly deep hollow about six or eight feet in diameter. Conveniently sheltered by the tree towering on the higher side, it is partly formed by two of the massive tree root's main limbs, as they delve into the ground. I would sit in there and listen for intruders. Miraculously other children never found this cowboy camp of mine. In the cooler months maybe I'd even light a fire like a real fur trapper. A playful passing breeze would rustle leaves and branches in gentle caressing waves. Rooks would squabble loudly high overhead occasionally intermingled by the just discernible, wavering chimes of Sherborne abbey clock.

On the other side of the 'canyon,' just off the lower footpath leading up to the playing fields, I came across a blackbird's nest that I'm sure was abandoned. When I came close the chicks' heads would pop up just like the ones Father had shown me in Castleton churchyard. I watched from afar for ages, first at mid-morning then again at midday. There was no sign of the mother bird or indeed the father. So I collected worms, chopped them up and fed them with great difficulty. I was aware that most mother birds sort of thrust morsels down their chicks throat. Despite my clumsy fingers inability to mimic a blackbird's beak, they seemed to take the food and I returned and fed them everyday for a week. Then one day I arrived and the nest was empty. Maybe they had flown, maybe a predator had eaten them. Either way nature had taken her course.

One afternoon near the 'canyon,' I heard the shouts of other children from up on the terrace playing fields. I cautiously approached and lay down in the undergrowth near the edge of the neatly cropped grass. A group of youngsters were playing rounders. It was quite organised and there were two adults supervising. It was quite pleasant in the fading afternoon sun. The excited shouts and laughter of the other children were intermingled with the complicated song of a nearby blackbird. I wondered if maybe it had started life as one of the chicks I had fed.

A couple walking hand-in-hand close by surprised me and I had to duck back down so as they wouldn't see me. I began to notice adult male battle cries from somewhere far away. When I changed to a crouching position I could see a serious football match in full swing in the distance way across the other side of the playing fields. Then there was a loud shout much closer and in a split second I noticed the rounders ball hurtling across the grass straight towards me. Before I knew it the boy chasing it was upon me.

"What you doing here?" he asked panting.

"Nothing," I said. He didn't seem particularly surprised and quickly gathered up the ball and ran back. Then I saw him with his arm held high signalling the adult. The adult approached him and it was obvious that the man was being told of my presence. Even though it was a public place and I wasn't doing anything wrong, I turned and ran for my cowboy camp.

Later in the evening I heard all the boys who had being playing rounders walking fast way down in the bottom of the 'canyon.' I went to my lookout and there was ten maybe twelve of them varmints, walking fast chatting and half of them had jumpers tied around their waists. I raced down the slope in front of my hollow to get to the gate at the bottom of the track before them. I intended to disappear down Gashouse Hill before they arrived but they were slightly quicker than I had anticipated. There was a particular boy I recognised, he always said he was my cousin, I don't know if he was or not.

"Why don't you join us on Tuesday evenings?" he said, "it's great fun …. and then we go for chips afterwards down Westbury." I shrugged my shoulders and all the rest apart from two, broke off and went separate ways. The idea of chips sounded good so I accompanied the two boys to the chip shop in Westbury where I experienced the delights of a bag full of salt and vinegar with a few chips floating around in it.

16

TLY69

And Todd's Morris 1000

Fed up with the cumbersome Bedford Workabus, Father sold it and bought a second hand Ford Prefect 100E. It was a noisy little car that constantly stank of vinyl upholstery, antifreeze and burning oil. A strange and annoying characteristic was the way its windscreen wipers operated. They didn't work on electricity, but on air from vacuum created by the car's engine. They could not be turned on instantly at the click of a switch; but had to be gradually coaxed into action by rotating a small pipeline valve in the middle of the dashboard, rather like turning on a miniature central heating radiator.

The strange system meant that the faster the car was driven the slower the wiper blades wiped. So when travelling on a main road in a storm, Father would be constantly dodging the barely moving wipers to get a less than clear view of the road ahead. To the other extreme, stuck in a traffic jam with the engine just ticking over, the wipers clattered away at such a speed that they often seemed to be driven to near self destruction. The frantic blades were often flung beyond their intended scope of travel, hence damaging the rubber seal at the bottom and side of the windscreen.

It did have its good points and I grew to like it as I became more interested in the serious workings of motorcars. In the place where the Spirit of Ecstasy would be on a Rolls Royce – out in front in the middle of the bonnet – was a chrome-plated icon of an aeroplane. Father worked on Spitfires in the RAF during the war and coincidently he had bought the car from a retired RAF pilot. The chap had fixed a tiny metal propeller to the nose tip of the plane, the rotation of which was of course directly related to how fast the car was driven. The car's registration plate read TLY 69. Unfortunately Father spent more time maintaining and repairing TLY 69 than we did travelling in it.

On freezing winter nights I would nurse a hot cup of tea for Father whilst following an old tangled electrical flex across the backyard and into the garage. I would find a yellow patch of light from an old inspection lamp glimmering in the icy, unheated darkness. Sometimes this light came from under the car, sometimes from under the bonnet but always accompanied by grunting, the mist of Father's breath and occasional muttered expletives.

Father would be determined to loosen just one last nut or something before grabbing the mug of tea. Although he insisted that the cold was nothing compared to what he and others had to endure during the war working on Spitfire aeroplanes, the mug was such an obvious comfort to his oil sodden fingers.

To the other extreme, on sticky summer nights trouble with TLY 69 meant that before I went to bed, I would take Father his beloved iced coffee or orange squash. A bothered, boiling face with thankful eyes, camouflaged with dark grease would eagerly down a glass in one.

The MOT test for motorcars over ten years old had not long been introduced, but TLY 69 was just young enough to escape it. In retrospect it would never have passed a modern day emissions test because it began burning more oil than ever. This was most evident when climbing a hill; clouds of blue smoke engulfed any following vehicles. As well as the visible smoke you could actually smell the sheer tiredness of the engine. I guess this tired smell came from the fusion of the smoke, exhaust gasses and antifreeze being forced out through the loosening joints of the engine and the perished rubber hoses; the concoction cooked by a constantly overheating engine.

TLY 69's last journey propelled with that particular engine was to a farm a few miles south of Sherborne to view a second-hand engine from a car that had apparently been in an accident. This meant driving up the long and sweeping Sherborne or West Hill. Father fiddled with his tie and gritted his teeth. I knew he was praying that the car would make it as he nursed it along and dared himself to press the accelerator pedal a little more.

A rusty, grimy cast iron lump of an engine lay at an odd angle in the entrance to the farmyard with a large territorial cockerel perched on top of it announcing ownership. The bird flicked its comb and ducked its head at each cock-a-doodle-do as we knocked on the backdoor. The farmer seemed to know who we were straight away.

"Well there it is," he said – roll-up cigarette stuck in the corner of his mouth. "I only took the bugger out this morning look." I was astounded when the farmer gesticulated towards the dirty iron boulder that his cockerel was standing on. Surely this wasn't the engine. A dribble of black oil trickled from it staining the dusty ground like blood from some monstrous alien's discarded, rotten tooth. The freshly crushed thistle under its sump cover seemed to be evident of an unceremonious dumping of what appeared to be scrap metal to me. As we inspected it further there was more detrimental evidence. Instead of undoing jubilee clips properly the rubber hoses had been cut, ripped from their housing for quickness.

"How many miles has it done?" enquired Father.

"Twenty," said the farmer.

"Twenty?" I asked myself. Then it dawned on me he meant twenty thousand miles. I'd heard Father say the present 'Prefect' engine had done two hundred thousand, so it wasn't too bad – if true.

"There's the 'Squire' up there, look." The farmer pointed to a Ford Squire up the other end of the yard lying on its side, "bugger rolled over see – in the ice last winter – insurance company wrote it off straight away." I wondered briefly whether the accident had actually occurred there where it lay. I eventually realised that the confines of the farmyard would have made it impossible to gather enough speed to accidentally roll it. It had been purposely tipped over there to enable the easy removal of underneath parts.

Father walked around the other side of the engine trying to think of what else to ask. He knew full well that there was no chance of analysing the condition of the engine without either taking it apart or running it.

"Why didn't you leave it in the car for us to see it running?" asked Father. Yeah that's a good one I thought.

"He wouldn't run see – 'cause the front were bashed in on the nearside wing an' the radiator were squashed right up against the fan."

"Would you guarantee it?" asked Father after a thoughtful pause.

"I ain't gonna write you out a guarantee to say that there engine's in a new condition, but what I can tell you is he come out of that car up there this morning and my son rolled that bugger last winter. At that time that 'Squire' had done about twenty thousand miles."

"But if I fit that engine in my 'Prefect' and find it's knackered….."

"It won't be knackered mate."

"But I've only got your word for that!"

"Look I'll shake hands with you now and I'll promise you that engine's only done twenty thousand miles."

Father and the farmer shook hands as the cockerel tore up across the yard towards another cockerel he had spied in a hay barn. Was that handshake a gentlemen's agreement that the engine was OK or had Father just made a deal? I asked myself.

"Will a 'Squire' engine definitely fit in a 'Prefect?'" asked Father with heavy emphasis on the word definitely.

"He'll go straight in – no problem at all, tis exactly the same under the bonnet see." I wondered how a farmer knew so much about which engine fitted which model of car if he didn't have more to do with dealing in motor parts than he was letting on.

"Would it include transporting it back to Sherborne for that money?" asked Father.

"You drive a hard bargain," said the farmer, "yeah alright go on then."

I'm sure Father had done far more difficult, or at least more fiddly jobs on TLY 69 in the past, but maybe not one so dangerous as to change a whole heavy engine without professional equipment. Father borrowed a block and tackle from somewhere and Uncle Todd came to give a hand one Saturday. I was forbidden to go anywhere closer than the garage doorway and Mother was banned from the entire area. No one was qualified in assessing the structural strength of roofs, but the garage timbers were definitely not designed to take the weight of a car engine. The timbers creaked and groaned with only the block and tackle attached, let alone the engine.

Jimmy arrived and two other friends. We stood gawping in the street by the open garage door while Father and Todd puffed and struggled under the bonnet of TLY 69. The roof timbers did more than creak as they took the full weight of the old engine. At one point it sounded like someone was intermittently banging on the corrugated asbestos roof with a hammer. With the old engine high enough to clear the front grill of the car Father shooed us kids further out on to the drive. Both panic-stricken, Father and Todd hastily pushed TLY 69 back out of the way towards the open doors. There were sighs of great relief as the two men gently lowered the offending article on to the floor just in front of the car. They stood hands on hips and then mopped brows before man-handling the lump across the floor out of the way. It took all day but they did it in the end. The 'new' engine was in place. All the bolts needed tightening up but they left all that until the next day.

Saturday morning had come around again and I was bored; Mother was shopping and Father was at work. By this time I was entrusted with access to the garage key, which was now kept on a hook by the backdoor. I would use the massive iron vice in the garage and Father's tools to make things like bird boxes, simple one-piece wooden boats and custom built battery powered contraptions. My latest project was an electric fan, which resembled a windmill. It looked quite impressive but the motor had burnt out when I had tried to operate it. I was beginning to realise that I had got the gearing wrong. I studied it in dismay. Realising I had no money to buy the required gear cogs I discarded it there amongst the menagerie on top of the bench.

TLY 69 was going quite well now. The engine always started and it didn't seem to burn oil excessively. I looked at the black and chrome vehicle standing there. To me it always seemed to have a peculiar expression rather like a forced smile. The grill for some reason reminded me of teeth – car teeth – it didn't really look like human teeth. And the headlamps with chrome surrounds were machine eyes that added to the overall polite looking, faint smile.

How I'd love to drive it myself. It suddenly came to me that Father would not be back for at least two hours, Mother probably the same and I knew where Father kept a spare emergency car key. I saw him put it back there the other day – under the bonnet next to the battery regulator kept in place with a self-tapping screw. I was overcome with excitement. Yes, I was going to start and drive TLY 69 by myself and who would ever know? But my heart sank when I thought of how to get the bonnet open. Then my heart missed a beat and I danced with uncontrollable excitement again when I noticed the bonnet was ajar. Father had not secured it shut properly when last working on it. I hoisted the bonnet up high, just managing to secure the catch. I fetched a Philips screwdriver and in no time the ignition key was in my hand. I caught a glimpse of Jill out in the backyard looking up at the garage door. She had a look of dismay on her face as if she was thinking: 'What on earth is he up to now?'

I climbed in and adjusted the driving position. I could just about reach the pedals with the seat as far forward as it would go. I placed the key in the ignition and then grasped the knobbly steering wheel with both hands. Subconsciously I suppose I was savouring the moment of anticipation before pulling the choke and turning the key. It started first time but seemed far more noisy than usual in the confined space of the garage. I forced the clutch to the floor and rammed it into first gear. The gears made a nasty grinding clunk, they always did. I drove forward three feet until the bumper touched the doors. Reverse was harder to find and made far more noise. I drove it back and forwards three or four times. I couldn't wait to get out there on the road one day.

Everyone said that Todd would never take to driving a car after years of pushing and occasionally riding a bicycle. However, he persevered and his brother eventually succeeded in teaching him properly. Todd now drove a milk-white Morris 1000 saloon with red upholstery that looked and felt like leather. For a while he kept it parked in the road outside Newland flats. But more recently he rented a garage for it down East Mill Lane just past Miss Carlisle's wilderness. Every time he walked from Newland Flats to take the car out – or on the more numerous occasions when he went to wash it, polish it, or maybe just to look at it – he had to pass right by The Corner House.

He started calling for me on Saturday mornings and we would walk down East Mill Lane together past Miss Carlisle's half-hidden chapel-like building nestling in the corner of her wilderness. Despite being accompanied by Todd, Miss Carlisle's garden was still extremely spooky, especially when we heard the rustling that always seemed to occur on the other side of the rusty, wrought iron fence. More often than not there would be an innocent blackbird totally engrossed in rooting through part of the tangled ivy and moss.

The peace of the dark, narrow lane and the gentle rustling in the undergrowth would occasionally be drowned out momentarily by an express steam train hurtling by just feet away on the other side of the prefabricated concrete fence.

Todd's garage was next to two or three others that never seemed to be used, all positioned around a small yard, which was covered in orange gravel. Todd gradually transported more and more things there like a little primus stove, teapot, kettle and a deckchair. It gradually took over from the allotment shed as the preferred home-from-home for Todd and a convenient facility for the general appreciation of the immaculate Morris. Todd didn't have a clue about the basic maintenance of cars like checking the oil, water, battery or tyre pressures. He didn't understand cars at all, but boy did he keep it sparkling clean and polished.

It was a solid well-built little car, the doors shut with a reassuring clunk and the seats were more comfortable than the Ford Prefect's. Sometimes, after he could clean and polish it no more, Todd would just start it up and let it tick over while he made a brew on the primus stove. Very occasionally we'd go on a test run around New Road and back. Todd was still fairly nervous about driving and would wait for ages at halt signs examining the area left and right meticulously, as if not trusting his eyesight. It was common for him to then wind down his window and listen for traffic. Sometimes he'd wear his glasses, sometimes he didn't. He really couldn't decide if he was happiest driving with or without them. Eventually, after convincing himself it was OK the little Morris 1000 would creep steadily out of the junction. Todd rarely drove faster than forty miles an hour, even on the new dual carriageway between Sherborne and Yeovil.

Then one day Todd asked me out of the blue if I wanted a go at driving his Morris – just around the privacy of the gravel yard. I was quite taken aback but eagerly accepted the offer. It was obvious Todd assumed I had no experience whatsoever of driving. I was bursting to tell him that I had in fact practised clutch control on Father's car but of course I dared not.

Todd's tuition was well organised. First he insisted on supervising a reflex exercise. I sat in the driver's seat, car stationary and engine off. I would grab the steering wheel and pretend I was driving along, Todd would then randomly shout "Stop!" I would have to ram my feet as quickly as possible on the clutch and brake.

With Todd satisfied about my coordination and reflex ability, I started the engine with the gearbox in neutral. I revved the engine a little.

"Steady!" said Todd. The gearbox clicked into first gear and I started to let the clutch out. "Hang on! Hang on!" shouted Todd, "you must look in the mirror first." I saw little point because we were only a couple of feet in front of the garage, but I suppose it was good practise.

"Nothing there!" I shouted. I revved the engine again and let the clutch out slowly. A rear wheel spun slightly on the loose gravel propelling a piece of stone up which hit the adjoining garage door with a metallic ping.

After three weeks I was getting on quite well. Then when Mother discovered that Todd was letting me drive the Morris around the private yard, there was a big argument and she banned me from visiting the home of Todd's car. She said that if I wasn't old enough to drive on the public roads, then I shouldn't be allowed to drive on private land either. I felt this was grossly unfair because I'd heard stories at school of boys from outlying villages who were regularly trusted to drive their father's tractors, often ploughing fields and towing trailers.

One Sunday Todd and Flo suggested following Father's Ford in their Morris on one of our seaside trips. Father was quite reluctant, he liked to be independent and hated driving in convoy, but he eventually agreed. Father was not a particularly fast driver but every so often he had to stop and wait in a convenient lay-by for Todd and Flo to catch up. Then the little Morris would come belting by us and we would have to take off after it and try and overtake it on a straight piece of road. If we failed to overtake, Todd would stop the Morris in the most ridiculous place on a bend or brow of a hill and wave us past; he would avoid taking the lead at all costs.

We never made the coast that day. Not far from Cerne Abbas Todd stopped on a blind bend blocking the road. He beckoned to

Father and shouted that he didn't fancy driving in the busy seaside traffic that day and suggested stopping off on Batcombe Downs not far away. We felt obliged not to abandon them and made for Batcombe Downs.

The downs were OK in those days. There was plenty of room to park, usually a couple of ice cream vans and funny little crooked, knotted trees that were easy to climb. There was also a thick bluebell woodland down across the valley not far away.

We managed to park right next to each other with windows wide open. Occasional words were exchanged between cars. But everyone except me, seemed perfectly content just to lay back and doze. When I'd got fed up with eating ice cream and climbing the small trees I wanted to go down into the cool woodland and explore. I was forbidden to go on my own but eventually Todd agreed to go with me.

We picked our way over the thick blue carpet with the smell of wild chives and garlic filling the air. As we strolled along Todd typically asked when I'd last had the slipper at school and if I had a girlfriend yet. Nobody – apart from other children and teachers – knew that I'd actually received the slipper nearly every week when at primary school. And I don't suppose Todd or my parents were aware that now the biggest threat at St Aldhelm's was the far more painful cane; I was too embarrassed to update Todd. I almost mentioned Kim and the mystery of crazy Miranda but felt it would be far too complicated; so I just said no to everything and made out I found it funny. I laughed like Todd.

When we were deep in the cool heart of the woodland with only pockets of sky visible through the canopy overhead, we heard a man's voice shouting and getting rapidly closer. We couldn't quite tell what he was saying but he was obviously very concerned about something. We both instinctively stopped dead as we heard the undergrowth and earth being disturbed by something bulky not too far away. It was then that a massive black and white bull emerged charging straight at us and trampling a path through the bluebells.

"Get behind a tree!" shouted a man now nearby, "get behind a tree and don't move!" Another man appeared with a large rifle and some rope. The animal was almost upon us and gathering speed. Todd grabbed me and we both stepped behind the nearest tree. I peeped from behind Todd to see the beast dig its heels in the ground and slide to a halt only feet away. The beast snorted loudly and I dared not breathe. The frantic animal seemed to look straight at us and in that split second its head tossed up and down in slow motion. It snorted again like something at boiling point and scraped at the bluebells with a hoof as if preparing to charge again. It suddenly took off to our right. The two men kept their distance and seemed quite shaken as they followed after it.

We stayed by the tree for a good ten minutes then cautiously made our way back up to the Cars. When we arrived Mother, Father and Aunt Flo were sound asleep and snoring. As Todd whispered that maybe we shouldn't wake them, a shot rang out down across the valley. Mother awoke with a start.

"Where've you been?" she asked.

"Down in the woods," I said, "we got charged by a bull!"

"Don't be so daft," said Mother, "there's no bulls around here!"

When we arrived back at The Corner House that evening we waited and waited for the Morris 1000.

"I didn't realise he was that far behind!" said Father typically fiddling with his tie.

"Perhaps they've broke down?" he muttered thoughtfully, "well I'll give them five more minutes then I suppose I'll have to go back and look for them." As Father finished speaking the little Morris appeared up over New Road railway bridge travelling at walking pace in a cloud of steam.

"Whas her on vire?" asked Mother straining for a better look.

"No that's steam," muttered Father under his breath.

The poor little Morris came to a rest outside The Corner House engulfed in white mist and hissing like a steam locomotive. The whole car, with little Flo sunk deep into the front passenger seat, disappeared completely in the swirling cloud. Todd staggered out.

"I thought I'd better keep going," said Todd, "but I knew there was something wrong."

"Get Flo out!" shouted Mother. Todd and Father struggled through the steam to help Flo out of her seat.

"Should'n think ee's much good now you know," Father stated as he fought to release the bonnet catch.

When it had cooled down Father confirmed a ruptured radiator hose. If Todd had only stopped when it had first happened he would have saved the engine. As it was he boiled it almost dry and completely ruined it. The little cream Morris 1000 was never the same after that.

17

Boys' Brigade, Girls

And Devastation

I started to join the gatherings of boys up on the Terrace Playing Fields on Tuesday evenings. If the truth were known it was the visit to the fish and chip shop afterwards that attracted me the most. The chips and scraps of batter floating in a bag of weak, watery vinegar with lashings of coarse salt, became the highlight of my week. Those evenings spent loitering in front of the abbey just up the road from the chip shop evolved to be a regular contest of who could stomach the most salt and vinegar.

But it wasn't only the satisfying of my unsophisticated palate that I came to enjoy. When the liquid in the greaseproof bags had penetrated through to each individual's newspaper parcel, horseplay often erupted. Handfuls of the resulting sodden mess would be thrown at each other. When bored with that sometimes we'd see who could throw a ball of mashed-up newsprint the highest up the nearest wall and hopefully watch it stick.

I discovered that it was in fact the recreational branch of The Life Boys and The Boys' Brigade who organised the Tuesday gatherings. The Life Boys were for younger boys and I had briefly attended one or two of their separate formal sessions as a sort of extension to primary school a few years before. I had hated the sailor's hats and had left when I had been heavily reprimanded for not polishing the soles of my shoes.

I was apprehensive about joining The Boys' Brigade but was eventually coaxed into attending more of their formal meetings. As well as the Terrace Playing Field gatherings there were three other sessions a week for drill, band practice and an optional social night; plus many church functions and parades to attend on Sundays. There were indeed a variety of things on offer and it was the chance to have a go at playing a brass musical instrument like a French horn or trombone that influenced my decision to join.

I attended my first band practice at the Rawson Hall, a green painted corrugated tin building, which is situated next to an alleyway known as Gravel Pits just off Westbury and not far from the chip shop. I soon discovered there were very few French horns or trombones available and instead I was handed a silver coloured cornet in a tatty black case and told to go home and 'muck around' with it.

I was initially fascinated by it. There was a book of music that had little diagrams drawn next to the stave in appropriate places indicating which valves should be pressed and when. Jill the dog and I were soon banished from everywhere except the topmost parts of The Corner House when I practiced the scales. It seemed it was only Jill the dog who could tolerate – in fact sometimes she seemed to even enjoy – the funny noises the cornet made. I often became incapable of blowing the instrument through uncontrollable laughter. Not only because of the ridiculous raspberry sounding notes I produced through not blowing hard enough, but also because these notes seemed to set off involuntary movement of Jill's ears. A new note might for instance cause her left ear to stand erect and her right to sag down. Subsequently an unexpected and uncontrolled change in tone would bring about a different combination. Then as my blowing diminished into laughter, Jill became very alert and seemed to regain control of her ears. She'd stand up ready to fend off this strange thing that I was battling with. Her look of embarrassment when she realised I was laughing at her just made things worse and I laughed even more until my stomach ached. Each session always ended with me discarding the cornet and making a reassuring fuss of her. Her tail wagging affected her whole body, so much so that she could hardly walk. She just wriggled around in my arms in an overflowing act of affection.

I returned to the Rawson Hall after just a week of mucking around with the battered old instrument to be told I would be playing it in a parade to Sherborne Abbey the following Sunday. When I protested that I couldn't play it, I was told to mime. I felt very self-conscious in the parade and was sure that everyone knew that I was miming.

I was approaching early teens and desperately wanted to break out of my cocooned existence, which was largely created by my mother. If Mother had her way my hair would be cropped short at the back and sides and I'd always be dressed in an immaculate Sunday suit. It was as if she'd like to keep me in a large, silent glass display cabinet with no hope of expressing myself or voicing an opinion of my own. As it was, Mother actively encouraged criticism and even ridicule from other family members if I dared to let my hair grow a little longer or if I wore tatty tee shirts or faded jeans.

Along with what must have been an early identity crisis, I had begun to notice girls in a different way. Kim had been my first genuine and true friend, but I now looked upon the opposite sex in a slightly more mature way; no longer as a 'cowboy' or 'sheriff' in an adolescent fantasy world, but as a real person in the very real 1960s. Gossip about who was 'going out with' who became rife amongst girls I had contact with.

My eyes often met with those of a particularly sweet girl who always returned my smile. By now I was probably in the third year at school and she was in the second, so I didn't see her very often; just occasionally we would exchange a fleeting glance, charging in different directions down a corridor – usually late for a lesson or something. More often than not she'd be in the back of a coach as I carefully cycled behind it down Bristol Road.

As Christmastime approached the only way I could think of getting closer to her was to buy her a box of chocolates. There was no way I could take a box of chocolates to school so I kept them hidden at home inside the pianola for ages. I suppose I must have I mentioned it to Mother who said I must get dressed up in my smartest clothes and ask Father to drive me to the girl's home out in the country. I somehow managed to find out exactly where she lived and my parents transported me there in the Ford Prefect one Sunday. I could hardly move in cardboard stiff immaculate clothes and a tight strangling tie.

The black 'Prefect' with its polite looking chrome headlamp eyes and slight car smile was a stranger to the inquisitive residents. This along with Father's driving – at walking pace like a funeral – made us quite conspicuous. As we approached the farmhouse I noticed the girl sitting on the fence with her two brothers.

"Is that her?" asked Father not knowing whether to stop and typically fiddling with his tie.

"Yes," I said.

"Go and give them to her nicely," said Mother. I felt truly sick as I got out of the car, partly because of Mother's nauseating instructions and tone of voice and partly because I was still so shy of other children; especially within situations that had been inflated into some pointless, ceremony by Mother.

As I approached her she recognised me and became so obviously dumbfounded – even horrified. I continued walking the few yards towards her in my trousers with razor sharp creases. The younger brother ran away towards the farmhouse.

"These are for you," I said. The other older brother laughed and poked his tongue into his cheek as a family of rooks not far away seemed to raucously share his amusement. He looked me up and down and smiled broadly. As the girl stood up in her gumboots, faded tatty jeans and torn tee shirt, her jaw fell open. I turned and walked away as quickly as I could back to the car. I felt an utter fool. I think they thought I was a lunatic delivering a box of chocolates out of the blue like that and looking like I'd just climbed out of a boys' outfitter's window. Back at school the following week the poor girl obviously thought I was totally mad and avoided me like the plague.

I had learnt that one way to ask a girl to go out with you was to pass them a note in class – this method lessened any inevitable embarrassment. I had made a new friend and he had done just that and was now seeing a girl from our form. He would share surreptitious moments with her behind the bike sheds or in the main foyer, providing there was no public punishment going on there. Then I discovered that a new girl I had noticed – again from a year below me – was in fact my friend's girlfriend's sister. The four of us began meeting sometimes at break times, but few words were ever exchanged; the environment was never really conducive to losing our inhibitions.

Then a note arrived for me in class one day, passed on via my friend's girlfriend. My friend and I were invited for tea at the sisters' home in a nearby village. It was arranged that the girls' father would pick us up in his car, and my father would collect us later in the evening. I was scared.

Mother insisted it would again be a formal occasion but I wasn't so sure. The sisters lived in a fairly large house set in its own grounds and their father was a successful businessman. There was a small swimming pool in the back garden and the two girls were lounging on deckchairs listening to a very impressive portable electric record player when we arrived. Everyone else was in casual clothes. They had a younger brother who had a proper little go-cart; everyone had a go except me – I didn't want to ruin my best clothes. Their mother served afternoon tea by the pool. I made an effort and removed my tie and threw my blazer off; but I still felt out of place, afraid of spoiling my posh trousers and shoes.

I felt like screaming 'I'm not like this really... I want to wear jeans and tee shirts like you.' Then I spilt jam on my trousers. Everyone else was lolling around on the grass by now and the record player belted out Dancing In The Street by Martha Reeves and The Vandellas. One of the girls made a sarcastic remark about me having to be careful not to ruin my expensive trousers. I smiled politely.

I guess it was these embarrassing encounters that not only made me hate the posh clothes that my mother seemed desperate for me to wear, but also made me increasingly rebellious of everything I thought posh clothes and formal occasions stood for.

My mother seemed oblivious to the fact that – except perhaps for Sundays, very special occasions and Boys' Brigade marches – other children did not wear smart clothes all the time. I guess because I began refusing to conform to her wishes she would seldom call me by my name; it was always 'stupid ass' or something. At kinsfolk gatherings – which usually happened on Sundays and often at relative's homes – she invited people to look at my 'filthy' clothes or my 'untidy' hair.

Teenage clan members' courtship statuses were also a favourite subject at these gatherings. This always started with a run-down on which youngsters had met a member of the opposite sex, when and where. It inevitably resulted in smutty 'Carry On Courting' type humour and ended with snide remarks at me as I sat silently in my torn blue jeans and flowing locks. I couldn't be bothered to participate or attempt to explain my feelings or opinions.

Mother insisted on encouraging further criticism of me.

"Colin has a girl for five minutes and then she do chuck 'im when she discovers how filthy he is!" Mother could not be told that times had changed drastically since her courting days and that she'd got things totally back to front anyway; it was in fact the immaculate clothes and formal rituals that girls found boring, or to use a new found term, 'square.' In any case I wasn't particularly desperate to participate in any sort of courtship and I found it irritating how Mother obviously felt I should be shoved headlong into a 'steady' relationship as soon as possible. I couldn't understand the apparent urgency. I hadn't had a proper girlfriend of any sort yet and I was certainly in no hurry for a so-called 'steady' type.

There would often be awkward silences at these family gatherings when people seemed to want a reaction from me. Then an aunt or uncle would apparently feel sorry for me and gently try to defend me by perhaps illustrating how times had changed since their youth and how the older generation should try to understand the youngsters more.

Once while having Sunday tea at Aunt Dorothy's she recalled how she'd met her husband Horace. Apparently she had been a housemaid for the lord of the manor and was expected to attend Sunday morning church with her employers.

"I'd only bin in the job a few days," she said. "It was the first time I'd ventured out in best clothes an' the first time I'd bin inside that particular church. I followed the family in an' took up my place in a pew. I knelt down when the rest did an' prayed. Half way through prayin' I opened my eyes just a liddle bit and noticed the big tall pipes of the church organ. All of a sudden the organ started for the first hymn an' I was late standin' up. A little way into that first hymn I noticed the dimly lit narrow bit behind the organ and I caught sight of a young man pumping the lever up and down. When I looked again he happened to glance up and across at me, an' our eyes met. I knew at that moment that I would marry him. And we've bin together ever since." She thought for a while, "but that was a long time ago and times have certainly changed .... and there's nothing anyone can do about it."

"Yes but you don't know him!" Mother said – referring to me, "he doesn't do anything he's told and just look at his clothes and hair – he looks like a tramp on the road." Father tried to intervene but was typically interrupted.

I had empathy for those bygone times and a respect for Aunt Dorothy's philosophical approach. But I was a young teenager in the 1960s and I wanted to be a part of it. Nonetheless, I didn't seriously rebel or misbehave at that time, even though I was so desperate to develop into someone Mother had no way of comprehending. After a while I guess I began to question my identity further. Was I really that stuttering, despicable creature with unimportant opinions not worthy of consideration that Mother seemed to want? All I really knew is that I wanted to be able to express myself; and perhaps more importantly I wanted to be on a par with young people of my own age.

Thankfully after I had started the fourth year at secondary school Mother didn't impose her rules quite as harshly. But she still telephoned ahead to the barber when she thought I needed a haircut. The barber would then want to carry out her instructions to give me a conventional short back and sides. On one such visit to the hairdresser months later, it was the barber's son – as opposed to the old man – who cut my hair. He actually asked *me* how I wanted it cut. I chose to leave it much longer and have it combed in a different way – with hair gel added. Mother was furious but eventually relented.

I suppose other boys were undergoing similar experiments. I remember a boy in our form who plastered so much hair gel on his head that he was given the name 'Grease Pot' which stuck for the rest of his schooldays and maybe into his adulthood.

After the psychological boost of a new, much longer hairstyle, I was told that a girl in the same year but different form fancied me. It was the first time I had been told that someone fancied me. Girls were quite good it seemed at organising foursomes.

On a freezing Thursday night – ironically up the dark gangway outside The Rawson Hall where The Boys' Brigade met for band practice – a friend and I made a rendezvous with two girls. We didn't even know which was which or who should go with who. But after an embarrassing silence kicking the gravel with hands in pockets we eventually paired off. I don't think the girls were actually bothered who went with who, but one of them seemed to choose me. Then my mate and the other girl walked away up the narrow dark footpath.

The girl drew me to her and into the darkest corner up the side of the hall. After a while she took my hands and placed them inside her coat. Her body heat radiated through her inner clothes, soft and warm. I undid my coat and we shared body heat for ages, just standing there with misty breath. I heard the chinking of someone placing milk bottles on a doorstep far away.

"You don't do much do you!?" she suddenly said. I groped her awkwardly and our lips met. I kissed her first softly then very urgently. We were then interrupted by my mate and the other girl who had done the circuit around the maze of footpaths close to the Rawson Hall. I felt very good.

I met her about twice a week. Sometimes by the hall, sometimes huddled in the bus shelter in Digby Road and occasionally up in the bandstand in Pageant Gardens. Nothing ever really happened. It was usually just sharing body heat, hesitant fumbling or maybe experimental kissing.

Then after two weeks I realised that I hadn't touched my cornet since meeting the girl or indeed attended any of The Boys' Brigade meetings. I postponed my meeting with the girl the following week and went to band practice instead.

"It's no good turning up here after two weeks absence and think you can carry on as normal!" said the bandmaster.

"But I…" I was going to say I'd been ill or something but he interrupted me.

"No excuses laddie… leave your cornet here." I dumped the cornet and turned to go. "If you make up for it and attend all the other meetings like drill and church appointments for the next two weeks then I might consider taking you back… it's up to you." I walked out.

I went to drill later the same week, it was held in a different hall that was part of Sherborne King's School for boys. After being heavily reprimanded I was told there was an important event at the abbey next Sunday and The Boys' Brigade and all its members must attend.

When Sunday came we marched to the abbey. Not having to concentrate on playing an instrument or indeed miming with one, I realised just how bad the band sounded. We filed into the massive, reverberant abbey and squeezed ourselves into the packed pews. All of The Boys' Brigade occupied the front three rows. We listened, prayed, sang and listened again.

In the middle of the service, with the vicar reading a passage, I suddenly inadvertently broke wind. I don't really know why I farted, except that it seemed a perfectly natural thing to do. However, I had no idea that it would be so loud or indeed heard at all. It was a little like the time years previously when I had farted in a craftwork lesson at primary school, but this time there was no bench to hide under. The fart echoed loudly around the expansive interior of Sherborne Abbey. The vicar stopped reading and looked straight in my direction. I kept a very serious face and turned to my right and looked directly at Paul from the potting shed gang who was standing there beside me. I frowned intensely at Paul who continued looking straight ahead. The vicar seemed to get the message and I was sure he now believed it was Paul who had farted. The vicar started reading again. I looked at Paul. That's for pissing on me, I thought.

After the service, milling around in the church porch Paul repeated over and over again,

"it wasn't me... It wasn't me." One of the loyal older boy members appeared.

"Who was it?" he asked frowning heavily.

"It was me," I said. Although I was never officially told, it was assumed that I would be thrown out of The Boys' Brigade. I never turned up again and left my uniform in a plastic bag on the steps of The King's School drill hall.

The meetings with that girl sort of fizzled out and I began to notice very attractive girls on my own doorstep so to speak – there in the same class. In a thoroughly boring and deathly silent history lesson I passed a note to Nicola. She was sat two rows behind me and the note was fed through three or four people. After I was sure she had got the note I made out I was scratching my head and briefly glimpsed behind me, she smiled at me. Back came her note: Yes she would meet me that weekend. I asked her where and sent it back.

"If that boy doesn't stop passing notes around he'll be in deep trouble!" said the teacher suddenly. It was obvious that other people were passing notes around too and I was sure that if I was extra careful he wouldn't see my particular notes being passed. But he did. At the end of the lesson no one was allowed to leave the room until 'that boy' had made himself known.

"He knows who he is," said the teacher, "now I've got all day and all night." I stood up and walked out in front of the class expecting a good telling off. Instead I was punched in the stomach and kneed in the groin. I never did get to know exactly where and when Nicola wanted to meet me.

I may have continued my quest to meet Nicola but my attention was diverted when Jill the dog became ill. She was off her food and just appeared miserable the whole time. She would sit in front of the fire at night and stare into it. Like me she never tired of watching the ever flickering, changing flames and glowing embers of an open fire there in her beloved Corner House; but her enthusiasm for human contact had all but disappeared. If spoken to or touched she would maybe just muster enough energy to poke a little bit of her pink tongue out to briefly lick your finger. Maybe a minute movement of her tail, just detectable.

Then one night just before I went to bed Father carried Jill to the vets again. After they had left the house I somehow knew that I would never see her again; I was devastated when this thought hit me and I realised that I hadn't even said goodbye to her. I didn't sleep at all that night.

Next morning I was up early and wandered downstairs. There was no Jill waiting for me at the bottom. She wasn't sitting by the newly lit fire and she wasn't begging for scraps in the kitchen. Mother and Father were both very quiet. I was halfway through a totally silent breakfast when I had to know for sure.

"Where's Jill?" I asked. Father immediately disappeared upstairs.

"She had to be put to sleep," said Mother, "she were very sick and it was for the best."

"Oh," I said. It was obvious from my parents' behaviour that they weren't sure of how I would react or how to handle any reaction that I might have had. I gritted my teeth and decided to put my back into the day. I intended to do my crying later on my own.

I don't remember the morning – it was all a daze. It would have been different had I said goodbye to her. I could not stop thinking of Jill's thoughts after Father had left her there at the vet's; how betrayed and deserted she must have felt – just when she needed someone the most.

I spent the lunch hour wandering around the playground occasionally being barged into by part of the milling mass. I guess one or two boys closer to me may have approached but they soon departed after sensing my need to be alone. I couldn't bring myself to tell anyone of my pain and grief.

It had turned into a fairly warm spring day and I had no idea that the headmaster had ordered that everyone should remain outside until the start of afternoon lessons. I was suddenly aware that I was bursting to go to the toilet so I let myself in and walked straight around the corridor to the boys' loo. Before I had finished relieving myself the history master accompanied by the science master came running in and one stood on either side of me. Their body language and stance reminded me of military police about to capture a soldier who had gone AWOL.

"You've broken the rule laddie," roared the history master.

"What rule?" I innocently enquired.

I was bundled down the corridor to the headmaster's office where I was made to stand outside for a half an hour until lessons resumed. I was not given a chance to defend myself or explain. The headmaster just briefly gave me all that rubbish about it hurting him more than it would hurt me. Then I was made to bend over his chair and witnessed by the science teacher, I was given six of the best with the cane. Boy did that hurt. They had achieved what they wanted; a poor frightened boy cowering; already lumbered with deep mental pain and now even more incapable of thinking for himself because of unbearable physical pain.

"Get out!" shouted the headmaster.

"Thank you sir," I whispered before running all the way to the changing rooms. I knew I had been made late for the next lesson – games. My head was a mess.

The changing rooms had two entrances side by side, boys on the left and girls on the right. As I reached the boys' door eager for a little private space I nearly bumped into Miranda of all people charging out of the girls' door, presumably late for her next lesson. We stopped and just stared at each other for a brief moment and I detected a slight smile on her lips before she ran away down the corridor.

Relieved at the temporary privacy inside the smelly changing rooms, I felt I was coping with the excruciating pain emanating from my backside. I frantically fumbled with my games kit. All the while I had an overpowering frustration boiling inside me. I was very aware that I had just been punished severely for something brought about by a genuine lack of proper communication, compounded by my pre-existing personal grief. I was also worried at having to explain to the dreaded games master why I was late. Obviously he would know I'd been caned, but I knew he would make a big thing about it. Then it just erupted. The shorts in my hands fell to the floor. I covered my eyes and started shivering. I lost control and cried and cried. I nearly sat down on the wooden bench but it hurt too much.

After the first five minutes of standing there gushing tears I felt a little better. I found it almost funny when it crossed my mind that someone may have heard me. I rapidly composed myself and asked myself why I was crying. OK so my backside hurt, that would get better I would cope with that. I've lost Jill. But she was only a dog I told myself. But my mind would not accept it; she was a very special dog and my only real true companion – I cried again. The injustice that had happened temporarily smothered my hurt with anger. There's nothing I can do about the injustice I have just encountered so just forget it, I told myself. The other problem was the games master. Well now he's going to be expecting a sad, quivering defenceless boy cowering before him. Well that may be the case but I shall hold my head high.

After a few more sniffles, I composed myself and dressed into my football kit. I washed my face, took a deep breath and holding my head high and proud, I jogged out on to the playing field. There were the familiar faces of other pupils, some friendly, some not. They were practising some tackling moves or something – I never did understand football. As I approached, the games master blew hard on his whistle and everyone stood motionless. I ran straight up to him and stood before him. I looked straight at him.

"Why are you late?" he bellowed like an ugly bull. I managed to smile which I knew would annoy him. Then I replied with as much confidence as I could muster.

"I've had the cane sir." There were a few shocked noises from some sympathetic classmates.

"Why have you been caned and made late for my lesson?" shouted the master. I smiled a broad smile again.

"For going to the toilet when no pupils should have been in the building sir."

"Did it hurt?"

"Yes sir."

"Good."

There was another poor little pupil who was not the healthiest person on earth. The master always, in the nastiest possible way, referred to him as 'Granny' and encouraged everyone else to call him that.

"You're not much good for anything are you?" the master continued. I smiled again. "We'll soon wipe that smile off your face – you and Granny run around the football pitch until I tell you to stop. Now!"

Later – after arriving home to the deathly silence of The Corner House – I tried my old attic den for grieving, but it was cold, dark and empty. I was so used to having Jill by the entrance guarding it for me. I went to my room. I huddled there under bedclothes until the night was over. Just like years ago when we lost Monty, my parents vowed never to have another dog because they couldn't handle the pain and mental upheaval of the eventual, inevitable loss.

We never did any open grieving as a family; I don't know why. I realised years later that my father was a very emotional man and he was quite embarrassed about it. Something life has since taught me is that being emotional and showing it is no bad thing. In fact it can only be good for everyone concerned.

I think partly due to Father's fear of exposing his emotional side for all to see, certain matters that could possibly induce such states were taboo in The Corner House. In fact the most fundamental human need of simple, acknowledgeable, communication was lacking, thwarted by the confounded generation gap. Therefore my parents had no way of understanding my deeper emotional needs at this time, nor me theirs. Despite this, in his own unique manner and characterised by ways of a past era, my father shone as a truly valiant man.

But I don't even know what happened to Jill's body. I hoped and prayed that she never ended up in a lorry load of discarded, abandoned pets buried deep in some awful godforsaken pit somewhere. Typically the subject was not mentioned. Notwithstanding Father's sensitivity, I had come to know that he didn't believe in souls or spirits and was convinced that death was a certain and definite end to a living thing; even though he sometimes told me otherwise as an easy option in-keeping with school teachings and as a useful remedy for quelling my inquisitiveness. Therefore I knew he probably didn't attach any importance to Jill's final resting place and would have gone for the cheapest, easiest option. But how I wished I could have buried her under the stone wall in the makeshift flowerbed in our backyard. Or maybe she should have been cremated and I could have scattered her ashes to the wind in her beloved Purley or up on the slopes above Sherborne town.

18

Fourteen Going On Sixteen

I was approaching the end of my fourth year at St Aldhelm's school and boys' playground activities could now be quite serious events with roaming gangs of dinner money thieves, blackmailers and kids who just liked to fight. Instead of swinging out against contenders with a satchel or giving a token swipe, quite serious brawls could now occur as we tried out our increasing physical strengths and toyed with new mental attitudes.

I somehow succumbed to the addiction of nicotine. My favourite foolish activity became having a fag behind the bike shed. There were occasional half-hearted, token attempts to curb the activity by prefects. We always had plenty of warning by posting younger boys as lookouts. The prefects didn't really care anyway and some would actually help hide the cigarettes for us or even smoke themselves.

I was now more aware of the strict unwritten hierarchy system and indeed couldn't help being part of it as I found myself moving up through it. Not surprisingly the situation helped nurture a feeling of authority over the younger pupils. But the pecking order had also begun to expand to become apparent between individuals within the same year, or even within the same class. Subsequently, camaraderie had developed greatly within certain tight-nit groups.

We were the rebel gang who didn't give a damn for anything or anybody. We played up teachers terribly, we let off stink bombs, and we wore high-heeled Chelsea boots. We would have the heels in the boots built up with metal and the idea was to see who could make the most noise marching into assembly on the wooden floor each morning.

These antics sometimes resulted in receiving the cane or worse. Although obviously frightening and very painful, receiving corporal punishment certainly gained points and a short-cut to promotion within the hierarchy stakes. We were on a blinkered, desperate quest for personal identities while trying to cope with the rapid chemical and emotional changes occurring in our bodies and minds. However, sometimes our wild behaviour was at least temporarily curtailed when basic human instinct surfaced from somewhere in our hearts.

Once a new, young female teacher tried to teach us. When she was reduced to tears by our rowdiness and bad language, we were shocked into becoming aware of our loutish, irresponsible behaviour. Two of us stayed behind to comfort her. Our inabilities and shortcomings were revealed when we couldn't find the words to speak soft and kind to a girl not much older than us who was sobbing uncontrollably. Even though we did eventually discover the simple virtue of saying sorry, we never saw her again.

To be honest there were a handful of teachers who were damn good at their job and earned respect from us all. We were able to talk to these people like fellow humans. There was no need for any punishment threat and we learned a great deal from them. Sadly most teachers were awful at their job; we played them up and learnt nothing. Then there were the two or three we were scared of to the point of panic. These teachers would not think twice about dishing out vicious, draconian punishment.

Apart from a certain teacher's public interrogations by the vending machines at lunchtime, there was another man who reserved his personal, ultimate so-called 'after caning remedy' for any boy for whom he thought the cane was not enough. Occasionally a hardened offender would be forced to partake in a public boxing match with him in the gym. The whole school would be made to watch the unfortunate victim get knocked around in a makeshift boxing ring by a man three times his age. However, our attentions were starting to be diverted to girls and their evermore noticeably attractive charms.

Our class – boys and girls together – had embarked upon a rare field trip to a seaside resort called Ringstead Bay. Elastic bands were flicked, pea shooters were shot and paper planes were launched around the interior of the brown and red coach as it made its way southwards. In an attempt to calm the horseplay we were encouraged to sing songs that we were suppose to know from our music lessons like Tom Brown's Body and My Grandfather's Clock. It made me think while I sang:

"My Grandfather's clock was too big for the shelf

So it stood 90 years on the floor

It was taller by half than the old man himself

Tho' it weighed not a pennyweight more.

It was bought on the morn of the day he was born
And was always his pleasure and pride
But it stopped short never to go again
When the old man died.
(Chorus)
Ninety years without slumbering
Tick tock, tick tock,
His life seconds numbering
Tick tock, tick tock.
It stopped short never to go again,
When the old man died."

We had not sung this song since the second year. Grandfather Frank's clock had indeed stopped short when he died – probably through lack of winding I thought. The next verse was started up hesitantly by two boys on the back seat singing, My Grandfather's COCK!

Ringstead was not a commercial resort and had a private beach; I guess it was by special arrangement we were allowed in there. The area was deserted; it seemed we had sole access to a mile long stretch of coast for the afternoon. The beach was a mixture of rocks and shingle and there were undulating sand dunes a little further back from the shore.

It didn't take long for me and three or four other boys to realise that a group of girls had turned a particular small dip between the dunes into a place to change into their bathing costumes. We crouched behind tufts of coarse grass eagerly trying to catch a glimpse of the girls in their secret hollow, but all we could see were occasional bobbing heads amid unintelligible murmurings and loud outbursts of laughter. Then Gordon decided to charge at the area and surprise them. The rest of us followed whooping and screaming all the way like cowboys and Indians used to do across Foster's School playing fields. We only actually skirted around the top perimeter of the girls camp, but three of them stood and screamed as loudly as they possibly could while one ran to the female teacher who was sipping tea back at the coach. I felt sure we would be punished, but no one seemed to mind.

Us boys eventually found a hollow of our own. With our clothes left in untidy mixed up piles, we ran for the sea and the rest of them. We frantically splashed each other time and time again. Even apprehensive little Timothy, in trunks many sizes too big and confined to the shallows, joined in. Philip the class athlete was soon on swimming endurance missions showing off his perfect crawl stroke while one or two girls tried to butterfly through the gentle waves. Despite numerous suggestions the teachers could not be enticed to swim; two of the three tried token little paddles in the shallowest trickles of surf.

Someone found a crab and I told them about the ones I'd taken home to live in The Corner House backyard years before. Girls were chased with seaweed and more crabs and someone produced a multi-coloured beach ball. Wild and furiously - and without any boring football rules - we headed, punched and kicked the ball around until it was partly deflated and we were exhausted.

The afternoon was almost over before I knew it. It was starting to get a little cold so back at our boys hollow after a little squabbling about whose towel was whose, we flung our clothes back on. Shivering slightly in the late afternoon breeze I sat by myself just feet from the sea, ate Mother's corned beef sandwiches and drank lemonade. There was a ship, way out to sea on the horizon. I wondered where it was going or where it had been. It reminded me of Radio Caroline. For a moment I wondered if it was Radio Caroline – it could be I thought.

I'd heard a story recently about someone who'd put a message in a bottle and it had been picked up somewhere across the other side of the world. What a fascinating thought. I looked at my empty lemonade bottle lying there beside me. I think one of the teachers was talking to us about a certain type of seaweed but I was totally oblivious. I fumbled for pen and paper in my duffle bag. I tore a page from my exercise book. 'To Kim – Australia,' I wrote in my best joined up writing. I wasn't serious. Even I knew that fascinating though the bottle story was, it would be nigh impossible odds for a bottle to reach Australia from the coast of southern England; and how many Kims would there be in Australia!? I scribbled and crossed out the words as if confirming the stupidity of the idea, then stared at the choppy surface of the water. I tore off a clean piece of paper and in large capital letters wrote 'If you find this please contact me at ……' below this in even larger best writing I included my name, address and Father's telephone number. I rolled it up neatly until it was pencil thin and thrust it in through the neck of the bottle. The note unravelled inside the clear glass thereby making the address largely visible from outside. I walked to the waters edge and threw it for all I was worth out into the vastness of the ocean. I watched it bobbing for a while; I wondered just where it would end up.

"Go and get it back Park!" I turned sharply to see the games master and the whole class watching me.

"Go and get it back!" he repeated typically emphasising each syllable.

"But sir it's a message in a bottle!"

"Go and get it back!" he said once again. There were sniggers from the rest of the class.

"But sir," I said, "I've got all my clothes on now."

"Well you'll have to take them off again .... *Go and get it!*" he shouted at the top of his voice.

I felt he was being thoroughly unreasonable. I was sure he just wanted to create a little entertainment for everyone at the end of the day and watching me struggle to get that bottle back would be great fun for everyone – except me. Surely it should be seen as an educational project sending forth a message in a bottle to bob its way to wherever. But I knew there was no point in arguing. I sat down and took off my shoes and socks and rolled up my trousers.

The bottle had now drifted further from the shore. I paddled out towards it to the cheers and whistles of the class encouraged by that awful teacher.

"The coach was scheduled to leave ten minutes ago," said the female teacher in a voice that seemed as though she hoped the games master would have second thoughts and allow my bottle to go where it would in the vast ocean.

The seawater was up to my knees and I just couldn't reach that bottle – try as I might. The other children cheered, screamed and whistled even louder as a wave surprised me and touched the bottom of my rolled up trousers. I stopped and tried to inch the tight, rolled up trouser legs just a little higher. The spectators started clapping. I thought 'oh sod it' and just waded out towards it grasping the neck of the bottle as waves saturated my trousers. Fun over, everyone made for the coach and left me struggling to dry my feet and legs enough to put socks and shoes back on.

Back on the coach I arrived beside the double seat I had shared with Gordon. Gordon had agreed he would sit next to the window on the outward journey and I would sit next to the window on the return journey. Gordon sat indignant by the window. When I reminded him of our deal he just ignored me. I chucked my duffle bag up on the shelf above the pair of seats. Gordon turned towards me laughing. I struck out with a half upper cut, half right hook. His head struck the headrest of the seat behind as he rebounded from the blow. There was a look of utter astonishment and disbelief on his face as he nursed his lower jaw and we changed places in silence. I fully expected punishment of some sort but the teachers seemed to ignore the whole thing.

My tree camp hideaway in the narrow strip of land between the railway line and Purley that I called 'no-man's-land' remained a secret. Later that same summer I was on my way there in a reflective mood. Souped-up pushbikes figured less in my life as did catching buckets full of gudgeon or bullhead there in the rocky shallows of the river Yeo. I remembered well pointlessly catching those little fish with my bare hands; I suppose it was the excitement I had felt setting them free again in a massive dark shoal and being able to witness Jill's fascination that had made me do it. I wandered along the bank murmuring the Fireball XL5 TV theme tune as I threw little stones in the river.

"What you doing?" My pondering was interrupted by a girl's voice some distance away across Purley towards the slopes. I turned and squinted in the sun. I could just make out the figure of Miranda in her typical tight shorts and loose top. I had scarcely witnessed Miranda utter more than few terse expletives before.

"Oh nothing," I replied politely while shading my eyes. She ran towards me trampling buttercups and celandines.

"You still got that snake?" she asked as she raced closer, frantically whipping thistles with a thin stick.

"I set it free," I said, "that was years ago."

"I wanna see it," she insisted out of breath.

"I set it free .. honestly............ anyway it was a slowworm not a snake."

"You're a clever bugger ain't you Colin?" she said as she reached me and playfully flicked her stick across the back of my legs.

"Ouch that hurt!"

"It was meant to...... you big streak of piss!" She paddled out into the river and started lobbing big rocks all over the place.

"Come on!" she shouted as she ran out past me and took another swipe with her stick, "I'll race you to the bridge." She ran off in the direction of the railway station.

I thought about chasing her but couldn't be bothered. I was eager to get to my tree hideaway on the other side of the river. I was thinking about paddling across when I heard the faint sound of other children a little further downstream. I didn't want to run the risk of revealing the location of my personal hideaway, so I decided to investigate the other children first.

There was obviously quite a commotion happening further downstream. I passed the massive bramble bush that overhung the river's edge where I'd sometimes seen a kingfisher and the bent tree that Jill had loved so much by the deeper water. There was shouting and much splashing around out of sight around the next bend in the river. As I approached closer I recognised Miranda's two wild brothers Stephen and Richard, they were waist deep in the river frantically shouting and dancing around like lunatics.

"I got the fucker!" shouted one, "hang on he's slipped away again."

"You couldn't hold a fuckin' party." Having enticed a jack pike from the reedy depths with a colourful, spiky lure, they were now trying to torture it. As Stephen managed to grasp it and prize its jaws apart, he nearly lost it again as he looked up and saw me.

"What you want you little runt?"

"Nothing," I said.

"Well fuck off then....... light the banger for fuck sake....... I ain't got all day."

"You're not gonna...?" I started.

"You gonna stop us then... cunt!" said Richard glancing at me and frantically trying to strike a match.

"I told you not to get 'em wet," remarked Stephen only just managing to hold the creature. Then a match was lit and Richard made a face as he brought the flame into contact with the firework's blue touch paper. Almost instantly a fizzle of sparks gushed out as Richard dropped it into the gaping mouth of the struggling fish. Job done, the matches were instantly forgotten. The discarded matchbox floated downstream as an elastic band was hastily stretched over the now closed jaws of the poor fish.

"Throw the fucker!" shouted Richard at the top of his voice, "throw the fucker!" Stephen held it by the tail and threw it upstream. As the current carried it back past us a muffled, deep explosion made it arch awkwardly upside down. It lodged in a nearby reed bed, half blown apart. We all gathered around it gawping saucer eyed until Richard fished it out and suspended it up high in a tree with a branch piercing right through its tail. It stayed there for months until it fell crispy dry to the river whence it came.

The brothers carried on their way upstream towards the lake. It was still far too risky to chance revealing my tree hideaway so I rather reluctantly continued downstream to where Miranda was waiting. Here 'no-man's-land' is cut short by the river twisting under a metal bridge, which carries the busy railway line into Sherborne station.

"Bet you can't do this then!" shouted Miranda as she launched herself to grasp on to and dangle precariously from a thin and badly rusted metal conduit. The pipe work spanned the river and was attached with equally rusty brackets to the main structure of the bridge. The pipe sagged as she propelled herself like a pendulum across the river. I shouted at the top of my voice that she was mad and that she could be killed. But an express steam train flashed by only a few feet from her head and drowned out my voice almost completely. The train gushed out hot steam and blew its whistle furiously. As the blur of carriages continued Miranda almost lost her grip as she turned her head away – her hair blown out straight behind her.

I realised that there was little point in telling her to come back now, because she was beyond the halfway point. She regained her confidence and inched her way to the other side where she dropped down on to the bank of 'no-man's-land' – out of breath. She stood there first bent over, hands on knees and then hands on hips upright and facing me. As she got her breath back she mimicked the sound of chickens and shouted that I was nothing but a little chicken myself.

At that point I very nearly walked away. I didn't mind being called a chicken by the likes of Miranda. Then I managed to decipher, amid her onslaught of abuse and threats, that she was referring to an owl's nest I had found up on the slopes. Was she bluffing? I had indeed last week found an owl's nest in a small ivy-clad tree half way up the slopes. I knew that word of such things spread like wildfire around the kids of Sherborne, but I didn't remember telling anyone.

"If you don't come across..." said Miranda, "when them white owl's eggs hatch.... I'm gonna take them chicks out 'an chuck 'em in the river." She waited for my reaction, "an' if they don't drown I'm gonna smash their bloody little........"

"Alright!" I shouted, interrupting her, "if you want me to come across, I bloody well will come across." Miranda sniggered to herself as I reached up for the pipe work. I swung my feet as hard as I could and, at the appropriate moment, inched my hands along holding on for dear life.

"Don't look down!" shouted Miranda, "don't look down!"

Luckily no trains passed by while I was suspended in mid air. I made it to the other side quicker than I had anticipated. Rather pleased with myself, but a little out of breath, I too dropped down on to 'no-man's-land.' When I turned to face Miranda she blew a massive pink balloon of bubble gum. When it burst she skilfully licked it from her lips.

"There!" I said, "happy now?" Miranda chewed vigorously and whipped her tee shirt off over her head and threw it on the floor. My first thought was that she must be too hot. She chewed even more vigorously and looking straight at me, she removed her bra and also threw that on the ground.

"Shag me!" she demanded – little breasts bobbing in the sun. There was another little pop from her bubble gum before a small steam train came chugging by.

"I can't.... not here," I stuttered as Miranda started waving at passengers in the passing carriages. I was furious.

I was unsure of the word shag. Was it like – all the way like a fuck?

"Well don't wave at them Miranda!" I shouted. She continued waving and smiled slightly at me.

"Right I'm having nothing to do with you," I said indignantly. My only escape was back across the river; immediately to the left was the railway, to the right and behind me the river and ahead the narrow strip of 'no-man's-land' was thick with impenetrable, matted brambles. The last carriages trundled by with people staring in amazement and disbelief.

"Shag me!" repeated Miranda, "or I'll tell my brothers that you raped I." I knew people had seen us but I guess I didn't want to reveal any panic to Miranda or indeed any inkling that I didn't have a clue how to shag someone. By now Miranda was sprawled on the ground, her back half supported by a small tree.

"Come here," she said in a much softer voice. I took a deep breath and turned towards her. As I approached I felt there was no way I could oblige her, no way at all; although she seemed less raucous now and spoke softly.

Nonetheless, I found myself kneeling then straddling her. I was suddenly aware of someone's presence. I turned sharply and there on the other side of the river was an old man in a trilby hat walking his dog. He looked straight at us.

"Don't be silly..." I said loudly so the man could hear, "put your clothes back on." As the man's Jack Russell started barking madly Miranda grabbed me where it hurt. The man's voice echoed slightly under the metal bridge as he called his dog.

"Rex!... Rex come here!" The dog still barked a little but the sound grew fainter as Miranda was eventually able to skilfully unroll a protective sheath on me.

Flesh on flesh, lips against bubble gum filled lips. The swish of undergrowth, the crack of a dry stick and the smell of strange shampoo was interrupted by a two-tone siren in the distance. I wasn't sure if I'd done it properly and didn't care. I ran to the fence right next to the railway line and squinted down to Sherborne station. There by the level crossing was the unmistakable revolving blue lamp of a police car.

"Calm down," said Miranda still half naked. I prepared to swing back across the bridge.

"Jump down in the river," said Miranda doing up her belt, "if we jump down in the river, we can easily wade under the railway bridge and come out in the engineering works."

"Yeah and there the coppers will be waiting for us," I said. In the confusion Miranda slipped down the muddy bank and grabbed hold of me. She clung to me and we both landed waist deep in the river. I wrenched myself away from Miranda and headed upstream to where the opposite bank was lower, allowing me to climb out.

"If you go that way you'll get caught!" shouted Miranda.

"I'll take my chances," I muttered. I glanced back at crazy Miranda, tee shirt chucked around her shoulders and carrying her shoes, battling to walk amongst the algae covered rocks under the railway bridge. Another train drowned out what she was saying as I managed to reach the far bank. New baseball boots slurping mud, jeans sopping and stuck to me, I scrambled up the bank. I ran for all I was worth upstream to where the river was shallower. I paddled across back over to the narrow 'no-man's-land' and quickly climbed my secret tree.

As darkness fell I cursed Miranda when I found pink bubble gum plastered in my hair. Soon I glimpsed torches and the glint of policemen's helmets on the other side of the river. There were dogs too. I stayed there in the moonlight until midnight, motionless and cautious about even breathing. After I had surreptitiously heard the intimate secrets of an innocent couple strolling by hand-in-hand and pondered over the barely discernible Black Horse jukebox pumping out rock 'n' roll, I ran home.

The following morning I had one of the biggest arguments ever with Mother when she discovered some of the pink bubblegum still caked in my hair

19

Approaching Manhood

I hardly saw Miranda after that episode – she seemed to avoid me. It was as if we had reached an unspoken, mutual understanding. She had perhaps satisfied her curiosity – and who knows maybe more – whilst at the same time she'd doubtless discovered that I wasn't the 'Clyde' she thought I was. And I certainly didn't want a 'Bonnie' who was into public copulation.

Ironically Father felt it his duty to explain to me about the facts of life or 'taking a fancy to a woman' as he called it. It was fairly obvious someone had been speaking to him about how he should explain it. He found it excruciatingly embarrassing and used the simplest, basic terms and it took no more than two minutes.

Father, and indeed Mother, came from a time when sex was never really explained to children, youngsters just found out for themselves. Indeed that's more or less what I had done without perhaps realising it – although I did have a reasonable idea beforehand. My parents had no idea what had occurred in 'no-man's-land' or that the media rumours of a sex maniac on the loose were totally unfounded and brought about by a train passenger's misinterpretation of my first fumbling attempt at sexual intercourse.

Life was now to be very different for me in every way. Not only had it something to do with that first bizarre attempt at sex and

Father's first man-to-man chat, but also there was the devastating news that we were to leave our home. The Corner House had encompassed my childhood. I knew every inch of its creaking roof timbers, crumbling walls and dusty, cobwebbed corners. The tumble-down old building had formed my very universe and had later become a hub as I explored beyond its spooky, yet strangely safe, framework.

Indeed for the first fourteen years of my life I knew no other home or way of life than The Corner House and its very basic facilities. At the time it never crossed my mind just how basic things were or to what extent the place needed renovating – I'd never experienced things any other way. It never bothered me that there wasn't a proper bathroom, or that the place was in urgent need of rewiring and plumbing. But quite apart from the lack of creature comforts there were health and safety and structural aspects to consider. The walls in the kitchen were literally disintegrating, ceilings needed replacing and the roof needed serious attention.

Father was not exactly well-off and came from an era when you only spent money that was actually yours. Therefore to someone adhering to these policies, The Corner House must have felt like a millstone around my father's neck. I got the impression that he found it impossible to reach any other decision but to put our home on the market. In 1967 The Corner House was sold. In many ways my boyhood as I knew it, was now to dissolve away leaving all those adolescent fantasies behind as I fast approached reality and – somewhere on the horizon – adulthood.

In retrospect I guess it was probably some kind of psychological attempt to cut all ties with The Corner House and forget about it and our basic way of life that made Father sell most of the house contents too. It was now common knowledge that I owned an air pistol, everyone seemed to accept that I would be responsible with it and not shoot garden birds or indeed any other living creature. Therefore, a secret hiding place was no longer necessary for it. This was lucky because in the commotion and confusion of moving, I realised my gramophone and the old Pianola where I used to hide the gun had disappeared. It was later when we'd been in the new house a few weeks that Father admitted that they had both been sold at auction. I was somewhat dismayed; I was actually developing an interest in playing the piano properly and I'd grown to like the strange charm of that ancient gramophone beast.

I had also developed a keen interest in sculpture, painting and sketching. I had acquired some books on these subjects and art in general. It was not until after we had moved that I discovered these had been given to the local charity shop without even asking me. Worse was the fact that some of my early pieces of work had been thrown out. I don't suppose it ever entered my parents' heads that their son might be interested in art. They didn't want to know about it. To my parents art was something that was now forced upon you at school – then you left and grew out of it.

While helping to clean out the old kitchen for the last time, under the cast iron bath amongst families of woodlice – or 'mother buttons' as Mother called them – I found new, still carefully wrapped, rolls of damp, damaged wallpaper. Apparently, using money she earned from cleaning, my mother had secretly been stockpiling this wallpaper for decorating The Corner House sometime in the future. I don't suppose she realised that the required renovation went far deeper than just the wallpaper or that the damp environment under the bath would ruin the paper.

I was reassured we were going to a 'nice new modern house,' that's all I remember being told. In actual fact we moved to Durrant Close, an old people's sheltered housing complex. We moved into the warden's house where my mother became warden in return for a rent free house and a small wage.

It was OK. There was hot water when we wanted it, central heating and wall to wall carpets. But there was no fun dodging creaky floorboards, I couldn't hear Castleton church bell on Sundays or the Black Horse jukebox in the evenings. However, there were compensations like a proper electric stereo system and the start of my vinyl record collection.

I still saw Jimmy from time to time but on our journey through puberty and beyond we had now taken slightly different routes. For some reason the recent the progression through school that seemed to instigate the restructuring of the hierarchy system, meant I found myself in a group that did not include Jimmy, or at least not on a regular basis. I soon struck up a new friendship with Robin. I'd known Robin since first attending St Aldhelm's but for some reason we'd never really been proper friends. I discovered we had similar interests and we got on extremely well.

Robin had an older brother and a younger sister and they lived with their mother in an isolated smallholding between Sherborne and Yeovil. Robin and I soon discovered a mutual interest in cowboys as portrayed in western movies. We made a real camp in the middle of a thicket some distance behind his mother's place. I would regularly cycle the two or three miles there and we'd light a fire, chat and act out cowboy fantasies.

Inspired by the rugged stamina and deep camaraderie dramatized in wild west films – typically years spent riding the range, herding dogies and looking out for your buddy – Robin suggested that we become 'blood brothers.' I was eager to partake and even though we both knew in our hearts it would only ever be symbolic, we took it very seriously. Acting out the scene, we even spoke in awful American accents as we synchronised the slashing of each other's right inner forearm with our bowie knives.

Before the trickling blood congealed we each thrust our arm hard to the other making contact wound to wound. Then using our teeth to tie binder twine, we bound them tight in position. We sat there for hours lashed together, smoking fags around the campfire.

Times were hard for Robin and his family. His father had left home years ago and his mother tried desperately to scratch a living from the tiny farm. Robin never had time to custom convert pushbikes like Jimmy and I. He rode an old, unconverted heavy machine rather like Uncle Todd's original Rudge Whitworth. He would cycle into town every Saturday to work on a fruit and vegetable stall on the wide pavement called The Parade next to The Conduit.

Father had now retired and had more money to spare from the sale of The Corner House. He sold the old Ford Prefect and bought an almost new Vauxhall Victor. He was very proud of it and decided to drive us to Scotland on holiday. To my astonishment he suggested that Robin came as well. It was rather weird, I was so used to three. Having a fourth person the same age as me who liked listening to Radio Luxembourg, fly fishing and seeing who could fart the loudest at night was fabulous.

Robin and I shared a room of our own. I had never actually lived closely with anyone of my own age before. It was a revelation. Not only through discovering true brotherly companionship from a like-minded person, but over the three weeks I gained a further insight into what someone else's life was like with brothers and sisters.

I suppose my 'lonely only' situation was just as strange to Robin as his tales of life with siblings were to me. I'm sure it was natural rivalry as opposed to jealousy that made Robin speak of his brother as a violent bully and his sister as a soppy, pathetic wimp. I'm sure he loved them both really. After years of not knowing anything else, I was beginning to get an inkling of how different my childhood had been from most others. Not unpleasant, not uncared for – just different.

One day at school having another fag in a hollow that existed between the perimeter hedge and the playing fields, Robin mentioned that his mother knew a chap who had two motorbikes for sale. I wasn't particularly interested because I hardly had any money. However, Robin insisted that they would be very cheap. So the following weekend I rode my pushbike over to Robin's place and together we cycled to the village of Nether Compton where the man lived.

There opposite the village green we found the old chap's house. He was expecting us and immediately beckoned us over. In the passageway that divided two cottages were a James 197 and a BSA Bantam 125.

"What do you think they're worth?" he said, thumbs behind his braces. We didn't have a clue and I was convinced that they would be far beyond our means anyway. We stood there in silence. I was thinking it had all been a waste of time when Robin enquired.

"Do they work?"

"Well I've not started them for months – well no years really but...."

"He's got to get rid of them!" interrupted his wife appearing at the doorway, "they've been blocking up the passageway for too long and it's such a struggle to get by into the backyard you see."

"Well it's true," continued the old chap, "I won't ever use them any more – not now." He held on to the handlebars of the 'Bantam' and tried the clutch lever. "Needs a bit of lubrication and cleaning up," he muttered. "But they should be fine, we could try and start them I suppose," he continued as he leant over the far side of the machine and tickling the carburettor. He struggled to wrestle the machine away from the wall, checked for neutral and thrust his foot hard down on the kick-start lever. There was one small explosion and a hint of smoke, but that was all. The old chap immediately pushed his foot down hard again, this time grasping the handlebars tighter. The engine burst into life. He revved it up and the passageway filled with choking fumes. As his wife shouted protests he let the machine idle to the telltale random pops and explosions so typical of a small, two-stroke engine.

"I used to work in Sherborne you see," he said shouting slightly above the din, "and they got me to work and back for years. I used this 'Bantam' mainly, but if anything serious went wrong with it I always had the 'James' to fall back on." He swung his leg over the saddle and sat thoughtfully astride the machine playing with the clutch again. The machine was somehow suited to the old man and he to it. This particular union of man and machine seemed familiar.

"Where did you used to work?" I asked. He just managed to hear me above the engine, the sound of which was much amplified in the small gangway.

"Oh down at The Silk Mills," he said, "shift work, two till ten and six till two." We all pondered without speaking for a good few minutes. Then he stopped the engine by stalling it, got off and carefully leant the machine back up against the wall.

"But then I had a part time job for twelve years," he continued scratching the back of his head, "only a couple hours a day, half twelve till half two at the boys' school."

"He should have given it up long before he did," said his wife – arms folded.

"Did you used to ride this bike up around New Road and up Newland every weekday?" I asked.

"Yes that's right," he replied, "and sometimes on a Saturday." He thought deeply before continuing. "Over the river bridge, over the railway bridge and past that house on the corner." He closed his eyes and thought again. "Quite often there'd be a young boy on a tricycle outside that house on the wide pavement – used to frighten me to death. I was always afraid he was gonna ride out in the road in front of me…..Then in more recent years there were a couple times when he pointed a microphone thing out of the window at me."

I leant on the 'Bantam' in utter astonishment. My other senses shut down as I stroked the drab olive paintwork of the fuel tank. I was lost in thought.

"Well I guess you'd better have 'em then!" the old man suggested.

"What?" I said.

"Well I guess you'd better have them!" he said again looking straight at me and obviously wondering why I looked so surprised.

"I ain't got enough money," I stuttered nervously.

"Well how much you got then?"

"I ain't got nothing – not at the moment," said Robin hesitantly.

"I got two pounds one and sixpence," I said boldly.

"Well give us a pound each for them – just to keep it legal." There was stunned silence. The combined astonishment and disbelief instantly turning to excitement made me breathe in deeply and momentarily my lungs were sort of paralysed.

"I'll lend you a pound and pay for them then," I eventually managed to say to Robin. None of us could control our broad smiles and we were so excited we had to use the old man's toilet.

"How we gonna get 'em home?" enquired Robin.

"It's all fixed with your mother," replied the old chap to Robin, "she said that if you bought them she'd pick them up in her truck."

We cycled as fast as we could back to Robin's place. But try as we might Robin's mother insisted that it was too late to pick the machines up that day and we'd have to wait until the morning. I never slept a wink that night and was itching to tell someone of our good fortune. I dared not mention it to my parents for fear of them confiscating them or something. Mother in particular was thoroughly anti-motorcycle and I was certain that she would hit the roof and do her best to ban the activity if she knew.

During the next few months – before leaving school for good – and unbeknown to my parents, the bikes were brought back to life and rode relentlessly around the fields next to Robin's place. The random pops and explosions of idling two-stroke engines often brought back memories of the approaching of mid-day at The Corner House.

But in 1968 I entered another very different phase in my life. I passed out through the school gates for the last time to 'enter the world of work' and sever all ties with carefree, childhood fantasies. Decisions had been made months before that I was not of the calibre to sit any sort of exam. It also soon emerged that according to the headmaster, I wasn't fit to hold down a job in a biscuit factory, let alone any other.

Therefore I was ejected from school with no qualifications whatsoever. In the many years since then I have encountered, experienced and indeed greatly benefited from a far more civilised educational environment.

There have been a few changes to The Corner House and the surrounding area since 1968. The allotments are now gone, replaced with neat little bungalows. Fosters Grammar School and St Aldhelm's Secondary Modern School are also gone – demolished in preference to bigger comprehensive schools. The wooden cricket pavilion will exist forever more in my memories, as will Kim. That headmaster died years ago but before he did, he had the decency to give me back my cherished penknife.

The Corner House itself is now proud and renovated with a proper bathroom and heating. I guess it never did have hippos in the backyard or bogeymen in the attic, but I wouldn't be surprised if the ghost of a little black dog now sometimes scampers through it and across Castleton, Purley and The Slopes.

Castleton's almost the same as it was all those years ago. My father's ashes now form part of the hallowed ground in the churchyard. The cottages 7 and 8 Castleton still stand down in the field near the railway line. Beyond them the only remaining evidence of Len Hart's footbridge is a solitary wooden post, now a shaky robin's perch. For me Miss Molly's spirit will forever preside over things around those parts protecting youngsters and fending off unmannerly men.

-----oooOooo-----

31384176R00190

Made in the USA
Charleston, SC
15 July 2014